Joel Dommett burst onto the comedy scene in 2007 and quickly established himself as one of the most exciting comedians on the circuit. He has become a regular face on TV, and in 2016 was a finalist in *I'm a Celebrity...Get Me Out of Here!* He went on to co-host the spin-off show Extra Camp, and co-starred with Nish Kumar in *Joel & Nish vs The World.*

JOEL DOMMETT

IT'S NOT ME, IT'S THEM

HEADLINE

First published in 2018
by HEADLINE PUBLISHING GROUP

First published in paperback in 2018

1

Cataloguing in Publication Data is available from the British Library

Paperback ISBN 978 1 4722 5130 5

Typeset in Sabon MT by Palimpsest Book Production Ltd, Falkirk, Stirlingshire

Printed and bound by CPI Group (UK) Ltd, Croydon CR0 4YY

Headline's policy is to use papers that are natural, renewable
and recyclable products and made from wood grown in sustainable
forests. The logging and manufacturing processes are expected to
conform to the environmental regulations of the country of origin.

HEADLINE PUBLISHING GROUP
An Hachette UK Company
Carmelite House
50 Victoria Embankment
London
EC4Y 0DZ

www.headline.co.uk
www.hachette.co.uk

Look, Mum! I wrote a book!

Contents

Acknowledgements

It's been an incredible slog of highs and lows to finish this book and make sure it wasn't utterly terrible. It turns out it's quite hard to write a book, especially when Instagram is so damn entertaining.

I am really very proud of it so I hope you like it.

I feel very uncomfortable about the word 'autobiography' because I don't feel like I deserve to write one of those. Instead I'll call it a 'memoir'. It's pretty much all true. Although sometimes two stories are combined into one to make them easier to swallow (like covering a pill in butter for a sick dog). I have changed the names and embellished from time to time like anyone does when they retell a good story. However, I promise all the diary entries are entirely real. I was a weird kid.

I wanted to write a book for many reasons: one, because I just bloody love stories, and two, you get a thank you section. So here goes.

Mum, you know you're the best: thanks for everything you've done for me. I love you more than you know. Thanks to Robert, Dad and Sarah, Brother Benj and Nicole: you are such a wonderful supportive family and I can be a real dick sometimes. Rick and all the people at Off The Kerb, this year has been amazing: thank you for making my wildest dreams come true. Steve, I couldn't have done any of this without you, you are incredible. Thank you Richard at Headline. Zade and Gareth for putting up with my moody days and my terrible snatch (it's a weightlifting thing). Thanks to Rikki Beadle Blair for giving me my work ethic. Thanks to Kim and my comedian-world friends: Nish Kumar, James Acaster, Nick Helm, Eric Lampaert, Ed Gamble, Tom Allen, Rebecca Austin, Steen Raskopolous, Stuart Laws, Stuart Goldsmith, Iain Stirling, Rhys James, Pappys, Suzi Ruffell and a million others I have forgotten.

And a huge thank you to the person this book is all about. I really bloody love you. You changed everything.

Prologue

15 April 2004

Hey JD
   I'm scared to have sex with someone else but I
want to get better at this. I think I just need to do it
more. Maybe forty people? More than forty people is
slutty. I definitely want to fall in love before I reach
number forty.
Sincerely, Joel

Have you ever had such a bad date that you end up telling
them about all the other people you've had sex with? I have.

I'm currently about twenty minutes into a first date. It's
going terribly and it's my fault. Her name is Hannah and

we're at a tapas restaurant in Shoreditch. It was my choice; it had a good TripAdvisor review but thinking about it there were only three testimonials so it was probably the staff. They've really pushed the boat out on the Spanish vibe. Next to the table there are some castanets hanging on the wall and a tanned man in the corner in an unbuttoned red shirt is plucking the tune of Enrique Iglesias's 'Hero' on his guitar. Hannah is so much taller than in her photos and judging by her expression I'm clearly shorter. When we greeted at the table she looked down on me and kissed my cheek like a lady giving a medal to a child.

I smell of stale boy BO. I'd picked up my favourite T-shirt I wore the day before and assumed it would be fine. It isn't. That, matched with some stained jeans and dirty festival-trodden trainers, make me look more ready for decorating than a date. By contrast, she is dressed perfectly, like she's been freshly lifted from a fashion blogger's Instagram photo. Every accessory and colour has been carefully considered before leaving her house. The only thing that matches on my outfit are the toothpaste stains on my jeans that look like sperm and the dried salty sweat marks under my armpits.

We met online a few weeks before. She sent me a cat emoji with the heart eyes when she was drunk. It's not a great story to tell the grandkids but it's how most people meet these days so it will have to do. If I'm honest, I forgot that I'd organised the date and when I remembered it was too late to cancel.

She's half Dutch and half Pakistani, which means she's tall, attractive and blonde, with some intensely dark bushy eyebrows. She's a glowing example of how wonderful immigration can be. They really should have made her the face of the Remain campaign for Brexit.

I always think a meal is a good idea for a date until you're sitting down and forced to look your potential partner directly in the face like you're at a flirty chess tournament. I really shouldn't be here. The memory of what happened last night is clinging to my mind like discarded loo paper on a shoe and I am not in the mood for polite conversation with a stranger. The conversation wades slowly through the muddy waters of my sulk. It's just . . . bad.

To break the tension the waiter finally arrives, wearing a tight red jacket and even tighter black trousers. He clearly wants to appear like he's come straight from the bullring but he looks more like a Butlin's Redcoat who's spent too long in a tumble dryer. He has the name 'Rodrigo' on his badge but I'm sceptical. I reckon he's called Rodney and got a spray tan and put on an accent to get the job.

When being served by someone with a badge on I love to throw their name into the conversation because there's a split-second moment when they think, 'How does he know who I am?', then they remember it's written in capital letters on their chest.

'Hello, Rodrigo,' I say expectantly. He looks at me, confused, then glances down at his badge.

'Hola,' he replies in a thick accent. 'Would you like still or sparkling water for the table?'

This is such a huge question to have flung your way early on a first date. Saying 'still' makes you seem boring, saying 'sparkling' makes you seem like an only child desperate for attention, and if you undercut both and say 'tap' then you're clearly an absolute skinflint. Everyone wants to say tap but it comes down to whether you have the balls to lay your cards on the table at such an early time.

'Tap,' I say. I have laid both my balls and my cards on the table. Figuratively. This date isn't going to last so there's no point in spending money on it. Rodrigo looks at Hannah as if to say, 'Why are you on a date with this guy?!' I am starting to ask the same question. He takes the rest of our order while giving all of his attention to Hannah, not once looking at me. It feels like I am the waiter at their date. He gives me one glance as he walks away as if to say, 'I can't help it, I'm flirty Rodrigo.'

I start panicking about things that I've never panicked about before. Like where should I look on her face while talking? Do I look into one of her eyes and swap every now and then or just focus on the gap between them? If I look at her nose does it look like I'm looking into her eyes? I've been having conversations almost my entire life; why has this all of a sudden become an issue? I then realise she's asked me a question but I haven't answered because I'm counting down the time to move to the next eye.

'Where do you live?' she asks a second time.

'Nunhead in south-east London,' I reply quickly, realising she has been talking to herself for a good while. She clearly hasn't heard of the place but nods politely. She asks another question and I give her another mundane answer, and we repeat this pattern a few times. I'm unable to muster the energy to ask her any questions back. It feels less like a date and more like a Spanish-themed *Mastermind* where my specialist subject is myself (why don't more people do that?).

She is really trying to get this bird off the ground and I am making it way too heavy to fly. Finally, she cracks.

'This isn't going well. What's wrong?'

I need to either leave or be honest.

'This is going to sound stupid,' I say.

'Try me,' she replies politely. Here goes. I tell her that I wrote a diary when I was eighteen in the form of a series of letters to myself, as you do. I found it recently and in it there's an entry where I wrote that I didn't want to have sex with more than forty people because I thought it would be slutty. Hannah puts her hand to her mouth to stop herself from laughing but it doesn't work.

'So I gave myself the challenge to find The One before I got to number forty,' I add.

'Why?' Hannah is still chuckling. It's a good question that I haven't really thought of an answer to until now. I think it's because I'm obsessed with stories. It would have been the perfect romcom ending to the tale. I wanted to tell my grandkids that I wrote in my teenage diary that I didn't want to have sex with more than forty people and your grandmother was the perfect goal in the ninetieth minute. Number four-zero. I wanted that to be the story, not 'she sent me a cat emoji with heart eyes'.

Hannah starts to speak, and I prepare myself for the worst. She is going to politely make her excuses and leave. I know it and I deserve it.

She leans forward.

'Tell me who your first was.'

#1 The Virgin at Virgin

I met Rose on an eventful day in 2001. I was a sixteen-year-old skinny goth mess of ripe zits and black nail varnish all packaged in an underwashed, oversized Nirvana T-shirt. I was working in the Virgin Megastore at the Mall Cribbs Causeway, a massive shopping centre that they decided to build on the edge of Bristol instead of the centre. If you don't know Virgin Megastores because you were born after the financial downturn, they sold CDs, vinyl and huge posters of marijuana leaves.

I started work there as soon as I was legally allowed, three days after my sixteenth birthday. It would have been fun but the line manager and I really didn't get on. He was skinny, tall and bald, and looked like a pencil. He was what Lex Luthor would have become without the inheritance. Retail line managers are always dickheads. They get paid 50p more an hour and only do the job because they love bossing around sixteen-year-olds.

I was so bored and pissed off with Lex that after only two weeks working there I set myself a challenge. By the time I was seventeen I wanted to:

1. No longer work at Virgin.
2. No longer be a virgin.

I will be talking a lot about both virgins throughout this chapter, so try not to get the two confused.*

Oh, my name is Joel Dommett, by the way. I'm not sure I need to say it because it's written on the front of this book, but I thought I would let you know just in case. Let's quickly go through the basics of me so you've got an image in your mind while reading these stories. I'm a stand-up comedian. I've been doing it for almost the lifespan of a goat (ten years) and I hope to continue doing it for plenty more goats. I'm also now a published author and I've been doing that for the lifespan of a strong fart, but I've been telling stories aloud for a while, so the fact that I have written some down isn't so different. I look just like the guy on the front of the book, unless you are reading this in 2027 in which case I now look like a wrinklier version of that guy, despite the industrial amount of daily moisturiser he applies.

Anyway, back to Virgin (the shop and me). Working in

---

* Imagine if suicide bombers actually received seventy-two retail branches of a rapidly declining industry when they died.

retail is tedious. You get to know the CD that plays on a loop so well that you can start singing the next song before it starts. The frustrating thing was, we worked in a CD shop. We were surrounded by tens of thousands of potential bore-dom-breaking albums. But we were only allowed the Same. Fucking. CD. Sometimes I think they were encouraging us to have a breakdown.

There was only one employee who seemed to have a sweet job at Virgin Megastores. The designated security guard. His name was Matt. He used to just stand at the front of the store with the walkie-talkie. I used to call him Matt Mat because his name was Matt and he used to stand on one by the door. Matt Mat. He was the coolest guy ever, like Shrek if Shrek had tattoos and piercings. He was HUGE* but he was a gentle giant. On second thoughts, I'm not sure whether he actually was huge. Maybe I was just small. When I was eight I went to the National History Museum, and all I can remember is the skeleton of 'Dippy' the Diplodocus in the foyer. It was MASSIVE and so were the security guards around him. I went back last year as a fully formed 31-year-old and it was so much smaller then I remembered because I had simply grown. Don't get me wrong; it's still big, it's just not BIG. Although the security guards had actually got bigger too, but I think that's probably due to the massive rise in obesity levels and terror threats over the last twenty-five years.

I loved Matt Mat so much. Watching him stand there

---

* I emphasised how huge he was there by writing 'huge' in huge letters, or 'capitals' as they are known in the literary world. I really hope it helped with the description.

guarding the keep was the highlight of my shift. Maybe if I could become a cool security guard like Matt Mat I would enjoy working at Virgin Megashit? It became my main objective. I wanted to stand proudly on the door as Joel Mat, the protector of all CDs. Most of all, I wanted a fucking walkie-talkie.

I asked Pencil Lex if I could go on security but he just laughed maniacally. He was so wiry that when he laughed he looked like one of those floppy inflatable people that flail around outside car dealerships. I sulked between the Soundtracks and World Music racks pretending to sort the *Fast and the Furious* and Enya CDs. An hour passed which included five lengthy toilet breaks where I just stood in the cubicle for a bit then headed back down. I waited till Pencil Lex was on a break and asked Matt if I could help him on security. He looked at me with his kind eyes and shook his head apologetically.

'OK, well, if you ever need anyone to cover for you, I'm your man,' I said, pointing at my chest with my thumb like I was advertising my services as a cheap lawyer in an advert.

Life at Virgin repeated itself over and over, just like the shit compilation CD that blasted out of the speaker, until the day finally arrived.

'I'm just going on my lunch break. You can take the radio if you want,' Matt Mat announced in his booming, bridge-troll voice. (I assume they teach you not to call it a walkie-talkie on day one of security school.)

I wanted to scream 'I'VE GOT THE WALKIE-TALKIE' but I kept it within and just muttered 'Ten Four' because that's what real security people say. Probably. I took my place at the door with the radio on my hip like a gun in a holster. I was like a cowboy in a saloon with absolutely no cowboy experience whatsoever – but finally, I'd made it. I was Joel Mat.

I felt on top of the world pretending to be someone who stops crime. That was until an actual crime happened about thirty minutes after Matt left me at his post. A teenager in full tracksuit* and baseball cap was standing at the chart section throwing Daniel Bedingfield CDs into his bag. I locked eyes on him. At first, I thought he was just a customer who really loved a bit of Bedders, then I realised he had no intention of waiting in line for ten minutes due to lack of staff because they were all taking fake toilet breaks. He turned and saw me seeing him. There was a moment of silence, pure calm before the storm, then like a slow-motion video before it returns to normal speed he let loose, bolting like a skanky horse in a grubby Kappa hat. I had no preparation or training for this. I was like a supply teacher on his first day. I could have just let him go; nobody would have noticed and the only person who would lose out would be Daniel Bedingfield. I wanted to let him run off into the metaphorical sunset of the indoor mall but I couldn't let Matt down. I'm going to make you proud, I thought. As Daniel Bedingfield would say, 'I gotta get through this.'

---

* When you see someone in a full tracksuit they are either a professional competitive sports athlete or an absolute scallywag. Why don't people steal things in a suit? They would get away with it so much more. On second thoughts, people do steal in suits; they are called BANKERS. *Am I right?!*

I gave chase. I was a keen after-school cross-country runner who would have been picked for the school team if three people fell ill. I caught up with him by Miss Selfridge and kept up the blistering pace. I pursued him right the way through the shopping periphery to John Lewis. He was fast but I was faster. His hat fell off and I grabbed it mid-run for DNA. I put it on my head. Backwards obviously. We ran past Topman, Route One, Fat Face then O'Neill. I saw security guards in the other shops watching us sail past, jealous that someone hadn't lifted something from their establishment so they could be the hero. I pulled out the walkie-talkie while running, making it a runnie-talkie. I pressed a button on the side to tell the first responders a pursuit was occurring. I had no idea who the radio actually communicated with. I assumed it was probably the government or the Avengers or something. It let out a huge shriek of feedback like a terrible open mic first-timer. It was clearly the wrong button. I'd been thinking so much about holding the radio I hadn't given a moment's thought about learning how to use it. I put it back in its holster. I'd just have to deal with this injustice alone.

We reached the outer door of the mall by Marks & Spencer. It was a large automatic rotating door. He stopped with his back against it. He knew he was caught. The Kappa horse had become a Kappa rabbit in the headlights. You could see he expected me to run into him and tackle him to the floor but I instinctively stopped three feet from him and we both simultaneously realised I was a scared sixteen-year-old with a spotty face like a bubbling bolognese who'd never fought a day in his life, whereas he was a post-spots teenager and he had clearly fought every day of his life. I was way out of my depth. I wanted Matt to run in and save me like Robin Hood Prince of Thieves hanging from a light fixture but I knew he wouldn't – Shrek loved his lunch.

We paused. We were back in the imaginary saloon again. He slowly started to walk towards me. I backed up. He kept walking. I backed up some more. He widened his eyes and I panicked. I bolted like a horse in a backward Kappa hat. He started chasing me but I really cannot be sure for how long because I never looked back. I ran past O'Neill, Fat Face, Route One, Topman, John Lewis, Miss Selfridge then back into the safe bosom of my Virgin mother. Matt was waiting at the door.

'He got away,' I said. I think Matt knew full well that by 'he', I meant 'me'.

I was demoted to stock room duty and was never given the runnie-talkie again.

After work that day I had some time to spare before my mum picked me up. I walked past the shops I'd raced past earlier, hiding beneath the new hat that I'd stolen from a stealer. I wandered into Fat Face, my favourite place for perusing things I couldn't afford to purchase. A mousey blonde girl was working behind the till. She may have worked at Fat Face but her face was of a beautiful normal size. She had jeans on that entirely covered her shoes and a lanyard hanging around her neck.* I glanced at the hanging ID. It said 'Rose'. She had brown eyes and a white vest top on which meant you could sneakily see an inch and a half of tanned belly. Those were the days, when the tiniest bit of skin showing

---

* Lanyards make anyone look cool. Rappers call their huge garish necklaces 'bling' but they are just massive sparkly lanyards.

was the most exciting thing ever. Nowadays Nikki Minaj is basically naked, thwacking you in the face with her big bits in every video, and as a result everyone generally tends to show more skin. I loved the time when people would get excited about sneaking a quick glance at a bare clavicle.

I'd had a few very innocent teenage holding-hands-type things before, and something a little more 'serious' with a lovely girl called Jenny, but I knew right then that Rose was the (first) one (that I would call the one). She looked perfect. She was studious but cool, like a skate magazine, and decked out head to toe in mandatory shopfloor staff-discount Fat Face. I stared at her from behind the espadrilles for fifteen minutes before she approached me to ask if I needed help. That inch of flesh was captivating when she walked; I was in a trance. Some might say hip-notised.* I was petrified. I held on to the espadrilles like I was clutching a lamppost in a storm.

'Did you run past the shop today chasing someone?' she said. I prised open my arid mouth and muttered, 'Yep.'

I expected a 'Did you also run back past the shop being chased by someone?' but it never came.

'Did you catch him?' My mouth became even drier. 'Yeah,' I said, while leaning on the rope-soled shoe display and praying that it would support my weight.

'Cool,' she said, then she and her hips and inch of skin walked away. I was unbelievably excited. What a day. I'd held the walkie-talkie and had a talkie with a lady.

'This is clearly the start of something incredible,' I thought.

---

* Absolutely superb stuff there, Joel.

I had to ask her out. And you know what? I did! I walked straight up to her, got scared, walked right past her, out the door, then returned and watched her three days a week from behind the espadrilles for around four months until eventually I uttered a teenage hello, and about a month after that, I asked her out.

I can't remember where we went on our first date but we used to mainly hang out on lunch breaks so it was probably Spudulike. My young heart melted like the cheese on my beans while I looked at her across the table.

My seventeenth birthday arrived. Still worked at Virgin, still a virgin.

I perked myself up by bouncing on my new present from my devoted mother – a massive garden trampoline. You cannot be sad on a trampoline; it's scientifically impossible. The bounce is medicinal and automatically turns your frown upside down. I'm aware that seventeen is a little late in life to be receiving playground equipment as a present but I was a tardy bloomer with most things: boning, birds, beards and bouncing.* So the weekend after my birthday, I had a trampoline party at my house (let's all still remember how old I was) and introduced Rose to my few friends and my mum for the first time.

My mother really is incredible. Sometimes I think she loves me too much, like Lennie loves the rabbits in *Of Mice and Men* (I'm trying to impress you with a literary reference but we all know I was forced to study it for GCSE). Although instead of killing the rabbits by holding them too tight, Mum

---

* A suggested, yet cruelly tossed aside title for this book.

would kill me by feeding me too much delicious home-made lasagne. It really is delicious. So many layers, so dense; I honestly don't know how she does it.

Mum is an excellent liar. She would lie to me as a child whenever it suited her purposes. I remember being twenty-three and suddenly realising that 50 per cent of people who get their ears pierced don't die from infection. By the time I figured it out I didn't want an ear piercing. Well played, Mother, well played.

Most comedians have an ingrained sadness that derives from some sort of childhood trauma. This festers inside them then reveals itself when they grow up and makes them want to bare their souls night after night after night, sadistically enjoying the solitary comedy deaths. I don't have any childhood sadness. If anything, I could say I was over-loved and that stand-up comedy was the only way of replacing the level of attention I gained from my mother's constant mollycoddling when I left the family home.

I wish my mum had forgotten to pick me up from school just once or failed to put my favourite chocolate bar (Rocky) in my lunch box, but alas, it all went frustratingly perfectly. The result is an entirely non-edgy adult. I'm a totally smooth human sphere. If you bought this book expecting a chapter where I suddenly go off the rails and start doing heroin direct from prostitutes' buttholes, you'll be sorely disappointed, but I'm not going to stop you if you want to head out and do it yourself.

My parents divorced when I was five but I was too young to be angsty, angry or sad because I was cleverly distracted by multiplied Christmas presents. Mum has that 'single mother' fire in her eyes. She's unbelievably caring, but if you hurt me or my brother she will fuck you up. She would, of course, find a delightful Penny Dommett way of doing it. Like poison a quiche* or something.

Once I got a tweet from someone saying:

@joeldommett your so unfunny I actually want to stab you #cunt

---

* Wow, I really had no idea how to spell quiche. I am going to take you through my attempts: keeche, kishe, keyshh and Ke$ha. In the end, I Googled 'middle-class savoury tart'. The first result was just a picture of Mary Berry. I'm sorry, Mary, blame Google.

Some people get so angry. They sit at home and shout with their angry typing fingers when their shit football team loses or their mum doesn't put a Rocky in their lunchbox. I enjoyed the additional hashtag as if he was trying to get it trending. I love an insult with a modern twist.

In my view, the worst possible action you can take in these online scenarios is to retort. If you reply it gives the uncouth cyberbully the attention they crave. Although I discovered first hand that there's one thing worse than replying. When your mother replies on your behalf.

@Pennydommett: I think you'll find it's 'you're' not 'your' #cunt

A small taste of some internet quiche poison.

The other important person Rose was to meet that day was Lily.

Lily had been my best mate since we were eleven years old. She was short and feisty with brown, bobbed, partially matted hair – like Dora the Explorer dragged through a bush. She was a real-life tomboy who was immediately better at all the clichéd boy things than me, including tree climbing, skateboarding, fighting, spitting and wearing your bag right.*

---

* Wearing your bag right was such an unbelievable pressure in our school. One strap, two straps, one strap diagonally, on the front like a baby carrier, maybe on your head like a Kenyan lady?! God, it was so stressful. If you were not ahead of the bag curve you were immediately branded 'gay', a word thrown around way too thoughtlessly in our school as an insult.

Lily was even superior to me at the ultimate manliness litmus test – football. She would throw herself around the pitch, weaving around the boys, stripping them of their masculinity as she evaded capture. I loved playing football in school but only because the football boots sounded like tap shoes on the concrete. I really enjoyed that specific part of the game that was post-changing room and pre-pitch. Most kids these days want to be Lionel Messi. I wanted to be Lionel Blair.

The classic, old-as-time story arc would see me and Lily end up together years later after a messy breakup and drunken heart to heart, but we have always been very clear on how much we disgust each other sexually. We became bestest amigos before I could even conceive that a lady was a desirable thing. We would run, climb, roll and jump together and I would feel completely numb to the fact she was a person of the opposite sex. She was just another human like me with slightly longer hair who went in a different football changing room before tap dancing.

We never flirted, fondled or French-kissed. However, 'almost kissing' was one of our favourite in-jokes. When one of us would happen to drop a rare compliment into a conversation the other would immediately undermine it by leaning in for a kiss, gazing longingly into the other's eyes, then when the distance between us was merely an inch, close enough to feel their breath on your lip, quickly retract and announce, 'Sorry, I completely misread the situation,' then laugh uncontrollably for way too long. This was nonstop fun for about three years of school. When the joke became less effective, we tried it on other people. It was odd to move in to intimately kiss classmates then pull away, at a time when everyone in our year was starting to kiss properly. There was clearly more fun to be had with committing and kissing someone but Lily and I wouldn't realise that until a few years after everyone else because we were too busy finding not kissing people hilarious.

I first met Lily when she bravely intercepted a fight between me and the designated school bully, Chris. By 'fight' I mean he was throwing punches at me while I stretched his jumper. That was my classic fight move: head down, eyes closed, hold on to their jumper and hope for the best. I didn't call them 'fights'; I preferred the term 'fisticuffs', which was much of the reason why I was a target in the first place.

Chris was one of those kids at our school who was on an entirely different level of naughty. He was never in any classes; he just seemed to wander into the playground at lunch, punch me then leave. That seemed to be the only thing on his curriculum.* He had the classic nineties bully costume – an undercut and a huge disregard for the formalities of the school uniform. The worst part was never the punching. Rarely would anyone in our school fights get physically hurt. The painful part was that everyone would gather to watch. There's nothing more exciting to lift the repetitive tedium of lunch and lessons than good ol' fisticuffs, complete with a large circle of jeering teenagers quickly developing around the altercation, baying for blood. If you see an excitable circle of people, it's generally either a fist battle or a dance battle. I was built to lose both.

---

* The joke was on him eventually because UCAS don't accept that as a valid qualification to gain entry into university.

It's sad when I think back. Chris's surname changed on four occasions in the time we were at secondary school so there was clearly some instability at home that led to him being frustrated and angry. I assume the dads kept walking out because they got fed up of buying new jumpers.

I'm making our school sound way worse than it was. It wasn't dangerous like ones in the films that have metal detectors and pupils calling the teachers 'teach'. It had an outstanding Ofsted rating, probably because we were pre-warned by a teacher that 'Ofsted are coming this week so you better fucking behave'. Occasionally it got a little edgy when a teacher would spin his chair around, sit on it back to front like the Britney Spears 'Stronger' video and talk about gateway drugs. I clearly didn't listen because it wasn't until I was twenty-one that I realised that a gateway drug wasn't a drug that you purchase in a gateway.

One day, after a good stint of Chris's abuse, I gazed into the mirror after washing my face like in a music video on Kerrang! TV, and said, 'Enough is enough! I'm going to stand up to this injustice!' This is another example of my fancy vocabulary that made me an obvious victim for fisticuffs.

I was not going to endure this any longer. I was determined to make it stop – but how?

Most kids would learn to fight or get an older brother to step in. Not me. I bought some nunchucks from a guy in school called Tim. He was a quiet boy and kept himself to himself but strangely at fourteen years old he had the body of a Greek god. I was inspired. For those of you less versed in films from the Orient, nunchucks are a simple device comprised of two wooden batons connected with a chain. They are a weapon. A deadly weapon in the right hands.

Unfortunately my tiny soft hands were not those hands. I spent countless hours alone in my garden devising and learning fancy new moves, spinning them deftly around and throwing them into the air. I became obsessed with Bruce Lee and would study his nunchuck movie scenes obsessively. The more time I devoted in the garden, the better I got at it. Mum used to call me 'My Little Ninja', which I felt somewhat undermined my aggressive intentions. I should point out these skills were completely untransferable in a fight scenario. It was more of a flamboyant display. It would be like a gymnast entering a street fight with their ribbony stick thing. I would make up elaborate stories while pretending to frighten people with my skills. I had a wonderful imagination and loved creating tall tales in my head.

It was perfect for me. It was a way to dance without anyone knowing you're dancing. It was the opposite of capoeira. Capoeira was a martial art developed in Brazil by slaves in the sixteenth century. They ingeniously made it look like dancing so they could practise without their captors knowing. They were pretending to dance but were secretly fighting. I was pretending to fight but secretly I was dancing.

One day I was out in the garden practising and the last thing I remember was passing the nunchuck under my arm and feeling a strong pain in the back of my head as the wooden baton struck my skull. I slowly woke up in the soft grass. As my dulled vision sharpened I saw my mum leaning over me. My head was thumping like a Slipknot kick drum and the pain was increasingly intense.

'Mum,' I whispered.

Mum smiled at me fondly. 'I think My Little Ninja assassinated himself.'

After a few weeks of intense dance practice I decided I was ready. I acquired my mother's new 'off-limits' JVC camcorder from the technology-themed cupboard in the lounge and on a rare, searingly hot summer's day, I took it out to the garden and made a makeshift tripod by nestling the camera between two boulders in the rockery. Then I pressed record and made a video of myself, alone in front of Mum's beautifully pruned bed of hydrangeas, going through a blistering display of my skills. Satisfied with my performance, I transferred the recording to a VHS tape, walked three miles to Chris's house and posted it through his letterbox. If that wasn't incredible enough, here's what I actually wrote on the front of the tape:

TO CHRIS – THIS IS WHAT I'M CAPABLE OF

It was written in thick, black, angry marker pen, traced over three or four times to gain the desired effect. I'm fairly certain I didn't put the apostrophe between the I and M of 'I'm' but I am trying to right my past wrongs here.

I ran home from Chris's house with a huge beaming smile from ear to ear, never slowing down, never frowning. This video was going to be the end of the fear, the closed eyes and the jumper clutching. I slept like a baby. Probably in my uniform.*

---

* That was a thing that I did. I would dress in my school uniform at night – everything but my tie and shoes – to save time getting

Lunchtime arrived. Chris marched into the playground right on cue. You could set your watch by his bullying. Then he cowered in my presence, knelt down and pleaded that I accept his humble apology.

Obviously that didn't happen. He punched me, I grabbed his jumper and he shouted at the top of his lungs, 'How the fuck do you know where I live?!' I could feel the usual crowd gathering around us as we tussled.

Then the battering suddenly stopped. It couldn't be down to the presence of a teacher because the human circle hadn't dispersed into every corner of the playground. I looked up tentatively, petrified that it was a ruse to land another punch, just in time to see Dora the Explorer solidly push Chris with the power of a *Street Fighter* Hadouken, both tiny hands on his chest. So much might came from such a small source, like pepper, or the British Empire. Chris's legs lifted high in the air and he flew backwards across the people circle. He travelled so far. It was just like a Bruce Lee one-inch punch.

Chris came crashing back to earth physically and metaphorically with a solid hard thump. It was going to bruise heavily. He clearly wanted to burst into tears but there were so many people watching. Small titters of laughter sprang from the gathered circle, growing steadily to a full chorus of guffaws. Chris's bully status was slipping through his tightly clenched fingers. He didn't just get beaten; he got beaten by a girl who was half the size of him, in front of the whole

---

ready in the morning. My mum would wake me up, I'd have some Frosties, then I'd jump on the bus, saving about four minutes' precious sleep.

school. It was perfect. I stood in awe, unable to process the last four seconds. I glanced at Lily like she was a firefighter who had just grabbed me from a burning building. She lifted the corner of her mouth in a half-smile, then winked, turned and walked through the circle, parting it like Peter parting the Red Sea (I haven't read the Bible). Chris got up and limped away and Lily and I stayed friends for the rest of our lives.

I would later find out that Chris didn't have a VHS player so never had the means to watch my video in the first place. He had four different dads *and* no VHS player. His troubled and aggressive nature suddenly made sense.

Anyway, let's bounce back to the trampoline party. Rose, the girl I wanted to be my girlfriend yet still hadn't kissed, was meeting Lily and Penny. The best friend and the mum. Big day. Lily brought the crash mats. Throughout my seventeenth year, the crash mats were a huge part of mine and my friends' daily lives. Once after a fairly standard school day we happened across the Holy Grail for teenagers with a penchant for danger: discarded crash mats. There were three of them: overused, underloved, me-ish in length and Lily-ish in width, all lying in the skip at the back of school ready for collection. They'd been cast aside because they were clearly not legal for children to use any more and had been replaced by mats that fitted the stringent school safety standards, but luckily we salvaged them on their deathbed. We discovered if you put all three together they provided enough sponginess to allow us to leap from huge heights off the stupidest of things, thus providing the best summer ever. We would tie them to the roof of Lily's car and drive from location to location, leaping and flipping off anything we could find: houses, trees, the school building (on weekends) and, after my birthday, my trampoline. On that fateful day we devised a game called Knifey Knifey Crash Mat.

To play this game you will need:

1 x crash mat
1 x trampoline
1 x knife
1 x friend whom you trust

How to play: Place the crash mats on the floor next to a trampoline. Jump as high as you can off the trampoline onto the crash mats in a belly-flop motion. Meanwhile, a friend holds a huge steak knife upright on the crash mat. At the last second the friend pulls away the knife and you land safely. As your belly flop flails through the air on a direct course for the knife you momentarily think you are speeding towards death, then – you don't. That's the game. I expect it's the same feeling you get from bungee jumping at a local fairground or having unprotected sex with a person from *Geordie Shore*. It's hugely fun because it's hugely irresponsible. Please DO NOT attempt this game in your local leisure centre or gym trampette class. Or in fact anywhere.

It was the birthday boy's turn to jump on the trampoline and play some KKCM. Lily held the erect knife firmly on the tired, deflated crash mat. The other partygoers crowded excitedly around the mat and started making a low grumbling 'oooohhhhhh' sound which slowly rose in pitch and volume. It's a popular phenomenon often seen in sport, for instance when a goalkeeper is about to do a goal kick. This universally recognised noise is a wonderful technique to get anyone to do basically anything. If you're feeling unsure or hesitant about doing something, maybe a bungee jump or having sex with someone from *Geordie Shore*, simply start a low and quiet 'oooohhhhhh' and build it to a high-pitched yell. I would also recommend it for marriage proposals. Pitch the question, then get straight in with the noise and the pressure to say yes will be insurmountable.

I climbed atop the trampoline and started bouncing, gradually gaining height. The group started their low persuasive chant, which slowly rose to a full, frenzied shriek. I counted down my bounces before lift-off, waiting to reach optimum height. My heart felt like it was on its own horizontal trampoline, bouncing at a hundred times the speed. One. Two. Three. One more. GO.

I put my weight forward and flew over the trampoline edge towards the mats. The knife stood erect directly below me as my body started to fall towards its tip. Take it away, Lily, please take it away. I closed my eyes and landed face first on the mats. I felt a sudden pain in my stomach. I was panting, breathless, with no air in my lungs. I panicked, turned over and glanced down, convinced I'd been stabbed.

Nothing.

Everyone cheered and Lily held the knife aloft.

Luckily I was just winded* from the lofty belly flop onto

---

* Come to think of it, I don't think I've been 'winded' since then. It's something that just stops when you become an adult. Like

non-regulation crash mats. The relief was unbelievable. What a rush. Still, don't try this at home.

I felt like a cop in a movie who gets shot then reveals a hidden bulletproof vest. I'd never felt so alive! Although let's remember I was yet to have sexual intercourse, so I only really had the elation of opening my Christmas presents and landing a skateboard trick to compare it to. Everyone let out a huge cheer. I looked up at Lily. She lifted the corner of her mouth, smiled and winked in the same way she did that first day we met. I stood up off the mat and Rose leaped in for a hug. I suddenly felt a tiny bit closer to that all-important sexual intercourse. I think I felt a tad cool. Although I think using the word 'tad' before cool entirely negates the cool.

However, the excitement was short-lived as a shriek was ringing out from the kitchen. Mum appeared, bounding out of the house to tell us off. I immediately felt further away from sexual intercourse again. She'd spied us from the kitchen window and was now shouting at us like we were seven. Through gritted teeth I uttered the classic 'Mum, stop embarrassing me in front of my friends' line, but it was too late, the damage was done. To this day I've never heard my mum shout like that again. Now of course I fully understand her anger.

My friends and I were not really into drinking so a quick game of KKCM was how we got our excitement. You could argue that it is dangerous but around 9,000 people a year die in the UK from alcohol-related deaths. You know how many people died of Knifey Knifey Crash Mat? None.

---

dead legs and playing the recorder.

Admittedly 697 died last year from stabbings but crash mat-related stabbings are zero. Probably. I have no proof to back that up.

I thought the stern telling off was surely the end of my chances with Rose but strangely she really didn't seem fazed by it. Maybe being told off by my mother in public made me seem like more of a bad boy. I don't know why rappers don't mention it more to enhance their hard gangster image: 'I did the crime, I've been inside, and I get told off by my mum all the time!'

Banned from KKCM, we spent the rest of my party lying on the crash mats, sharing stories and laughing heartily until darkness fell. Eventually, Mum called from the kitchen that she was going to bed, adding, 'Don't touch the knives!'

Slowly my friends started to leave in their low-category-insurance cars until only Lily and Rose were left. I remember feeling like Lily was perhaps staying a little too long. I never thought about what that meant until I was older. Eventually she said, 'I'll leave you two alone.' We fist-bumped and she left.

The two remaining partygoers sat on the steadily damp-ening mats in the evening dew. I remember thinking there was so much space now that everyone had gone. Now Rose and I were alone, this was technically our first non Spudulike date. The sag of the ancient crash mats may have worked against school safety standards but it worked in my favour that night because the dip in the cushion pushed us young lovebirds together. It was as if the mats were encouraging us to kiss for the first time. We chatted for what seemed like hours. We didn't want to chat, we wanted to kiss, but neither of us were willing to step up to the face and make the first move. Instead, over the few hours that we conversed, we gradually leaned in at terrifically slow, glacial pace. We carried on talking until our faces were stupidly close like two boxers at a weigh-in, pretending to still be caring about our conversation about the merits of the new Green Day album while half an inch away from each other. Our first kiss didn't start with either of us making the first move; it started by both of us talking on each other's lips. We were discussing our top ten Limp Bizkit songs with our faces touching and it seamlessly transitioned into a kiss. It started with a closed-mouth, pursed-lips affair, which very quickly escalated to a disturbingly sloppy teenage snog. At that age you don't yet understand the subtlety of delicate kissing so just go at each other 150 per cent, the way you attack a dripping Mr Whippy.

I felt unbelievably alive for the second time that day and both scenarios involved a hard erect object that's illegal to get out in a school.*

This wasn't my first visit to Snogsville. I don't mean to brag but I'd touched lips with some girls pre-Rose. My first ever non-pillow/hand kiss was with a girl in school everyone called 'Big Chin'. She was named Big Chin for two reasons:

1. Kids are brutal.
2. She had a fucking massive chin.

_____

* I'M TALKING ABOUT MY DICK, EVERYBODY.

Honestly, you could hang baubles off it like a Christmas tree branch. It was insane. It was odd because she had an attractive face, but there was just this unfortunate hook at the bottom of it, similar to one you might find on the back of a toilet door. She was oddly beautiful. Like a Picasso or James McAvoy. 'BC', with her ski-jump face, wasn't a girl of many words, but those she did choose to utter were strangely cutting and cold. She was wonderfully friendly and smiley in her silence then she'd carefully pick a couple of words to destroy your day. We used to do after-school cross country together and she used highlighter pens to colour the front of her long blonde centrally parted hair. It was the coolest thing I'd seen since I saw Lionel Blair live at the Hippodrome. It was creative with an edge of wayward naughtiness and I found it utterly intriguing. I was still at that age that I didn't understand my sexual feelings.

We first talked at cross country. I say talked, what I mean is I rambled at her like Forrest Gump on a bench. She was at the head of the pack and I was very much the least talented of the runts. If we were wolves I would have definitely been killed by a raccoon or the cold.

When you're a teenager you approach relationships in an entirely different order to fully grown humans. I was obsessed with holding hands. It was such a huge deal. If you held hands you were going to be together forever. Holding hands was first base and then kissing was second base. It swaps round as an adult. If you try to hold hands before kissing, the lady will quickly cut loose and run in the opposite direction, assuming that you are trying to kidnap her.

One night after cross country, I plucked up the courage to grab BC's hand. It would have made more sense if we were together, scared on a roller coaster, or if we were brother and sister at our dad's funeral, but in reality we'd just finished running four miles and were waiting silently outside school for our parents to pick us up. (We finished early, my mum wasn't late. Of course she wasn't.) Amazingly she didn't pull her hand away, scream like she was on a roller coaster or cry like she was at her dad's funeral. She just held on. We didn't move or speak until ten or so minutes later when she saw her dad's car pull around the corner. She let go, slid off the wall and said, 'I think my dad would hate you.' There were those ice-cold words I had forgotten to expect. I didn't really care. I'd reached first base.

We graduated to holding hands in silence at lunchtime.* Still no kiss. I was petrified of that second base. I was practising 'snogging' my pillow most nights and would maybe have a lick of my hand a few times a day too. I once kissed a closed door. I had no idea whether the real thing was more pillow/hand or door so I tried to cover all manner of materials in preparation. We were not kissing, not talking, not having sex. We were like an unhappily married couple in their seventies, not teenagers at the start of an unknown journey into all things exciting and tingly. I had no idea what she was thinking while we were standing with our palms locked. As for me, my inner monologue was constantly telling me to

---

* This book seems to suggest I only court women over lunch. I promise later in life I learned to woo while not holding a stackable wooden tray.

just lean in and kiss her, but my body didn't seem to want to listen. We would eat in silence then when the lunchbreak was coming to an end my mind would start to race and I'd repeat to myself, 'The bell is about to ring, just do it,' until the bell rang, at which point she would say something like, 'You look ugly today,' then leave.

After two weeks of zero kisses and her chipping slowly away at my self-esteem, I decided today had to be the day. Lunchtime arrived. We held hands in the queue as per usual, we ate in silence, then, finally, the bell rang out. We stood up, I looked at her, I locked in and went in for the kill. Her high-lighted hair acted as a runway light to guide me in to a successful snog landing. My fresh tender heart was beating so hard my school tie was flapping. 'Just do what you've practised,' I thought. 'Commit.' I leaned in. I kept leaning. I leaned further. I had to take a step forward. I had started the lean too far away. I took a step then continued the lean.

I opened my mouth wide and unleashed my tongue too far away from her face, giving her an unfortunate amount of time to decide that she didn't want this wet jellyfish stinging her mouth. I committed too much. I went in all gums blazing. She didn't seem to be reciprocating with her kiss prep. 'It's OK, Joel, commit,' I continued to repeat in my mind. Her eyes began to widen in disgust as I got closer. 'COMMIT, JOEL, COMMIT!' After what felt like an unbelievably long approach, contact was finally made. Although by the time I got to her she had decided to not open her mouth at all and I simply licked her along her lips like a cow cleaning its newborn calf. She was rightly disgusted and used her massive chin to shoehorn my face off hers. It was just like how my mum used to flick the dog poo over the garden fence with a spade. It was a disaster. She walked away to her lesson. She dumped me the next day and told the whole school I was a terrible kisser.

Technically it was more of a non-consensual lick but I still count this as my very first kiss.

Between then and my seventeenth birthday party I had to prove to myself and the entire school that I wasn't orally inept. I will entirely blame Big Chin for my poor GCSEs performance. I should have been at home revising but instead I was panicking about kissing and finding more objects in my room to lick.

I would love to say I lost my virginity that night Rose and I kissed for the first time on the crash mats but alas I didn't. That night was three long snog-filled months later.

Rose had already had sex with one guy so that made it slightly easier, as it wasn't an entirely clean sheet. (Metaphorically, not physically. In reality my sheets were perfectly clean because Mum wouldn't have it any other way.) I was happy that at least one team had some past experience. When playing chess it's preferable that you both know how to play but it's doable if only one of you knows because they can teach the other. However, if neither of you knows, then you're probably playing Snakes and Ladders.

Rose and I had become very much a couple in those three months after my seventeenth birthday. Gradually, she started to stay over, but I, like in most youthful relationships, was made to stay in the lounge. Yet in the night I would sneak into my room where Rose was sleeping.* I would tiptoe to my own boudoir, push the door ajar and slip inside the room I knew so well. The walls were splashed with large aggressive posters of bands, films and skateboarders, all of course bought from Virgin Megastore at a sweet 25 per cent discount. I'd squeeze into the skinny confines of the single bed, breaking the one rule that the name advises. We would feverishly kiss, lying on top of each other like two stacked lunch trays, locked in to each other, unable to move for fear of falling out. For the first time I was in my bed kissing something that kissed back. I couldn't help but think my pillow was jealous. I would turn it over the way an adulterous husband would turn over a bedside family photo.

During those first months we moved slowly and steadily from first base to second, then second to an unsure third. The bases had moved now to the more traditional sense. They shift as you get older and your moral compass changes. Every night we would adventure slightly further than the night before, then quickly return to home base to ponder on our findings before heading out once more the next time, incrementally further again. It was like *The Shawshank Redemption*, where every night he tunnels further away from the cell, then returns unnoticed before the morning. During one midnight

---

* That sounds creepier than I meant it to. I promise I was asked. Everything is creepy if one person isn't into it. The more romantic it is if they are into you, the creepier it is if they are not. Turning up at someone's house unannounced, buying them a stuffed animal, skywriting and getting a tattoo of their name are all excellent examples of things you should only do if the person loves you, otherwise you'll just look like a serial killer.

mission we landed just shy of fourth base and agreed to make the leap on our next rendezvous. The next night the big evening had arrived. It was time to climb through the sewer pipe of excrement (that is what happens in *Shawshank Redemption*; I am not insinuating anal sex was in any way involved. It would be a bizarre turn of events if we decided to skip fourth base and go directly to fifth).

I performed a faux yawn while saying goodnight to Mum as a realistic flourish, then went to the lounge for pretend sleep. I waited for thirty minutes, twiddling my thumbs and imagining Rose was doing the same, then I grabbed my Velcro Megaphobia wallet and fished inside for the lonesome condom that lay nestled amongst the needless receipts.* Lily had sold this condom to me for 50p before swimming on a Friday because she had spent her locker money on a new drink in the vending machine called Red Bull and now she couldn't stop shaking. It seemed to me like a very reasonable price at the time and, thinking back now, that is an absolute bargain. I think the never-before-experienced level of caffeine had affected her negotiating skills.

I hadn't taken the condom out of my wallet since I put it in. It was waiting for the right time before it was to be used, like a latex superhero in hiding. I sat up in my boxer shorts, my hairless thighs stuck to the clammy leather sofa.

---

* Megaphobia is Europe's largest wooden roller coaster. It's a cool coaster name but ultimately it just means 'fear of the word mega'. I got it from Oakwood and I think you will agree it was a very cool place to keep baby stoppers.

I took out the condom and made my move from my temporary lounge bedroom to my real bedroom where a real person awaited me for some real-life, real sex. On the royal blue packet it said 'Durex', then below that 'Extra Safe', then below *that* 'Best Before 02/01'. Wait, what?! Best Before? Condoms have a Best Before?! That means Worst After! It's made of rubber; it's not whole milk or freshly sliced ham! I panicked and assumed it immediately turned to dust as soon as you put it on your penis. The good price suddenly made sense. Lily had sold me a perished prophylactic. Did she want to ruin my first sexual experience on purpose? No, I doubt it. I'm sure she just wanted to eat fifty penny sweets or five pre-inflation Freddo's. The virginity would have to wait untaken until another day. I crept like a cartoon burglar into the bedroom to give Rose the bad news.

'You'll never guess what,' I whispered.

'What?' she answered.

'My condom has gone off,' I said, assuming she was going to be utterly frustrated at my stupidity and tell me to run back to my sofa. Instead she said, 'I have loads, do you still want to do it?' in a calm manner. It definitely sounded like I made up the excuse. I think she thought that I was scared. I mean I was, but that's not the point. I barked 'YES!' while making a fist and pulling my elbow back in a classic teenage celebration.

'Shhhh.' Rose looked beyond my shoulder through the door crack, listening for Mum's footsteps. Nothing. She delved into her bag and revealed what looked like one condom, then unpinched her back finger and ten or so connected clones fell from beneath it. A swinging line of baby preventers that looked ironically like the kind of reel of boring baby photos that adults like to produce from their wallets.

We de-clothed. I ripped open the condom and unravelled it. First mistake. You are really not supposed to unravel it. I should have read the instructions but as a man you are not supposed to read the instructions on how to put together an Ikea cupboard let alone how to put a dick-shaped thing on your dick. I proceeded to try and pull it over my penis like a doctor pulls on a rubber glove before surgery. Eventually it was on-ish.

Then – it happened. We did it. Sex actually happened and my God it was efficiently brief. I had no idea what I was doing. I was literally taking a stab in the dark. It may sound silly but until then I honestly assumed all men had sex with their hands behind their heads like the way a policeman asks you to stand when they arrest you. I don't really know where I got the idea from – maybe I saw it in a film or it was in a sexy science textbook – but I thought that was meant to be the comfiest position. Now I was doing it for real that seemed hugely impractical. It is incredibly difficult to do sex hands-free. It's like being on Megaphobia; you need to grab on to something otherwise you feel like you're going to fall out and if you do, it means you're too short for the ride.

Afterwards, I lay down on top of her because the single bed gave us very little choice. I was out of breath. It was like I'd run a full cross-country in fifteen seconds. My thudding heart was blending with Rose's, creating a cluster of out-of-time beats like rain on a tin roof, or the transition between two songs performed by a shit DJ. As my breath returned, so did a wave of intense elation. If could sing I would have belted out a tune, if I could dance I would have pirouetted from the sheets. Unfortunately for me my only talent was nunchucks and post-coital that didn't seem appropriate.

I immediately jumped to conclusions and assumed this profound euphoria must be the thing that everyone talks about in songs and movies – so the words 'I love you' spilled out of my mouth directly into her ear. I now obviously know that it wasn't the feeling of love at all, it was just the feeling of sex. She smiled and didn't say it back. Rightly so, really.

I never told Lily, or anyone really. I was never someone to talk about my sexual experiences. I didn't really have anyone to tell. I always felt it seemed braggy, like the day after a lad has had a night out and they list off all the drinks they consumed.

She would say those all-important three words a few months later and we stayed together for two years before she left me for James, a guy who was effortlessly cool with bleached tips. You just assumed he had a leather jacket even if he didn't. That's how cool he was. It broke my tiny undeveloped heart into smithereens.* I drove in circles around town in my beloved Citroën Saxo** with Lily, listening to ear-blisteringly loud music,

---

* Nobody can be sure how big a smithereen is but it is implied that it is lots. You can't break something into two smithereens.
** I spent most of my Virgin earnings on my car. By Virgin earnings I mean my salary from working at Virgin Megastores, not my earnings from simply being a virgin. Unfortunately for teenage me there wasn't a virginity bursary. I had the car lowered closer

crying my eyes out. Most people with deafening stereo systems in Bristol listened to jungle. By this I mean the music, not the relaxing sounds of endangered frogs or me and Carol Vorderman having a natter (I will talk about that more later). I listened to metal when I was feeling upbeat, but when I was heartbroken it was musicals. Imagine hearing the booming bass from a lowered, glowing sexy-mobile half a mile away, then as it crawls closer, avoiding any speed bumps or potholes, you realise it's playing 'Do You Hear the People Sing?' from *Les Misérables*. Welcome to eighteen-year-old me. I was devastated. Rose didn't stay with James for long and we started hanging out again every now and then. We would have sex sometimes too which was great for me because I was petrified of having sex with anyone else. I wanted to get back together but Rose said we had just drifted apart.

I was at the lowest ebb of my very, very easy eighteen-year life. Rose had become the thorn in my side.* What do you

---

to the floor, replaced my fourteen-inch alloy wheels with seventeen-inch ones and put green lights beneath the car which perfectly lit the potholes that would pop my stupid, impractically thin tyres. None of this made it go any faster but it looked like it could and that's all that mattered. I installed a subwoofer too. This makes your stereo sound ridiculously loud, deep and bass-y, all for the small sacrifice of £300 and the entirety of your boot space. From inside the car the songs blasted out full of bass; from outside the car you just heard every loose nut and bolt on the vehicle vibrating. It sounded like a moving, throbbing Nokia 3310. It was so almost cool.

* Great stuff there, Joel.

do when you're feeling frustrated at the injustice of the complicated nature of love but you have no creative talents to express those feelings? I could see no other option than to report the inner anguish in a written diary. I bought a thick-lined hardback notebook from WHSmith on my lunch-break from Virgin Megastore and started writing a stream of nightly adolescent ramblings. I clearly thought the inner anguish was going to last longer as the book I bought was massive but I ceased after a few months when I'd started to recover from my relationship torment and buried the diary in my plethora of unread books and unwatched VHS videos. I forgot about it until thirteen years later.

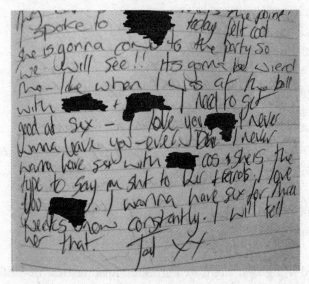

Every entry starts with 'Hey JD' and most end with 'Sincerely, Joel'. I was writing letters to myself. The letter format is a nice one, I can't fault young Joel for that, but when the serious formatting of a Jane Austen-style letter to a lover away at war (I've never read Jane Austen, has it got a war in it?) has the ramblings of an Emo eighteen-year-old between its hello and goodbye, it's truly fascinating.

I knew that there was more love to come. I was ready to settle with the first but there was so much more out there. I'm glad Rose broke up with me, otherwise I wouldn't have written a diary and this book would be worse. I wasn't a teenager any more – I was a man. This relationship had pushed me into becoming an adult and as a result of the breakup I decided to move to where all the adults live – London. I had to stop being pushed around and stand up for myself.

In 2012, Chris – the bully – got in touch via Twitter:

@Chris_3433: Hey do you remember me? We went to school together. Tose were the days. [sic]

@Joeldommett: I remember you used to punch me lots. Tose were not the days.

@Chris_3433: ha! We were kids. You kinda deserved it tho right?!?!!?!

I had a gig that night at Latitude music festival in Suffolk. Four thousand people were in attendance and I got the whole audience to scream, 'Chris is a cunt! Chris is a cunt! Chris is a cunt!' I filmed it on my mobile phone, then sent it to him on Twitter with a caption that read:

TO CHRIS – THIS IS WHAT I'M CAPABLE OF NOW
#CUNT

30 April 2004

Hey JD,
   The most mental two days of my life to date. I
found out that Rose had sex with James, BITCH. So I
went a bit mental and me and Rose had a big talk. I
pretty much just numbed myself to her. She said it
meant nothing to her, but it meant a lot to me and
showed me how much I meant to her. I wish you
were with her last. I needed to write so badly. I
fucking hate the fact that I still write about her and I
can't just be myself again. Just me and Taekwondo. I
don't need a woman, Taekwondo is more than
enough DEAL WITH IT BITCH.
Sincerely, Joel

'That was longer than we both were anticipating,' says Hannah after politely weathering the lengthy tale.

'I wish Rose could have said the same,' I say. I've never told that story about Rose to anyone before, let alone a stranger (and by proxy an entire readership). It's not that I was embarrassed about it, it's just – nobody really asked. Maybe I should just tell her about last night? Rodrigo has been ages with the drinks. I'd picked a random gin-based cocktail that had the least amount of things I hate in it and Hannah picked some margarita hybrid. I am seconds away from giving the castanets a click to get his attention when I see them start to arrive from the bar on a tray, courtesy of Rodrigo. One cocktail is packed with accessories – celery stick, tiny umbrella, fruit and a sparkler that is lighting up his stupid face. Can you even buy them outside of gunpowder plot season? The other is very plain.

Rodrigo sidles closer, throwing his hips from side to side at every step, knowing how tight his trousers are. He places the tray gently on the table and hands me the drink with ADHD. Of course it is mine. How was I to know? If the menu had pictures I would have ordered a cocktail that represents me: laid back, chilled and weak. Not an ostentatious drag queen on fireworks night. I swear Rodrigo has done this on purpose. He is sabotaging the date. Little does he know I am sabotaging it myself by telling Hannah lengthy stores about my virginity.

I take a sip. It tastes of bonfire night. I take the sparkler out, feeling naughty holding it without a glove. I am very excited about the tiny umbrella. It's impossible to not be excited by this thing, with its tiny moving parts and thin paper canopy.

'Who was your first?' I ask. It only seems fair to ask since I've just given her a lengthy virginity TedTalk. Hannah doesn't hesitate and it is a good story. She really knows how to structure a tale. She also knows how to edit it to a decent packable date size, unlike me. I've never been this candid with a stranger before and it feels so . . . strange. I assume that's going to be it, but Hannah has other ideas.

'OK, who was your second?'

#2 The Difficult Second Album

After sixth form I was a little lost. I didn't have any particular flair for any topic in school. There was no glaringly obvious career route. I also didn't fancy university because I didn't love anything enough to study it for the minimum prison sentence for kidnapping (three years). But I had to do something. My friends were a creative bunch; they were all foregoing university to pursue their dreams of being photographers and musicians. So I thought I would move to London and give acting a go. I know. I was one of those pricks. I thought it was that easy. I thought you just moved to London and started immediately being in movies, snogging Sienna Miller. I had no idea how hard it was.

I signed up to the National Youth Theatre and travelled up to London as a naïve Bristolian for its reputable summer course. Three weeks later I returned, pretending to like red wine, Shakespeare and vocal warm-ups.

I'm easily swayed. I was an intensely insecure young person and my way of dealing with it was to emulate anyone who seemed like they had their shit together. I was like Mystique in *X-Men* but less sexy, blue and flexy.

The person who had the privilege of me latching on to them at NYT was Toby. He was my newest friend, the ship to my barnacle. He was a tall Caucasian concoction of edgy urban rapper and holistic, yoga-obsessed actor, all bundled inside a name suited to a posh royal baby. Toby grew up in south-east London so was gifted with a beautifully thick Stormzy accent (or 'Grime-zy' as my mum calls him), yet he meditated every morning and loved listening to Etta James.

He had a past filled with the street-based japes you would expect growing up around an area of London only now starting to find its feet, most of which I could not comprehend having grown up around a provincial village farm. He came to visit my mum's house once and made her stop the car so he could get out and look at a cow. That is a true story.

By the time I met Toby he had almost completely shed the edginess. The only element that remained of his old self other than his cool-as-fuck accent was a blurry, old tattoo on the nape of his neck that spelled 'MC'. He'd got it because, literally, he was an MC. In the endz it's that simple. I'll assume the other members had 'bassist', 'backing singer' and 'guy who pretends to DJ' tattooed on them.

I really wanted to be an edgy actor like him. Unfortunately for me I didn't have the upbringing to make it possible. It was too late for me. The worst thing that had happened to me in my life was when my mum didn't give me a lift into town. I was destined to be an actor bereft of edge.

After the summer course, Toby offered me a room in his house for £60 a month. A MONTH. IN LONDON. That's how much it costs to live in Gravesend. No offence, Gravesend, but your town is a bit shit. It combines two utterly joyless words, Graves and End, and when I went there I was like, 'Yeah, that fits.'

I foolishly still thought £60 was too much because anything more than a gratis room in your mum's house feels expensive. I'd never really bartered before but I plucked up the courage to give it a go and asked, 'Can I barter?' 'No,' he replied. My debut barter was a disaster.

I agreed to the £60 and we shook hands awkwardly. I wrongly assumed Toby would expect more than a standard handshake so I went in with the classic 'clenched non-violent greet fist' (or CNVGF as they call it on the streets). He went straight in for a hug instead and we embraced with my arm awkwardly caught in the middle of us like it was hanging on a sling.

I moved to Toby's house in London shortly after. I had one small suitcase full of a few clothes, a pair of pants, a pair of socks and a pair of nunchucks. It wasn't really a case of packing light, I just packed badly.

With my countryside roots and Toby's urban edginess, living together felt like the plot of a sitcom that would be promising but ultimately get cancelled after the first series because the commissioner of the channel changed and nobody would vouch for it.

Toby wouldn't be there for long. He got accepted into the

prestigious LIPA, the Liverpool Institute of Performing Arts. Of course he did. How could any panel of industry experts turn away such a rare gem as the T-Dog?

I auditioned too but didn't get in. In fact, I didn't even get to the second round and there were four rounds which means I was not even a quarter of the amount of great as Toby. Now I think about it I was more upset about losing my barnacle buddy for three years than not being accepted. I didn't even get to the round with the judges' houses (it happens in X Factor so I assume it happens at drama school too).

Before he left I asked him for some acting advice.

'You can never find a character until you have found yourself,' he said seriously in his low rumbling south-east London tone. I wanted to paint it on my wall as a proverb. He was so damn wise.

Finding yourself was hard and I didn't really want to find me 'cos I was boring. Why not find the nearest cool person and be them instead? Maybe while Toby was away I could simply adopt his persona for a bit and people would think I was talented like him.

He left for LIPA and I began my transition while still living in a small room in his house. I dropped my Bristolian accent and laid on a really thick London twinge. I had a full wardrobe upheaval and began dressing like Toby too. He always wore tracksuit trousers, white T-shirts and trainers, the standard attire for a UK prison inmate or a Sunday hangover. I assumed that's what successful actors dressed like so I made a trip to Primark and grabbed everything I needed from the pyjama department. I began trialling my new persona at acting classes and, you will never believe it, but it honestly bloody worked! I was feeling so much more confident as . . . not me. I was method acting an actor to be better at acting. I suppose to a degree I do it onstage as a comedian now, pretending to be a more confident, more energetic, more outgoing person who is, well, funnier than me, but adopting a persona offstage is much stranger. They were teaching me acting in the acting classes but they had no idea I was acting already.

I slowly started slipping into my new persona when I was alone, shouting 'Nah, blud' when someone made the wrong choice on *Who Wants to Be a Millionaire?*

You would think I would drop my schiz-faux-phrenia when I met with people who knew the old legitimate Joel, but I didn't. I returned home for my twenty-first-birthday party, which was held in a marquee in my mum's garden. It was basically a wedding without the relationship commitment. We did speeches. I'm not even kidding. I have a recording of it and it is an incredible thing to behold. I command the room confidently in modern urban cockney dialect while my Bristolian friends and family around me smile and nod, assuming it is a joke. You simply cannot pretend you're edgy while you are doing a speech inside a marquee in your mother's garden.

Even my later diary entries changed from 'Hey JD' to 'Yo JD'. That's how committed I was to faux-Toby.

Then the unbelievable happened. Me and my fake persona got a job. It was a play at the Theatre Royal Stratford East called *Bashment*. I played a gay, Bristolian, white (obviously) rapper (less obviously). It was a complicated month for me personality-wise as I was a Bristolian pretending to be from London who was pretending to be from Bristol.

I made the bold decision that my character would don the traditional African hairstyle of cornrows. When white people do it they sometimes rebrand it 'boxer braids' and it is usually met with an acceptable level of criticism. It worked in the confines of the play, but it obviously wasn't something I could just remove after rehearsals, so the cornrows remained, secured on my scalp for the remainder of the play's duration. My edgy persona had tipped over the garden fence from a harmless impression of a white urban friend into full cultural appropriation in a matter of months. The rows had to be painfully redone every three days as my soft, straight, Caucasian barnet would slip out of the weave very quickly. You know why? White people are not supposed to do it. It's almost like my hair was trying to push it out to save me from the embarrassment but little old me would ignore all its sensible efforts and just get it redone.

Not long after I debuted my cornrows I started kissing men. It was a big month for Dommett. It was in the play, I should say; I didn't swap sexual preferences that quickly. Although having said that, if Toby was gay I would have already blown fifty dudes in an alley. That's how committed I was to becoming him to become a good actor.

Preparing for my debut man-kiss had me riddled with anxiety. It wasn't going to be a peck on the lips. It was the crescendo of the play, the moment the audience had all been waiting for, when two unrequited admirers of the same gender passionately threw all caution to the wind and showed their intense love for one another, so it would be a huge anti-climax if we just shook hands. A full snog was absolutely necessary and that's what I was going to bloody do. I started to worry that men maybe did it differently. Did they rotate their tongues a different direction to 'the straights' the way water disappears down a plughole anti-clockwise in Australia? These were unchartered saliva waters and I was about to jump in head-first. When the first rehearsal for the play came I was back in the panting panic of the playground with Big Chin. My mouth was suddenly devoid of any moisture. Luckily I knew seconds later someone was going to lick my mouth wet again. The last pre-smooch line was uttered and I went in. It was normal. With added stubble. It was like locking lips with an unshaven lady leg or astro turf. We grabbed each other's faces and licked the shit out of each other (I mean that figuratively, obviously). The actor on the receiving end was called Vince and he was a real-life actual, living, breathing homosexual, so he was a dab hand at it and I just followed his vibe. He was driving the bus and I was happily sitting at the front on the top deck pretending to drive.

I really enjoyed it, it was beautifully liberating.

It did make me realise, however, that at that particular point in my life I wasn't of a homosexual persuasion. I'm still not, but I don't want to completely rule it out just in case one day it rears (pun intended) its rainbow head. I watch gay pornography every six months to see if it's my thing. I call it my biannual bi-anal. Until now it's not really been my vibe so I just finish watching it and say 'see you in six months, Pedro', or whatever their name is. It's good to look at the gate and realise you don't want to go in. Most people won't even approach the gate. How do you know you don't want to live in Soho if you've never been? I walked around a bit and wandered back to south-east London, discovering that I liked it in Soho and I loved the people there but I wouldn't want to live there. That was all a metaphor.

During the *Bashment* tech (short for technical) rehearsal, we slowly but steadily mapped through the performance move by move while the technical (long for tech) staff programmed the array of lights to make sure we didn't act in the dark. It was hot and boring. I leaned against the proscenium arch like anyone in the background of any scene in *Grease* waiting for my next instruction. A tall, slender figure walked towards me, silhouetted against the bright lights, which illuminated her from behind and emanated around her outline, like an angel welcoming me to the gates of heaven. I lifted my hand to shade some of the light to make out who the angel was, like the way you look at an eclipse if you've forgotten to wear the special glasses. As she stepped outside the light, I could see her for the first time. She was dressed entirely in black like a ninja. She was the sexiest Milk Tray man I'd ever seen. She knelt down next to me and fiddled with a coloured light near my foot.

'I'm Joel,' I said, my voice quivering like I was answering a question on the first day at school and I'd just accidentally shouted 'Mum' instead of 'Miss'.

'I'm Iris,' she said. I searched deep into my mind pockets to find something interesting to say but all I could find after a lengthy silence while she fixed her light was: 'Cool.'

She was hot, I was boring.

For the next few days I went about trying to spend as much of my time as possible casually bumping into Iris for a chat. I discovered quickly that it's frustratingly challenging to let a lady know you have feelings for her while constantly kissing men in front of them. I would go as far as saying it was problematic. How did I let her know that I was actually interested in the people with nipples that work?

I tried casually being good at opening jars around her and talking about football but I knew gay people were capable of opening jars perfectly well and also enjoy football. The other flaw in this plan is that I am terrible at opening jars and hate football so I was just digging my own sweet gay hole a little deeper. I was the perfect clichéd undercover redundant nipple lover.

After opening night, while tipsy on red wine that I was still pretending to like to fit in with the actors, I decided to take the leap and tell her once and for all that I was interested in her kind, by creating another entirely different problem.

'I have a girlfriend,' I said nonchalantly at a place in the conversation that didn't make any sense whatsoever. I'd jumped out of my homosexual hole and immediately into a new heterosexual one.

'OK,' she said, frustratingly unfazed.

The play remained at the theatre for a full month, which I was very glad of because it took so long to get the lights right each night and it was enough time to pretend to break up with my imaginary girlfriend and tell Iris I was back on the market.

I hadn't imagined a scenario this complex since I was six. Most children that age have an imaginary friend. I had an imaginary married couple. They were called Mr and Mrs Moncaster and they sat in the corner of my room and ignored me. The beauty of a faux friend is you can imagine anything or anyone you like. I chose to imagine an African couple that just didn't like me. Yep, they were African too. I felt like my mum was a little jealous of them as I basically imagined an African family had adopted me. The exact opposite of Madonna. Essentially this was the first time in my life that I started making up stories and since then in one way or another I've never really stopped.

Why couldn't I just be honest? I was sure this new friendship was not going to lead anywhere further because steering around a complete fabrication is an awful start. I continued the deceit for a while, planted some tiny little made-up seeds that it wasn't going well, then eventually I told her I had broken up with my imaginary girlfriend – by which point I had made up a name, where she lived and why we were not right for each other. I made it an unnecessarily epic breakup. It ended with her shouting, 'You aint' wurf it, Joel!' in an empty London square at night outside a pub. I almost definitely lifted it directly from *EastEnders*.

After the final night of the play, my tolerance for red wine had increased and Iris and I chatted in the theatre till the bar closed. Iris was unfathomably calm about absolutely everything. You got the impression if you told her aliens existed she would shrug her shoulders and say 'cool'. She never got excited or frustrated or angry; she was always composed. If she were in a horror movie she would just tell everyone to not go back in the house in a really carefree manner and calm everyone's screaming.

She didn't smile much but when she did, it really meant something, like when the sun comes out in Scotland.

I waited for her bus with her and when we saw the N4 approaching we finally, after a month of setbacks and stupid dishonesty, kissed under the shelter while the light east London rain fell around us. I'd become used to kissing the scratchier faces of men so her skin felt odd and smooth like when you stroke one of those bald cats.

I still had my London accent, by the way. She was kissing a guy in cornrows, who had spent a month kissing guys, who had a false accent and who'd been in a false relationship, while waiting for a bus in the rain. What a lucky girl.

The play finished and I figuratively and literally let my hair down. I was now an out-of-work actor, or, as they are known in the business – an actor.

My second audition was for the pièce de résistance of the pretending-to-be-other-people business: a feature film. In the casting I was required to say one line and I don't want to blow my own tuba but I spoke the shit out of it. I was fantastic at auditions with not many lines to learn and even better at the ones where there was nothing to say at all. My character was called 'Train Soldier' and that tells you everything you need to know about the person I was playing. I was an army man whose primary mode of transport in the film was aboard a locomotive. I was sent the script which had 'TOP SECRET' written in large letters across every page. This of course is entirely counter-productive. It makes anyone who happens to find it think it's hugely important, instead of assuming that it's a sheet of noth-ingness paper. If it's truly top secret just write 'Tax Return 2015–16' on the cover and nobody will ever pick it up.

I got the part. This was two out of two. A 100 per cent success rate for me and my fake accent. This acting malarkey was proving wonderfully easy. I was to be involved in two pages of scenes. Train Soldier meets a lady (I can't remember her character name but it was more subtle than Train Girl) in 1940s Wales. He flirts with her, they have a chat – or as actors call it, 'dialogue' – then they go to the back of the train, have some more dialogue then they 'entwine in passion'. WHAT DOES THAT EVEN MEAN?! Did it mean full sex or just a hug?

They also didn't specify who was playing the part of the lady so I sent an email enquiring. They replied. In the subject line it obviously said 'Top Secret'. Any hacker casually browsing my inbox for juicy info would immediately be drawn to open it. They should clearly title it 'Money from Nigeria', 'Joel Dommett Mailing List' or 'Groupon'.

Below the subject line it said: 'The lady in question is Sienna Miller.'

WAIT, WHAT?!

Was I going to have a faux fuck with Sienna fucking Miller?! I started acting so I could have a sex scene with someone like Sienna Miller and a paltry* two months later I was having a sex scene with Sienna Miller. I didn't think it was going to come true so bloody quickly. I couldn't believe my luck.

However the excitement was short-lived. The fear and self-doubt suddenly swooped in.

She'd been in many sex scenes, so I dreaded to think how many times she had done it in real life. Probably at least four. I'd only done real sex with one person and now I was going to be recorded doing it. But what if I'd been doing it weird? My odd technique would be captured on film forever. Surely she was just going to laugh at me and my inexperience? Also, was I expected to get a stiffy?** If I wasn't supposed to but I did then that'd be hugely embarrassing. But then again if I was but I didn't that would surely be worse. I couldn't even Ask Jeeves*** because people on the internet ask questions like 'How do I tie a tie?' not 'Am I supposed to get a boner when I have fake sex with Sienna Miller?' It's too specific. I couldn't ask anyone due to it being top secret so I just had to suffer in silence. Maybe I was worrying for nothing. I could be

---

* I just realised that word is not spelt the same as the collective word for chickens.

** I have not used the word stiffy since I started getting stiffies, and it feels wonderfully nostalgic.

***If you do not know what Ask Jeeves is, he was the predecessor to Google until he died in 2006 due to being asked too many stupid questions.

misinterpreting 'entwine in passion' and it just meant a round of jiu-jitsu.

In preparation I watched *Layer Cake* where she walks in with her boobies out and practised pretending I wasn't that into it. It was really difficult. I was really into it.

The big day arrived. We were filming on location in a beautiful part of Wales. There aren't actually many ugly parts there apart from maybe Chepstow but that's because it's just over the Severn Bridge so it's been tainted by ugly England. I was wearing clean, unbranded, potentially 1940s-esque boxer shorts from H&M, just in case they were to be exposed. Jeeves couldn't tell me anything about the underwear gentlemen wore in the 1940s. They probably wore none but I wasn't going to take that risk, plus the World War Two costume trousers were 100 per cent wool so would scratch the bejesus out of my bell.

I had a trailer! Admittedly it was about a third of the size of Sienna's and rightly so. Come to think of it, mine was actually more of caravan. I thought I should pop in to meet Sienna, so I wandered over to her gigantic trailer next door. How the hell was I supposed to introduce myself? 'I'm nunchuck silver medallist in the Bristol and Gloucester area' maybe? Or 'I'm obsessed by you'? Or 'I'm scared I might have been doing sex wrong'?

I knocked and a voice I recognised all too well said, 'Come in.' There she was. Sitting on the sofa (there was space for a sofa!) reading her lines. She was far more beautiful in real life than in the films. She was glowing. She radiated confidence with an edge of approachability. She had that ungraspable, invisible film star quality. She had the X factor, a phrase that has been utterly ruined by *The X Factor*. She wore bright scarlet lipstick which glinted in the sunlight from the massive French windows (there was space for French windows!). Her hair was perfectly preserved, not a follicle unkempt or stray. I instantly understood why everyone wanted to work with her, because you just simply fall in love with her. Not in the way I would with a girlfriend but in a pathetically-obsessed-from-a-distance way. Even though she was right there I wanted to send her a fan letter.

I unoriginally uttered 'hi' shyly and introduced myself. It was fairly humiliating to have to say, 'Uh, I'm playing the Train Soldier?' but it was better than nothing and she seemed happy to see me even if she was pretending. She was a BAFTA- and Golden Globe-nominated pretender after all.

I blurted questions out about the filming which I inter-spersed with compliments about how large her trailer was. She was really quite lovely. You assume film stars who are as enticing and fantastically famous as her would be horrible people but she was so calming and polite. I was so relieved. I didn't have to potentially have pretend sex with a prick.

She had a serene quality similar to that you might find in a yoga studio. I felt so soothed in her presence I had to fight the urge to lie down and savasana.

'What do you think "entwine in passion" means?' I even-tually asked.

'I have no idea,' she replied. 'Let's ask the director.'

The man at the helm of the film was a nerdy, flamboyant American.

'What does "entwine in passion" mean?' Sienna asked.

'Whatever you straight people do!' he said dryly. It really

didn't help. I wasn't experienced enough at sex to confidently know what straight people did. I had spent the last six weeks hanging around and kissing a gay cast of gossipy actors so if anything I only confidently knew what non-straight people did.

'Let's just play it by ear,' Sienna said. What does that mean?! I couldn't believe everyone was so fucking blasé about which base we were going to pretend to get to.

The time had come for our first scene, the less confusing chatter scene in the first train carriage. It was a real steam train on a real steam train track which would only go one way until the track ran out, then the driver would have to saunter to the other end and we would return to the beginning and go again. It was such a logistical hassle to move the train back and forth they counted on the actors to get their part of the deal correct first time to save time, money and coal.

My directions were to lean forward give Sienna 'flirty eyes' and light her cigarette. Apparently assisting a slow death was how people flirted in the 1940s. The renovated train jolted down the track to nowhere. The director yelled 'Action!' Oh my God. It suddenly felt real. I was in a movie and I was sitting opposite my film star crush and in the next scene I may or may not be smooching her.

I lit the match and held it to her cigarette. I started to shake. The size of this moment felt heavy on my shoulders and it made me more nervous than I had ever been. Shaking hands are my first sign of nerves and when I have to concentrate on something accurate or precise it makes my tremors worse. I was horrific at the board game 'Operation' when I was younger but it did actually help when I was a teenager and started fingering.

The match wouldn't connect with the end of the cigarette while Sienna's eyes followed it. The fast-burning timber was shaking around the end of the rolled tobacco like the way you tease a dog with a treat. It was requiring the concentration and effort of getting a thread through the eye of a needle, but the increased frustration only made me shake more.

I started doing my concentration tic of pushing my tongue out of the right-hand side of my mouth. I had almost forgotten about the scene; it now was firmly about the challenge of lighting this goddamn cigarette. Wait. Almost there. DAMN IT. Closer. Closer. Closeeeeeerrrr. YES. But by the time I got it we had strayed too far down the short track and we had no time left for our lines. You could sense the disappointment of the whole crew. The extra fifteen minutes it took to change around and go back to the beginning was wasted post-work drinking time in the local pub or precious time with their family.

I apologised. 'I'm not nervous, I've just had too much Haribo,' I joked. Nobody laughed.

The director appeared from behind the camera and asked Sienna to light it herself. He was courteous enough to make it sound like it was a suggestion born from a character decision.

'I think she would light it herself.'

I was devastated. I had such a tiny amount of tasks to perform in this film and I was already having them swiped from me. If I was shaking trying to light her cigarette, imagine how much I would shake when I was trying to touch her nipples. I felt myself suddenly sweating heavily. Not just a moist glow but actual beads. If this was real life, Sienna would have obviously moved elsewhere to find a steady, unclammy man to rut with.

The make-up lady kept returning to powder my brow to give the impression I wasn't such a moist mess. The viewers needed to believe I would be in with a fighting chance with this overly lusty locomotive lady.

The train started its second short voyage. It went way smoother this time due to the small amount of physical directions I had to concentrate on. Sienna lit it first time like a person would with a normal level of hand-to-eye coordination and we moved on to our lines. I have no idea how they went, I really couldn't concentrate because the entire time my brain was shouting 'THAT'S SIENNA FUCKING MILLER!' over and over. I was slightly afraid that I was actually saying it out loud which would almost definitely not make it into the film.

I must have announced the prescribed lines adequately because after a couple of goes down the track we moved on to the scene we were 'playing by ear'.

We moved to a more private carriage towards the rear of the train. The make-up girls returned for one more mop of the now gushing forehead. We had three lines before the 'entangling'. I decided I would just follow her lead. Wherever she went, I would follow.

Line one.

Line two.

Line three.

I froze. What's going to happen? I was waiting for the ear

to be played. Suddenly and quickly she leaned in for a kiss. I kissed her back. She used her tongue. I used mine. She bit my lip; I bit hers. She started undoing my shirt buttons, then with a couple left to go, ripped the shirt apart, flinging the buttons across the carriage.

I tried to unbutton the buttons at the back of her dress. It became clumsy. We were locked in a hug while I fiddled with her tightly fastened 1940s garb. I felt my concentration tongue slip outside the corner of my mouth again. One button done, two buttons done, last one, DONE. Her dress fell off one shoulder to expose her 1940s bra. The teenager in me was so excited to see her clavicle.

The magic was ruined a little bit when she kissed my ear. I can't stand anyone kissing my ears even if it's cinema's Sienna Miller. It's lovely to kiss an ear but if you're having your ear kissed yourself it's utterly disgusting. A tiny peck to the kisser is amplified to a thunderous clap and a minute sexy moan sounds like a busker's digeridoo.

To shift away from my ears I began to make my own moves instead of following hers. No more playing with ears or playing by ears. I kissed her neck. She didn't even think of that! Then she kissed mine. 'She's following me!' I thought. I felt like it wasn't going terribly. I was having pretend sex with my dream Hollywood person and it was far superior to real-life sex. I didn't have to go through the crippling insecurity of thinking I was horrific at it and the obvious awkwardness of me saying 'I love you' immediately afterwards. We were in full flow and the playing by ear was going wonderfully. I felt her hand grasp my thigh tightly and squeeze. She then slowly edged her palm upwards, dragging her nails over my coarse costume towards my awaiting groin. I had a full 100 per cent erection. There was no doubt about that. The flag was at full mast at Buckingham Palace and the Queen was home. I was still hugely uncertain whether I was supposed to or not. Her hand crept further; it was mere centimetres away from the crown jewels. This is happening, Sienna Miller is about to touch my—

'CUUUT!' the director shouted from behind the camera.

I was out of breath. Surprisingly for an actor I'd never actually done cocaine but I assumed that this was the racing, pumped feeling it feeds you with. If Sienna could bottle and sell that feeling, she would be a millionaire. I mean, she probably is already but if she wasn't and wanted to – she could be.

I couldn't wait to do it again, surely we were going to do it again? Please say we were going to do it again?

We didn't do it again.

I pretended that I was happy that we got it in one take.

'That's a wrap, Joel,' the director hollered.

'Great work, guys!' I said through gritted teeth.

Sienna said goodbye. It felt odd formally shaking the hand and delicately kissing the cheek of someone I'd just wrestled passionately with for three minutes. I said namaste to her and a standard goodbye to the crew all while trying to hide my ceaseless erection.

A month later I was sitting in my flat in London when my phone vibrated on the coffee table. I glanced at the glowing screen which said 'Private number'. I hate private numbers. It's either someone really important, or someone asking if you have PPI, never anyone in between.

I answered, hoping I wouldn't hear the hubbub of a call centre in the background.

'Hello?' I said.

'Joel!' came the distinctive voice of the director.

I didn't expect to hear from him again. I immediately got excited at the prospect that they wanted me to do more. Maybe a bigger part? Had the lead fallen ill and I had impressed them so much that they wanted little old me to take over?!

'Most of your stuff has been cut,' he said calmly and confidently as if he wasn't delivering a sizeable chunk of terrible news.

Did I shake that much? Did I actually say 'THAT'S SIENNA FUCKING MILLER' aloud?!

He said he was sorry and thought he would do me the courtesy of calling. I now know this was a lovely thing to do and that most directors would not bother.

My two pages of scenes were replaced with me looking at her, no dialogue, before it cuts to us walking through the train on our way to the sexy carriage and then the slow steam train with plumes of thick white smoke disappears into a brick tunnel. My sex scene was replaced by a classic boning metaphor. I consoled myself with the thought that, somewhere on a cutting room floor, is Sienna Miller almost touching my bulge.

Iris and I eventually entwined in passion. Your second sexual partner is like the difficult second album for a band. You really want to make sure you make Nirvana's *Nevermind* not The Darkness' *One Way Ticket to Hell . . . and Back*. Second albums more often than not have an air of arrogance because the band's done it once and think they know all there is to know when they should always remember Johnny Cash made ninety-six. Strangely I'd learned quite a lot from the almost pretend sex with Sienna. I was more confident in my foreplay fumblings. This, combined with my discoveries from the real sex with Rose, made me feel like I was a little improved. I was starting to realise that the more confidence you have, the better it goes. Just like stand-up comedy or backflips.

Iris and I started seeing each other. 'Seeing' is an odd phrase but it fills a necessary gap in what I call the 'Companionship Scale'. It's a complicated beast so I've gone to the trouble of writing it out for you.

1. Just friends
2. Sex friends
3. Seeing each other
4. Dating
5. Relationship
6. In love
7. Engaged
8. Married
9. Divorced
10. Widowed
11. Dead

It's like a game. If you make it to the end happy with your companion then you win. Unfortunately millions of silly people forget the 'happy' part and just think it's important to get to the end.

Iris and I rose to Level 5 very quickly and pretended we were on 6 but I don't think you can say you are in love when you are still pretending to be a different person. She thought I was this cool London-accented confident actor man, when in reality I was from a village outside Bristol and felt insecure when I tried on a hat in a shop.

Nine months in, things started to get strained and I could tell we were just not that into each other much any more. It's hard to not get bored if you are not being yourself. You run out of things your character would say but if you were just you, you could keep on rolling forever.

I tend to realise I'm not fully invested in a relationship any more when Christmas or birthdays come around. I'm aware that's a horrific thing to say, don't shit on the book and tweet a picture of it to me just yet – but it's true. It forces me to a) write a romantic message in a card, and b) buy a meaningful present.

Now, writing a soppy card message to someone you love is such a wonderful concept. It's the closest we get to harking back to the ideals of our romanticised past where our ancestors asked their partner's parents before kissing them and wrote letters back and forth for twenty years while the man fought in a war somewhere with a sword. Nowadays people send aubergine emojis to strangers to express their 'love' and give out blowjobs like Tic Tacs. Writing a card gives you a taste of that romantic former glory.

If you send cards and only write 'To person' (insert relevant name), then let the pre-written generic card message do the talking and only add 'From (your name)' at the bottom, I'm about to save you a lot of time at Christmas and on birthdays – don't bother. Nobody cares. The only cards I am happy to receive are those from relatives I assumed were deceased. If the recipient is not worth writing a proper message to with some form of actual handwritten content then just put a message on their Facebook wall. If you do that in a Valentine's card, you probably don't love each other and it's probably best you break up with them via their Facebook wall too.

The problem with sweeping long card messages explaining your devotion is that when you stop feeling those feelings, those passages become frustratingly hard to pen. You can breeze through a relationship pretending to love someone but writing in detail how much you love them is really quite tough when you don't mean it. When written down it feels strangely contractual, like the message will be used against you in Relationship Court during the breakup.

Buying a meaningful present for someone you've fallen out of love with is similar. It makes you realise that you simply haven't listened for three months. When you're in a relationship with someone you are interested in, you listen. I'm not saying you listen all the time, but you at least care and remember the things that matter. If you watch a comedian you like, you listen and quote their bits badly in the office on Monday. If you don't like them you stop listening, talk through the show and tell them afterwards that they're 'brave'.

Iris's birthday arrived, I had done both a) and b) really badly. My card felt so forced. It read like love song lyrics written by a sixteen-year-old. In fact it may have just been the words to a pop song that I'd just listened to and subconsciously copied down. I would love to be able to find the card now, it probably said something like:

> I don't know where to begin, baby. I got one thing I want you to know, wherever you go I want you to tell me because I want to go. We have found love so don't fight it and life is a rollercoaster you have just got to ride it (all night long).
> Love from
> ~~Ronan Keating~~
> Joel

Now Iris was due to arrive at my flat in a matter of minutes after a night working at the theatre. I had my try-hard card and a few presents that meant nothing to either of us lying on my bed. It suddenly became blisteringly obvious that it really wasn't enough. I should have been taking her out for a planned night of surprising romantic twists and turns or at least be staying in the flat and making it into a cosy love nest in which we could cuddle and celebrate in comfort with sweet seductive sexiness. I had done none of the above. I had made no plans. The worst part was I hadn't even thought about it. I was standing in a dull, cold, grey flat which I should have cleaned weeks ago and I hadn't showered in days. No signs that it was a birthday at all. It was like an apartment shown in an air-freshener advert before they spray the product and it suddenly brightens up the space and smells delicious.

I had to find a way of salvaging this disappointing mess. Iris was always prompt to get to my flat; you could set your watch by her arrival because she finished at exactly the same time every night and jumped on the same train. I only had six minutes.

I grabbed some deodorant from the chest of drawers and made myself not smell of smelly boy. Good start but not enough. 'I smell of Lynx Africa' is not considered a gift.

Five minutes.

I took my clothes off. All of them. It was a bold move. It wasn't even a bald move (this part will be hard to do on the audiobook) as I hadn't had the decency to prune my private part shrubbery into anything less than an absolute disaster. It was long enough to weave into corn rows which, to be fair, would stay in place longer than my straight head hair. In a blind moment of panic I thought nakedness was the correct way to solve this mess. I think I believed it was potentially romantic, or at best slightly sexy, but in reality it was just a cold, naked, skinny, blindingly white man, standing in a disaster area of a room. I didn't look like a sexy, thoughtful boyfriend; I looked like I'd been kidnapped.

Three minutes.

'Light some candles, Joel!' I thought quickly. I'd seen the episode of *Friends* where Monica proposes to Chandler and sets up hundreds of candles in the flat. Let's do that.

But I then got distracted and started thinking about how weird the name 'Chandler' was. The other Friends had fairly normal names: Monica, Ross, Joey, Phoebe and Rachel. He was called CHANDLER. *Nobody* is called Chandler. If there are a few adult Chandlers (God, I've said it so much it's getting weirder), there surely haven't been any post-*Friends*

Chandlers? Chandler killed off the name Chandler just like Adolf before him. To make things worse his surname is 'Bing'. He's made up of an unknown name and a noise, poor guy. Don't even get me started on Gunther.

One minute. Fuck! I'd been standing in the nude for two minutes thinking about Chandler and wasting valuable time.

I ran with my appendage slapping against my upper leg (it was cold) to the equally chilly kitchen. I looked under the sink that was piled high with dirty dishes and bowls and waded through the avalanche of hoarded plastic bags. I found one candle and one tea light. This amount of non-matching candles does not make the atmosphere sensual, it just suggests 'power cut'. I lit them regardless, ran back to the bedroom and placed them without care or thought on the bedside table beside me. Then I lay on the unmade bed, splayed like a crime scene picture of a dead body. This was disgusting.

I was a terrible boyfriend. I'd written a terrible card, bought terrible presents and I was lying here naked and awkward in a desperate attempt to seem like a better boyfriend. In truth I didn't want to be a better one. I didn't want to be her boyfriend at all. It took me till now to realise it. I should put my clothes back on.

I heard the front door unlock. It was too late. I had ten seconds till she reached the bedroom door. I looked like I'd been cheating on her and my mistress had just leaped out the window into the street.

'Look sexy,' I thought. I pointed a Fonze finger towards the door and waited.

Five seconds.

I looked to my right at the bedside table and saw the sad candle. I looked to my left. There was the deodorant can.

Candle. Deodorant can. Candle. Deodorant can.

A memory flashed into my mind of science lessons when the teacher would turn his back and we would gleefully put a lit splint in front of a gas tap – creating an unbelievably dangerous arc of fire. I grabbed the candle in my right hand, the deodorant in the left and just as door opened I sprayed the deodorant over the naked flame and my naked body. It created a huge gust of flames that shot across the room. Iris threw herself back against the wall, understandably petrified. I sprayed again. It was working way better than I could have imagined and I started to feel powerful. I moved the can down to my genitals as if my penis was emitting the fire and swayed the flames from side to side. I shouted 'HAPPY BIRTHDAAAAY!' as I threw out wave after wave of flames for a good couple of minutes. It was no longer for her; I was purely doing this for me. 'MY DICK IS A DRAGON!' I shouted at the top of my intoxicated lungs. I only stopped when the fire alarm went off. The smell of singed pubic hair was thick in the air. 'Happy birthday?' I said, more feebly this time. She looked at me, disappointed, then walked back out the way she came.

We broke up with each other the next day – on her birthday boxing day.

Toby got home from his first year at LIPA soon after.

It was embarrassing. It's fun doing a Robert De Niro impression until you have to do it in front of him. The persona had grown slowly while he was away, like the acceptable level of fake tan in the UK, and I suddenly realised how ridiculous it was.

When he went away he said, 'You can never find a character until you have found yourself.' I was further away from myself than I had ever been. I found out who I wasn't and that was gay (for now) and Toby.

How would I find me? I went where most young people attempt it. Abroad. Apparently I thought I was hiding in the Alps.

3 May 2004

Hey JD,
    Not going to ring or txt her today. It's up to her to contact me. If she doesn't then I'll move to London and it'll be cool. Ten press-ups. GO. Done. Gotta look good for the fifteen women I need to sleep with to get over Rose. First, I need to get good at sex.
Speak tonight.
Sincerely, Joel

Hannah leaves a silence as she takes it all in. 'I'm just trying to imagine you with cornrows,' she says, squinting at me to help her brain picture it. 'Do you tell all the ladies you kiss men on the first date?' she adds with an intrigued smile on her striking foreign face.

'No, you're special,' I reply, embarrassed. Rodrigo returns to take our food order. I really don't like tapas but I keep coming back because I bloody love ramekins for the same reason I love those tiny cocktail umbrellas.

'I recommend you have three or four plates each,' Rodrigo says. Well, I recommend that you charge three or four times less for each plate please, Spain. Sushi is expensive but I don't mind paying for it because it looks like it's taken some sort of expertise to make and the chefs can't just get a cheap easyJet home. I can only assume tapas is Spanish for expensive starters. How about we make them all mains and call it a meal?

While we are choosing, Rodrigo decides to spout off a fact. 'Did you know "tapa" is the singular for "tapas"?' Oh fuck off, Rodrigo. I am really holding back from shouting 'Rodri-go fuck yourself.'

We order our three or four miniature meals. Roddy of course remembers them instead of writing them down, to impress Hannah. I really hate it when waiters try to remember orders – just use a tiny notepad like everyone else (I love these too). You're not impressing anyone, you're a waiter, not an Egghead. He walks away arrogantly.

It is my turn to ask a question of Hannah. You would usually not 'take turns' and just 'have a conversation' instead but this has clearly become the structure of the date.

'Tell me about your first one-night stand,' I say. I know it's a good question and I can tell she's frustrated she hasn't got there first.

'OK,' she says, accepting the challenge, then she begins weaving a wonderful story with nail-biting jeopardy and twists. I'm obviously avoiding telling you any details of her stories as they are not my tales to tell. If you want to know the details you can buy her book that she hasn't written yet but definitely should or just go on a date with her yourself.

Her stories are so concise. They are tiny tapas size and mine are massive mains. Usually someone wouldn't be able to stomach more than one. Hannah is clearly different because after she's finished she asks me the same question back.

'Tell me about your first one-night stand.'

#10 The First One-Night Stand

After I started being myself again and the nervousness crept slowly back into my life, unsurprisingly the acting work started to dry up. I peaked really early. My wide-eyed naïvety worked in my favour in the beginning but the longer I did it the more the nerves slowly seeped into my auditions when there was more at stake. I fell out of love with it. I realised I loved creating stories but I didn't love pretending to be in other people's. I'd fleetingly dated a few semi-willing people since Iris, and in contrast to acting it seemed to go better the more I was myself.

In order to be able to afford my ludicrously cheap living quarters, I began working in my dad's smelly cheese shop. Yep. My dad owned a cheese shop. A shop entirely dedicated to the selling of coagulated milk protein. It was in Surrey and I used to get the train down from London every Saturday. He used to own a dairy farm which he inherited from my grandfather so he basically just moved further up the milk chain.

My dad is an interesting little plum. My mother gifted me with my talkative social side that wants to constantly put on a good spread (the food kind) and my dad gave me my determined, loner edge. He was the typical clichéd father figure from one of those eighties sitcoms who buries his emotions deep inside the cellar of his emotionless man-husk soul, never to be seen by the world until he stubs his toe.

I remember once asking, 'Dad, do you love my brother more than me?' I expected him to answer in the way that all parents do and say, 'No! I love you both equally,' but he simply replied, 'I've just got more in common with him.' I really laughed. He didn't intend it in a mean way, it's just he has no understanding of sugar-coating something. If he was an Instagram photo he would be a #nofilter photo, which is a reference he obviously wouldn't understand.

I'll never forget the first time we hugged. By that I mean as an adult; I'm sure he hugged me as baby, but that doesn't really count because he was probably technically carrying me. It was when he'd bought me an iMac after I first moved to London and when I said goodbye I leaped in. I'm unashamed to say he bought my affection with a cool computer.

He sent me on a week-long cheese course to learn about, well, cheese, so I was better informed on the shop floor. Due to me not going to university, to this day cheese is my highest form of education. I didn't even like it. (Not the course, I strangely loved that, I just don't like actual cheese.) Customers would buy cheese from me on the strength of my recommendations, despite me having absolutely no knowledge of what the stuff tasted like. It was probably a good thing – if I ate cheese all day I could have put on a lot of weight but luckily I didn't get high on my own supply.

Slowly, over time, I got used to the overwhelming pungency in the shop air, much like a podiatrist must have to. After a while you don't smell it at all because you are now part of that smell. I had blended in with the cheese. If one day a Tyrannosaurus Rex stormed in looking for human meat, it would leave thinking there was only Brie and Gorgonzola Dolce there.

It almost definitely wasn't worth it financially for dad to pay my train fare and a wage for a shop assistant he didn't need but I now understand that he was doing it to see his son. Essentially he paid to see me which I was very happy to encourage.

While I was failing auditions in the big bright lights of London and commuting on weekends to sell cheese, my friend Lily was left alone in the dim flicker of the peripheries of Bristol. Just like me, she didn't have a particular vocation in her sights. Maybe that's the reason we got on so well; we shared a lack of focusable talent. She pottered around, eventually getting a temporary job at Topman in the Mall Cribbs Causeway amongst the pre-sex teens. She only lasted a few months and eventually she decided a solitary life in the dim peripheries was not suited to her and that she was destined for greater things, if only slightly.

She informed me over the phone that she was heading to

the big gay lights of Brighton to study 'Business Management' at university. I laughed, assuming she was joking. She had absolutely no interest in Brighton, Business or Management.

'Why?!' I asked.

''Cos rich people do business and are managers,' she explained. I laughed harder. Her logic was faultless.

It was fortunate for our friendship at least, because Brighton was only an hour's train journey from south-east London and I was bored of the acting bunch by now. I'd left the protective shell of Toby's personality behind and had reunited with the artist formerly known as Joel. Everyone was just so serious in this odd realm and I missed the fun of Lily being around.

That autumn, she set off to Brighton for the rut fest that is Freshers' Week. She was to be one of thousands of young adults marking their territory and establishing their embryonic personalities while away from home for the first time. Student life is like Battersea Dogs' Home with WKD and herpes. It's important to make sure you don't do something stupid that makes everyone remember you for the next three years as 'that boy who pooped himself on the dancefloor during R Kelly's "Ignition"' or whatever.

I told Lily to have a blast and remember to let loose a little. She can often be standoffish with potential new amigos and automatically gives off a negative vibe. I knew it was important for her to open up a bit.

I called her after a week.

'I've got a boyfriend,' she blurted out immediately.

Oh Christ. I hadn't meant open up in that way . . .

His name was Peter and they'd immediately hit it off while

doing beer pong and other games that heartily encourage not drinking at your own steady pace. She described him as tall, dark and handsome with glasses. I was picturing Clark Kent but I assumed I was probably way off.

'Does he slow-dance with you?' I asked. He didn't. One of the strange things about Lily is that even though she is proud of her tomboy persona she has an underlying femininity that would occasionally show itself. She loved to slow-dance and thought it was the epitome of romance – proper hug-and-slowly-move-around-in-circles stuff. When we were kids I would always mock her for it and she would grab me in a headlock and wrestle me to the floor. It was essentially an aggressive romantic manoeuvre.

Sadly, Peter thought slow-dancing was stupid but I was happy for her nonetheless. They moved up the Companionship Scale at a rate of knots. By the way, why does that phrase not specify the amount of knots? It's just a unit of speed. I know from a personal experience of punting that you can still travel slowly in a boat. Anyway, my point is they moved fast.

By the end of Freshers' Week they were staying at the companionship hotel on Level 6. The love level. Fuelled by free Freshers' Week jelly shots they said the 'L' word within a couple of days. That's way too soon. At that point you have no idea whether the person you're saying it to squeezes toothpaste from the middle of the tube, sleeps loudly or kills people recreationally. She was clearly making the same mistake I'd made with Rose and to honest it was pretty cute.

They connected over their colossal lack of enthusiasm for business management and happily missed all the lectures. If they'd bothered turning up they would have learned that the most important part of managing a business is learning how to manage a business.

After a semester of hating the learning and loving the yearning for each other they both decided they would forgo the rest of the degree and quit university. It would be a tough decision to make by yourself but as a duo it was easy. They spurred each other on like Sid and Nancy or the Chuckle Brothers.

They'd got what they wanted out of it. Each other.

'What are you going to do?' I asked her on the phone. By this point I was not surprised by her decision. Every time I spoke to her since telling her to open up she had leaped recklessly towards another unstable lily pad in the pond. It was quite exciting really.

'We are going to do a season,' she said with a level of excitement in her voice I'd never really heard before. I assumed she meant watch a season of a television show and they had left the relaxed schedule of university because they simply couldn't juggle four lectures a week and the box set of *Lost*.

'A ski season!' she clarified. Oh fucking hell. It was worse than I thought.

'A ski season' is when white people spend six months in white weather. You work for little to no pay and are instead rewarded with cheap drinks and a free pass to slide down a mountain on an expensive plank/planks. It's basically Freshers' Week on fresh snow.

She was unbelievably excited. I was a little apprehensive because this was all happening with a guy I'd never met. It's hard to trust someone in that situation. This is something

I wish I had remembered later in my life when I was catfished by a stranger and pictures of my penis were put on the internet. We will chat about that in detail later, don't worry.

Peter and Lily were not the most organised of individuals. It was all game and no game plan. They both fed each other's impulsive nature while forgoing the admin required to make sure it wasn't an absolute fucking disaster. Frustratingly, for someone like me who enjoys figuring out if I'm on the right road to the right destination, somehow – without a map or a clue where they were going – they always turned out OK. Like the Chuckle Brothers and unlike Sid and Nancy.

I should also point out that neither of them enjoyed winter sports. Neither of them partook or had ever partaken in the act of being on snow for fun. It made this sudden decision an even stranger choice and I personally thought it almost certainly meant it was going to be a disaster.

'I've always wanted to do it, so I reckon I'll be OK at it,' Lily told me on the phone. I informed her that's almost exactly not how things work. I've always wanted to go to space, but that doesn't mean I automatically have the necessary talents and intelligence to do so. Unlike Lily I had been on snowboarding holidays a few times and knew that most of the first few frustrating trips involve sliding down the mountain on your derrière like a dog with a dirty backside. Regardless, Lily and Peter headed out on their fearless adventure. She invited me out there for the whole season but they were a new couple and I didn't really want to be a third ski.

I perhaps foolishly thought I would go out and join them

on their frozen escapades for a few weeks as I'd never met Peter and I'll admit it did sound like fun. I was also desperate to get better at snowboarding. I was absolutely terrible at it due to my severe fear of heights and general snow-based death.

I thought two weeks in France was enough, as I had to be back in Blighty to fail dismally at more auditions. I also thought leaving in a couple of months was enough time to let them settle in. I *also* thought an egg was *un oeuf* in French and I checked and it is, which helped make this paragraph wonderfully funny.

I spoke briefly to Lily when she arrived and told them the exciting news that I was coming to visit.

'Great! Fly to Geneva – it's closest – and we will pick you up from there. I can't wait for you to meet Peter!' she said excitedly. She told me not to book accommodation as when they got a job they would get given an apartment for free. I thought it was strange that they didn't have jobs already but before I could say anything she uttered, 'I have no credit so I gotta go,' and hung up.

In preparation I bought a brand-new snowboard that I had saved up for with all my cheese money. I was so proud of it, it was stunningly beautiful. It was certainly more beautiful than my snowboarding but I would look cool holding it at the bottom of the mountain and that's what counts.

Lily had been hard to communicate with due to her frustratingly frugal credit use but the sporadic one-word txts I did receive seemed to indicate things were going OK. I stayed at my mum's house the night before I left due to flights from Bristol being less pricey, although I didn't factor in the travel cost from London to Bristol so it ended up being a £30 difference, which I should really have given to my mum for picking me up from the train station, housing and feeding me for an evening, stealing her big leather passport holder and then driving me to the airport the next day.

I sent a text with my flight details to Lily.

'SHIT. OK, I'll be there,' she replied: a text full of mixed messages, I think you'll agree.

I flew in clutching my beloved new sharpened shiny snow-board baby and my lift was there – three hours late, obviously.

There's no lonelier feeling than when you get to an airport and nobody is there waiting for you. Even if you haven't organised for someone to pick you up, a part of you always thinks, 'Maybe someone will surprise me?' If you ever wonder what it is like to be a stand-up comedian who's just told a joke that doesn't work, it's exactly like the feeling when you get to an airport and nobody is waiting for you and the people lined up waiting for other people don't give a shit.

We hugged tightly like I'd just bought her an iMac and she whispered, 'I've got so much to tell you,' in my ear. I quickly assumed the worst and thought the relationship with Peter had returned back down the Companionship Scale as quickly as it had shot up it. I was ready to mop up the tears or at least throw a snowball in her face to help her disguise the fact she was crying.

We sat in Peter's tiny Nissan Micra full of what felt like everything, including the kitchen sink.

'Buckle up, it's a five-hour drive,' Lily said.

'What?! I thought this was the closest airport?'
'Roadtriiiiip.'

Usually, when embarking on a six-month stint away from home in a mountainous winter wonderland, people organise a prospective job before heading for the hills. You know, so you have an income and somewhere to provide walled protection from the elements that kill you? It turns out Peter and Lily did not do this. Armed with no money and a month of Business Management knowledge they made the lengthy schlep to the French Alps in a car ill-suited to the long distance, winding snowy roads and the sheer amount of disorganised hoarding they considered luggage thrown in the back.

They assumed that the hotels, resorts and ski companies would be waiting with open arms for two useless untrained English people. It's safe to say they were not. They found that on the contrary everyone had very closed arms. Obviously all the companies had already organised a full rotation of staff because running a business requires organisational skills greater than that of a ten-year-old. I can only assume they learned that doing business management at university for the full three years.

After landing in their resort of choice, Tignes, and being told by almost all the season-based employees that they were idiots, they ended up sleeping in Peter's car and simply woke up and put the heaters on every few hours to stave off inevitable death from hypothermia – but not for too long due to lack of petrol funds. After a few cold weeks they found a large chalet that never locked its balcony doors so they would scope out the unused apartments within it during the day, then Lily would use her tree-climbing skills at night to scale the side of the building and break into one of the empty flats. They would leave in the morning before anyone noticed. All this while living entirely on dry baguettes. But it was OK; they had each other. I should add that somehow they were still finding the time and money to go out every night. They were swerving death from the cold, starving themselves and breaking the law every night in favour of alcohol-based japes.

The day before I arrived they had somehow managed to find a job. A way to stop sleeping in their car and breaking and entering. Unfortunately they were told they would have to move away from Tignes to a tiny family resort called Puy-St-Vincent, far, far away. Five hours from Geneva to be exact.

'Anyway, to cut a long story short, we moved,' Lily said after not stopping talking for about two hours. I explained to Lily for the millionth time that she was using the phrase 'to cut a long story short' wrong. That's one thing that's always frustrated me about her. You can't tell an unfathomably lengthy tale then tell the short version *after* it. You are supposed to just do the short version. She should say 'to make a long story slightly longer'.

Peter had to work his first day at the new resort so that's why he wasn't with her to pick me up. I think it may have been the first five hours they had spent apart in six months or so. This was all on the day that Lily was supposed to start work as a nanny but, touchingly, she'd asked to have her first day off so she could come and get me.

The idea of her being a nanny made me choke with

laughter. I've never seen anyone be less impressed by children. Once at a family birthday gathering, her young niece read a book aloud while the rest of the family surrounded her, amazed by her incredible new talent. Lily waited until she'd finished and then just said, 'It's not that impressive, everyone can read.' I assumed she would be applying this wonderful gentle approach when looking after strangers' children as their parents slid down a snowy slope, blissfully unaware of the psychological damage being done.

We finally arrived at the tiny resort with our snow-chainless tyres skidding past the hundreds of signs that read 'CARS MUST HAVE SNOW CHAINS'. The place really was small. It looked like where you imagined Father Christmas and his elves would live when you were a kid. Unlike a lot of other resorts it was quiet and serene. All you could hear was your footsteps crushing the deep snow beneath you. Snow makes everything look so beautiful. It covers up imperfections like a thick layer of make-up and automatically brings out the child in you. It's nature's toy; you can't help but run, jump, roll and throw when you're in it. It's so fun, but let's all remember that like Knifey Knifey Crash Mat it will kill you if you disrespect it.

It was so late it was early. We shook off the snow and crept up an echoey stairwell that led to their new flat. It had a bed and a cupboard and that was it. There was no space for anything else, especially extra people. It was a prison cell but colder.

'Shhh, he's fast asleep,' Lily whispered with her finger on her lips. Peter was wrapped up warm in the single bed they shared.

'Why is it called fast asleep?' I said. It was a good question.

It's the only time you can guarantee that someone is being the opposite of fast.

'I don't know!' she said, then added quietly, 'Why is it called sound asleep when you don't make any sound?'

At that point, like a gift from the comedy gods, Peter moved and let out a tiny sleep fart. Lily and I cried with laughter until we couldn't cry or laugh any more. It was good to be reunited. These two weeks were going to be packed with fun (and occasionally looking after other people's children).

I laid out some pillows, thick coats and salopettes on the only available thin strip of cold tiles that wasn't taken up by a bed or cupboard. The only thing worse than sleeping in a prison cell is sleeping on the floor of a prison cell. I whispered goodnight then eventually fell 'rate of knots asleep', only to be woken up the next morning by Peter accidentally kicking my cheek as he got out of bed.

'Shit, sorry!' Peter said.

'Nice to meet you finally!' I whispered, quite politely considering he'd literally just stood on my face. He grabbed some clothes and tiptoed around me to the door and to what I assumed must have been a communal bathroom, because there was certainly no ensuite to be found in this place. To be fair to my imagination, he did actually look like Clark Kent.

Lily and I went for breakfast later that morning and I was introduced to the long-standing resort manager, Laura. She was a harsh, blonde northern lady of probably around forty-five years old who clearly started on a season several years ago and simply never left. Her face seemed frozen in anger by the bitter weather. Laura loved her managerial role and relished being stern to excitable university drop-outs.

'You can't sleep on t'floor, it's against company policy,' she barked in her northern accent like a disgruntled *Game of Thrones* character. It was clearly a policy that she herself had made up but you could see that argument was futile.

'An Asian family ain't turned up if you want cheap rate on t'room? It's the only room left in t'resort.' Her eyes softened. I could tell that the cheap rate she was offering me was clearly going straight into her pocket. I had no idea why she found it necessary to tell me the family were Asian, but I assumed it was somehow important. It was €200. That was so much money. Three-point-three-recurring months' rent, to be exact. But it was that or sleeping in a car with intermittent heating intervals so I said yes to the four-bedroom family apartment for two weeks at a slice of the price it would usually be, but a chunk more than I had anticipated for sleeping on the floor of a happy couple's bedroom.

That afternoon, after Lily had finished her first half day of nannying, we went snowboarding. Frustratingly, she was a bloody natural at it, not disproving her 'I've always wanted to do it' theory. She'd obviously managed to practise while she was jobless on her ex-rental board that she had clearly stolen but insisted she had 'acquired'. Snowboarding suited her tree-climbing tomboy fearlessness and after a few sessions she was already far superior to me. I was superb at looking like I was good at it when holding my snowboard but terrible at actually being good at it once it was strapped to my feet and I was letting gravity hurtle me to the bottom of the slope.

As well as my impressive new snowboard I also had my white Apple earphones in which were attached to my white 100GB iPod in my pocket because all the cool snowboarders listened to music while they did flips and 540s. I just loved listening to tunes while I fell down repeatedly.* The snowboard was my pride and the iPod was my joy. These were the only two things I'd spent my minimal money on in the last few years with the exception of my new Asian apartment.

After a few basic runs, Lily led me off-piste. I wasn't good enough to enjoy the pristine on-piste let alone the rough, unflattened, unpredictable stuff, which, I should add, voids your insurance as soon as you go on it. Which reminded me.

'Ah fuck, I forgot to get insurance,' I said to myself inside my coat which was zipped up tightly over my mouth.

Piste or off-piste – I was uninsured. I was also almost certainly running before I could walk and I was very worried about breaking my spine so neither of those things would be an option. I would also then have to destroy my family

---

* I was terrible at making playlists because I was so indecisive, so I would just put the iPod on shuffle. However, the problem with that was about half of my iPod was taken up with audio books. I may have looked cool with my earphones in but I was actually listening to a chapter of *Lord of the Rings*.

financially due to the huge French medical bill that they would be lumped with.

This is why I'm not good at brave, gutsy things like snow-boarding. While Lily rushed down the slope enjoying the sheer adrenaline caused by the simplicity of going so incredibly fast, I was focusing on insurance and paralysis.

We followed the path of the ski lift down the bumpy, treacherous slope. I the scaredy cat was hesitating instead of letting gravity do its part, Lily the gutsy dog was gliding effortlessly from side to side, letting out the occasional joyous 'Wooo!'

She was pulling further and further ahead; I had to get a grip and catch up. I pointed my pride down the steep white abyss that was below me. I was telling myself aloud inside my coat to relax and enjoy it. The speed was increasing and I felt in control. Skiers and boarders slowly ascended the snowy cliff face above me, watching from the chair lift. I think I may have looked like I was good at it . . . dare I even say it, I may have looked cool. The onlookers craned their necks as they scaled past me towards the summit, like when you see someone attractive on the opposite escalator of the Underground. I was flowing effortlessly from side to side like a waterproof pendulum wearing a bobble hat.

Then, as if someone had pulled the ground from under me like a magician with a tablecloth, I was suddenly airborne. I was falling fast, instinctively circling my arms as if in my moment of need they would turn miraculously into wings and I would fly safely to the village below. Alas, my arms were just shit arms and I hit the slope with a thud. Then I was in the air again, rolling. While all of this was happening

I had the sound of Frank Skinner's autobiography in my earphones. I could see sky then snow, sky, snow, tree, sky, snow. My earphones were ripped out and I finally came to a halt gazing wearily at the sky. I felt like I'd been in a soft car crash. I took a second to collect myself, just lying there silently in the deep white Slush Puppy. I looked up at the huge cliff I'd just fallen from. It felt like I was OK. I was in no pain, so I was either lucky, or dead. Either way the insurance wouldn't be needed. Silence. Lily was long gone. I was alone.

'Plank prick!' Three ecstatic skiers on the lift were sticking their middle fingers up and shouting gleefully. It turned out I wasn't alone. I was actually providing the entertainment for a hanging conveyor belt of laughing snowgoers travelling up the mountain. I went from off-piste to pissed off in a matter of seconds.

I lay there for a while, slowly gathering my senses and dignity, then headed immediately for on-piste ground, weaving my way to the bottom like a fragile leaf falling from a tree.

Lily was of course waiting for me at the foot of the mountain in pristine condition without any covering of sweat or snow, wanting to go again. 'Where have you been?' she shouted, waving her neon arms to get my attention. My grey jacket and overly baggy beige trousers were covered head to board in white. I looked like a Mr. Whippy ice cream that had been carelessly dropped on the pavement. 'I hate off-piste,' I said to Lily, brushing myself down. I was so cold yet so sweaty at the same time. 'If you're not good enough for off-piste don't do it. Just be patient,' Lily said. Apparently in her few months away she'd become the Mr Miyagi of snowboarding.

I wasn't going to go again. I wanted to nap in one of the four rooms in my Asian home. I went to fish out my apartment keys from my pocket, which I had carelessly left open. They were missing. I checked all my pockets even though I knew it wasn't in any of the others. I love the feeling of finding something you've lost. It's almost worth the gamble of losing things just for when you occasionally find them. But in this case they were definitely gone. Fuck. Laura was almost certainly going to charge me for it. As if I hadn't paid enough for that room already. Wait! No! My iPod was missing too! I'd LOST MY JOY? Double fuck! It must have been flung from my open pocket while I bounced down the cliff. I wanted to run up the mountain to save it but Lily held me back like in a war film when a soldier tries to run back onto the battlefield to drag the body of a wounded comrade to safety. I was so sad and I couldn't even listen to sad songs to help me cope with the sadness. It was so depressing to imagine the iPod repeating the Black Eyed Peas to itself on the mountain alone until the battery ran out.

We called Peter to let me in. He held the master key because the glorious job he had been given was hotel cleaner.

It was the first time I'd seen him without him being slow asleep or standing on my napping face, and he really was quite a charmer. You immediately trusted him and wanted to be part of his tight gang. He was tall and handsome, but in an unconventional way, like an attractive short person that someone had stretched into a slightly less attractive taller one. He shared Lily's nonchalance; it seemed like nothing fazed him. He always had one cool eyebrow raised like the

Rock in his wrestling days and you imagined him with a cigarette in his hand even though he didn't smoke.

He wasn't the sort of person I thought Lily would end up with. I thought she would end up with more of a geeky, creative troubadour instead of a coolheaded charmer. I guess I'm saying I thought she would end up with someone like me but, you know, just not me.

That evening I bought some cheap travel insurance online and left the chalet for my first night out on the town (village). I had no meticulously personalised playlist to listen to after all so I might as well listen to it from a DJ or a pub stereo. I don't know whether it was the altitude, meeting Peter for the first time, not seeing Lily for ages or me mourning the loss of my personal music hard drive but we got druuuuuunk.* It seemed the unanimous vibe in the bar. Everyone was hammered. Maybe they'd all lost their iPods too. The legendary triumvirate of Peter, Lily and I were definitely some of the worst off, apart from a stag do in the corner who looked like they had been drinking solidly for four days straight. The stag, who was dressed as 'Where's Wally?', was intermittently vomiting outside and returning for more. He was very easy to spot.

I was knocking back the OranGINas. It's Orangina mixed with gin. Oh, I didn't need to explain? OK. I made it up that night and it really is quite delicious, although you have to take the Orangina out of its bottle and that's where all of its power lies. It's like Samson's hair or Alex Ferguson at Manchester United (I'm in a realm I don't understand there but I think

---

* There is roughly one 'u' for every three alcoholic units consumed.

that was a good simile). After a few hours of friendly fun I noticed a lady standing at the bar and uncharacteristically I wandered over to strike up a conversation with her.

I've never been a 'talk to strangers in bars and clubs' person. My courting technique is to assume everyone has a boyfriend and not really bother. However, on this night I was fuelled by the loss of an old 100GB friend and OranGINa.

'Tonight I stumbled upon the most excellent drink,' was my opening line.

'What's that?' she replied, already looking bored of my slurring.

'OranGINa, It's Orangina with—'

'Yeah, I get it,' she said. I would normally walk away after such an immediate burn but the overload of gin and vitamin C made me persevere.

'You are dishy,' I garbled.

'Can women be dishy?' she asked, noticeably more coherent than me.

'Why is it just men that are described as dishy?' I enquired, ready to dazzle her with my thoughts about the phrase 'fast asleep' as the next point of conversation.

'True, I've never seen a plate and thought, "I want to fuck that crockery,"' she replied. She said the 'f' word in such a sexy way; she really elongated the 'f' sound then snapped the 'k', making 'fuck' sound like the long sweep and crack of a whip.

'Either way, you're dishy.' I pointed at her and tried to raise my eyebrow like Peter.

'Do you want to fuck me?' she said calmly, like she was saying, 'Can you pass the salt?' I almost fell off my chair like she'd one-inch punched me in my chest. She said it like she just couldn't be bothered to have to go through the rigmarole of talking to me any more. She was unbelievably forward. Like Wayne Rooney for Manchester United (again delving quite fearlessly back into a metaphoric realm I don't fully understand).

We'd reached Keen Town and she was buying up property like nobody's business.

'I have an Asian four-bedroom apartment to myself,' I stuttered, realising I really didn't need to say the Asian part.

She grabbed my hand and led me out. This felt too easy. It's not meant to happen like this. I would usually undergo a month of txts, flowers and impressing mothers before even approaching a smooch. Clearly I'd been learning my courting techniques from a period drama (and I hoped tonight she didn't have one of *those*, AM I RIIIGGHHHHT?*).

I walked her home, veering around under the influence of the GIN, leaving a wavy snow track behind me on the concrete. Her footprints, by contrast, were dead straight parallel to mine.

We reached the level of my abode and I walked along the corridor, squinting at the door numbers to make them unblur and stop moving. This next part sounds ridiculous but I am going to throw it out there and hopefully you will choose to believe me.

While taking this bold lady back (bold not bald. Oh God, not again. Sorry audiobook), I tripped over a naked man in

---

* That was a lady parts bleeding joke and I am ashamed of it. I really am. I'm sorry but it's still staying in.

the corridor. It was Where's Wally? with his willy out. Frustratingly, I hadn't seen him this time. His friends had clearly stripped him and left him outside as the final punch-line of the night. He had a hotel door sign hooked over his penis that said 'Do not disturb'. To be fair to the stag do, that was hilarious. I turned the label over so it read 'Service me' instead. I kept on thinking about the fact Peter had to clean this all up tomorrow.

I eventually found my Maison d'Asian and we pretty much got straight to it, having sex in the lounge. I don't really remember it but I do remember thinking it was a complete waste of the four bedrooms.

The next thing I knew, I woke up, throat dry and bleary eyed. Where was . . . the lady? Did I even know her name? We had got to it so quickly we didn't exchange the basics. I was such a blooming floozy. Just like my iPod, she was gone. She had disappeared like Batman does when Commissioner Gordon glances away. Although she had nine hours to do it and I assume Batman and Commissioner Gordon sleep in separate bunks.

I got up and started to piece together the events of the night before in my head like when you lose your wallet and someone frustratingly sensible says, 'Well, when did you last have it?' I looked and felt like a zombie in any zombie movie ever.* I peered in all the bedrooms to make sure she hadn't angrily moved to one of the spare rooms like we were a turbulent couple who'd been married for forty years.

---

* Has anyone thought about the fact that zombies are just hungover people looking desperately for hydration?

She wasn't there. I remember thinking, 'Oh, this is what a one-night stand feels like.'

I felt mildly excited about it. But I also felt like something was missing. Aside from my dignity and one-night stand cherry. I paced around looking at the flat like a 'spot the difference' picture. My snowboard. Where was my snowboard? I ran from room to room to double-check. It wasn't anywhere. My dream, my pride, bought with hard-earned cheese money. I smelled like Brie for months for this – where was it? The lady, the keys, the iPod and now the snowboard were gone. So much loss in so little time.

She must have taken it. It suddenly all made sense. She was the only sober person alone in the bar and she was overly eager to return to my apartment. She was a sex burglar.

I assume she thought that more treasures awaited in the four-bedroom apartment than a mid-range used snowboard. If I hadn't lost the iPod she would at least have had a slightly better yield. Even my phone was still in my discarded jeans, which I assume she didn't steal because it was a Nokia 3310 and had the value of a mouldy conker. I felt a bit sorry for her. I wished I had a bit more stuff for her to steal.

I had traded a new snowboard for a one-night stand. It was like prostitution mixed with ebay.

Not to worry, I thought. I would tell the police, get a crime report, claim the snowboard on my new insurance, borrow one for the remaining twelve days and still enjoy my holiday, even though my possessions were depleting at a rate of miles per hour (fast).

I met Lily and Peter at the bar that we'd been to yesterday, which felt like four months ago as so much stuff had happened since then. I didn't tell them. I never really shared my sex stories with Lily and I was kinda embarrassed. I just said my snowboard had been stolen from the locker room. Lily persuaded me to report it to Laura the resort manager.

'The nearest gendarmerie is thirty minutes' drive away in the next town,' Laura stated in her relentlessly humourless northern tone.

'What's the gendarmerie?' I asked. With my lack of French knowledge I could only assume it was a quick way of saying Jean-Claude Van Damme.

Laura didn't laugh, of course. She had nothing but hate in her heart. 'It means "police". I'm driving to the town now, want a lift?'

Halfway on the trip to the Jean-Claude Van Damme I was leafing through the massive passport holder I'd taken from my mum's house – which I'd brought with me for police ID purposes – when she happened to call me.

'Joel Dommett, have you got my passport?' she asked in a very serious tone. I thought it was odd that she full-named me, especially as half of that name is also her own.

'Yes!' I said playfully.

'Have you got our tickets for our holiday to the Maldives TOMORROW?'

Oh God.

'Yes,' I replied meekly. This was the first time I'd heard her angry since KKCM. She explained that I needed to get back to Bristol immediately as it was the most expensive holiday they'd ever undertaken and, at this point, my shitty easyJet endeavour to the Alps was obsolete in comparison. I'm paraphrasing but you get the idea.

I hung up the Nokia 3310, which was by this point my only remaining possession.

'I have accidentally brought my mum's passport. She is going on holiday tomorrow, I have to fly home,' I told Laura solemnly. She finally let out a genuine laugh. Huge misfortune was clearly her chuckle vibe.

I went straight to an internet café and booked an unbelievably last-minute, extraordinarily expensive flight home for that night. I then got a crime report from the Jean-Claude for my stolen pride and drove back to ask Lily to give me another five-hour lift back to Geneva due to all the flights at closer airports not getting me back before Mum left.

Lily said yes. I would like to think I'd do the same for her but I probably wouldn't. She really is the best.

We got back in the car and Lily prepared for another ten-hour round trip only two days after she had previously done one. She had to ask Laura for another day off work (that was two out of four).

I flew into Bristol Airport and waited for another five hours to meet my mum and exchange the package.

What a trip. I tried to claim everything on the insurance but apparently it was invalid as I bought it when I was already there. Of course it was. In less than forty-eight hours I'd lost a £400 snowboard, a £200 iPod, a £177.68 four-bedroom apartment (at the current exchange rate), spent £30 on pointless insurance, booked a £250 same-day flight and done twenty hours of driving. But I suppose it was slightly worth it because I'd had my first one-night stand.

What Lily told me about off-piste patience stuck in my mind. Good things don't come without working hard and deserving it. With snowboarding, planning holidays and relationships. I wanted everything now – the sex, the off-piste and the holiday admin – and I was falling over every time. This newfound patience proved to be hugely important when I spent the next ten years learning stand-up comedy, only to be called an overnight success.

9 June 2004

Hey JD,

Met up with Rose for the first time in ages. Guess what?! Just had wicked sex with her!!!!! The condoms worked!

It was the first time she nearly ejaculated from penetrative sex and it was wicked. Just wanted to say that and write with my new pen.

Sincerely, Joel

'Piste off was definitely the highlight,' Hannah says and she is right. I've never shared so much with a complete stranger. It's free therapy. Well, therapy at the ludicrous cost of six small plates of tapas. I'd still much rather have one big plate of tapa.

The noise from the guitarist in the corner is becoming unbearable. He's treating it as an open mic night instead of background restaurant music. He's definitely slipping in some of his own creations.

Roddy returns with the ramekins and places them on the table. There isn't enough room for the thousands of mini dishes so we have to Tetris it all together and put the multitude of different-sized redundant wine glasses on the next table. Of course he forgets one item because he didn't fucking write it down. I can't tell whether he did it on purpose or not. If I say something I have no proof, it's my word against his with no mini notepad. He's still only looked at me once, at the start of the date when I said his name; ever since then he's been exclusively focusing on Hannah.

I politely remind him of his mistake. 'You forgot the chorizo,' I say. He rolls his eyes and makes out like I'm the one at fault for complaining. He looks at Hannah as if to say, 'What do you see in him?' Little does he know how little she sees in me.

'It's pronounced *choreetho*. You forget it's a Spanish word,' Rodrigo says, overly pronouncing the lisp part. Strong words coming from a man who forgot the dish entirely.

He sways off to tell the kitchen. 'Are you piste off?' Hannah asks. I smile. God, I love a callback. We grab our napkins and I wait to see how she wears hers before I place mine. I want to tuck it into my collar but feel like that is the uncool cartoon-character way to do it. I don't want to seem too Winnie the Pooh. She places it over her lap gracefully like a magician covering up an audience member's watch and I copy her.

Now, do I go straight from ramekin to the mouth? (That phrase has a real ring of a disgusting porn site to it.) It seems so stupid to put things momentarily on a big plate like an annoying flight layover. I'd rather go direct but I understand there's probably some kind of protocol to this. It's a terrible decision to eat on a first date. Watching someone ingest food is just too intimate. A first date is about getting to know someone and you can't do that if the hole that is used for the majority of communication is filled with meatballs. Although you do get to find out early doors whether someone eats with their mouth open or leaves their knife and fork non parallel after finishing. I simply couldn't be with someone who doesn't adhere to these simple culinary rules. It would be a frustrating waste of everyone's time to find these things out on a fourth date. I pointlessly put some meatball on the layover plate and then put it straight into my mouth. It tastes like dog food. By the look on Hannah's face her choice isn't much better.

'It tastes like your shirt,' Hannah says jokingly with an undertone of absolute seriousness. Rodrigo comes back quickly with the missing 'choreetho', proving that it doesn't take that long to make the dishes. They just drag it out normally to make it seem like they put some care into it.

'Do you have Orangina?' Hannah asks Rodrigo.

'*Non*,' Rodrigo replies. To which I say, 'Isn't "*non*" French? And he replies, '*Sí.*' I am so confused. He leaves and we are both ready for another salacious story. I want to tell her about last night but it feels a bit much to tell a date that you had sex with someone else the night before.

'I've got a good one,' Hannah says. 'Who's the oldest person you've slept with?'

#21 The Mysterious Older Lady

In the intervening few years since #snowgate I'd jumped from date to date, occasionally dipping into a short relationship. I tended to shy away from one-night stands as I had too many things in my house to lose.

At the beginning of 2007 I flew to Los Angeles to stay at a friend's house while he was away. To be honest he wasn't really enough of a good friend to warrant me staying in his home for a full month but I think he felt rude saying no. He was a friend of a friend. A friend squared. I told him if he ever wanted to stay in a tiny untidy box room in an uninteresting suburb of south-east London he was always welcome. The currency rate was beautifully favourable to the UK at the time, making everything basically half price. USA was basically BOGOF for Brits. I was still cheesing on weekends and somehow became an untrained garden landscaper during the week, which I would do if I wasn't acting – which was all of the time. You wouldn't know it to look at me but I know how to lay a paving slab or two. That sounded like a euphemism but I promise I meant it in the literal sense.

My plan was to go to LA, the Mecca of acting, and give it one final push. So far I'd only been in London, the Mecca Bingo of acting. If it didn't work out then I was resigned to the fact that I would just become a full-time landscaper and carry on erecting gazebos with a slight lean. Again, not a euphemism.

I settled into the friend of a friend's flat and made myself at home. It was a large studio, with a wooden floor that you could sock-slide effortlessly on, which was fun and cleaned the floor at the same time. It had a gargantuan grey sofa that was to be my bed for the month. Everything is bigger in America. The country itself, the apartments, the sofas, the roads, the cars, the egos . . . the beautiful people are taller, the fat people are fatter and the muscly people are musclier. I was just a middle-sized, little-egoed, 21-year-old with size six and a half feet which by now I was frustrated to realise were not going to grow any bigger. I'm six foot tall; I can almost guarantee no other six footers have size six feet. On a windy day it's hard to stay standing up.

I naïvely arrived with no car and no friends. I couldn't afford either. You need a car to go anywhere in LA, it's nigh impossible to live without one, it's like living in Scotland without a coat, or London without an underlying sense of anger.

I walked everywhere and it took hours in the blistering

heat. Public transport in LA is as effective as a clingfilm condom. Nobody else walks. Nobody. People look at you from their air-conditioned cars and restaurants like you're homeless, or worse – an out-of-work actor.

Within a mile radius of my friend of a friend's flat there was a gun range, a golf range, a TGI Fridays and a comedy club. I approached my leisure activities like a Grindr date: I made my decision based on what was easy and close. I thought I would take advantage of their non-taxiable close proximity and pay a visit. Not understanding the benefits of moderation I decided to do them all in the first couple of days.

It's difficult to dress for both a gun and a golf range. Nobody wants to undermine the aggression of shooting a gun by wearing chinos and golf-club rules are firmly against the wearing of camouflage because it makes you look like the rough.

Why are they not in the same venue anyway? Rich Americans could hit the balls and angry Americans could shoot at them. I made a mental note to take the idea on *Dragon's Den* or, as the Americans call it, *Shark Tank*, the weirdos.

In the end I decided to wear jeans and a polo neck, hoping that both parties would welcome me into their antisocial groups.

The gun range was closest. I wandered in soaked head to toe in sweat from walking outside for twelve minutes. Luckily everyone else in there was sweaty too, most people sporting a damp vest. People who love guns hate sleeves.

The place had the musky smell of a vintage shop on fireworks night. There were guns everywhere. Hanging on the walls like sweeties in a newsagents. They were just out and looked so easy to steal, then I realised the reason people don't steal guns from gun ranges is because they are full of people who are desperate to have a reason to use their gun and they will definitely shoot you.

Three bulky, hairy men sat behind the counter.

'Excuse me, I was wanting if possible to shoot a gun,' I said meekly, not really knowing how or what to ask for. I'd never sounded more English in my life.

The man at the desk reassuringly asked for ID. He had maybe five or six guns strapped to various parts of his body, as if one wouldn't be enough to do the job. He was like an Action Man with way too many accessories.

I passed over my English driver's licence. He glanced at it and returned it. It makes sense. If you're trusted to drive a massive metal killing machine you are trusted with a tiny metal killing machine. Though they probably should have asked how many points I had before giving me the thumbs up.

'What do you want to shoot?' Action Man asked.

'8mm?' I said, thinking I could impress them with my casual firearm knowledge.

'9mm?' he replied. I realised that an 8mm is a camera.

'Yes please, sir,' I said. I'd seen enough cop shows to know that you call someone 'sir' to prevent them from shooting you in the face.

He gave me a gun and I walked into the back room where the killing-people practice happens. The gun was heavier than I imagined it would be but I was comparing it to those plastic ones that shoot fluorescent darts.

The range consisted of a large shed with booths, almost like urinals, full of freedom-filled Americans shooting their chosen enemy paper targets. I picked a kidnapping. It was a drawing of an innocent lady being held at knifepoint by a gleeful, sinister-looking man. I wanted to save the paper lady like a knight in shining denim.

I pinned the paper hostage situation to a peg and sent it on a pulley system to the back of the room. I got myself into the position learned from people in films and got ready to fire.

Suddenly I started to shake. There's always a moment in every action film when someone who's never shot a gun before picks one up, points it at the baddie* and starts shaking. I always thought if I were in that position I would just confidently shoot the guy who just tried to blow up the world and slapped Halle Berry. Alas, here I was, shaking like a soldier on a train trying to light a cigarette.

Strange thoughts whirred through my head as I cradled the gun. What if I suddenly snapped and shot everybody? Obviously I never would but I could do if I wanted to and that scared the shit out of me.

I really wanted to stop the paper kidnapping – but I just couldn't.

I didn't shoot anything and returned back to Action Man behind the desk. 'I couldn't do it, I'm sorry,' I said and made to leave.

'Hey, I'll help you,' he boomed in his Texan twang. I felt like a toddler who needed help at the potty. He took me back into the range. The kidnapper was still there. Obviously. If

---

* 'Baddie' is such a good word. So much of a better than 'villain', but I feel like it slightly undermines how bad one is because it just sounds so darn cute.

this was a real kidnapping he would have lost interest by now and killed the hostage out of pure boredom.

'Raise the gun,' Action Man demanded.

'Take the safety off.' That was the first time I realised the gun had a safety. I wouldn't have been able to shoot the first time even if I tried. Turns out guns are really safe. I flicked the safety off and pointed the gun at the static kidnapper.

The fear set in again. I started to shake. Action Man, sensing the gun fear, slid in behind me, spooning me and holding my hands steady on the gun. It was like the famous sexy scene in *Ghost* but instead of harmless clay we were holding a killing device. With the bloody safety off.

I think it's the most sexual thing I'd ever experienced, and I'd had real sex. I could feel his guns pushing against the back of my legs. I really wanted to say 'Is that a gun in your pocket or are you just pleased to see me?' but I didn't. The Venn diagram of gun-loving Americans and homophobic people is basically one circle. If I were to make a joke to suggest that he was sexually aroused by this human contact there was a huge probability that he would simply shoot me in the head and claim it was self-defence.

He started whispering things in my ear.

'Shhhhhh, relax.'

I haven't had gay sex but I imagine this is exactly what someone would say if they were having sex with someone who had never had gay sex before.

'Breathe, focus on the target and pull the trigger.'

I took a deep breath and squeezed my index finger. The gun kicked back. I think I would've fallen over if it weren't for GI James. I couldn't believe I'd done it. My heart was pumping. 'That was incredible. I want to do it again,' I said. I haven't had gay sex but I imagine this is exactly what someone would say immediately after the first time they'd done it. My heartbeat settled and I looked at the target.

I'd shot the innocent hostage lady right in the face. I shot a few more times and finished the box of ammo. I was glad I did it but I'm very happy to not do it again.

The golf range was surely more my cup of tea. Strangely, the staff there were less friendly. I was terrible at it but nobody came to my rescue and spooned me and held my club. At one point I sliced a ball right across the golf range completely perpendicular to the way it was supposed to go and narrowly missed a staff member. Imagine if I went to a gun and golf range and killed someone at the latter.

The next day I went to the TGI Fridays for lunch.

If you're ever lonely and want to be cheered up, head to

your nearest Thank God It's Friday alone and tell them it's your birthday. It's a sure-fire way to brighten your day. I promise.

'How many of you will be dining with us today?!' The red-and-white-striped cheery waitress asked excitedly.

'Table for one!' I replied.

Her cheeriness transitioned momentarily to worry then snapped back to a false smile.

'Come right this way?'

I don't think they had many tables for one there but I didn't care. The more odd it seemed to the staff, the more I started to enjoy it.

'Can I have a booth please?' I asked, pointing at the huge booths meant for birthday parties, hen dos and family get-to-gethers.

'Yes, of course,' she said begrudgingly.

I felt like a king. I could see the staff chatting to each other about the loner in the booth. A waitress came over to take my order. Remembering everything was basically half price I ordered a booth king amount.

'That is lot of food, sir!' she said, continuing her faux cheeriness.

'I'm treating myself because it's my birthday,' I said proudly. She looked genuinely sad for me and left with her tiny notepad in hand.

I sat back in my big booth unbelievably excited for what was about to happen. Nobody can disprove your birthday lie if you're alone. Every day is your birthday if you have no friends to tell you it's not your birthday.

The food arrived. I ate as much as I could then reclined back in my seat like a medieval lord at a banquet.

Then it happened. The moment arrived.

The lights turned off. 'Happy Birthday' played out from the speakers and all of the staff appeared together from the kitchen holding a cake topped with candles.

The whole restaurant all joined in as their eyes followed the snake of red-and-white-clothed staff weaving slowly through the tables. Where was it going to stop? It can't be the guy sitting by himself in the huge booth, surely?

The whole TGI workforce stopped at my table while I sang 'Happy Birthday to MEEEEE' then blew out the candles. The entire restaurant looked utterly confused.

Everyone clapped, but not in a congratulatory way, more the way people clap when an easyJet flight lands.

What an experience. It really cheered me up. I urge you to do it. It's almost medicinal.

That night I went to the comedy club, the last of the proximity pastimes.

'Ticket for one please?' I asked at the door, handing over some dollars, which still to me felt like Monopoly money. The woman handed me my change and a ticket, not caring that I was alone. No TGI judgement was placed.

I'd never seen live comedy. I'd been enjoying it for years on DVD, VHS and the interweb but I'd never thought of seeing it in real life.

My VHS of Ade Edmondson and Rik Mayall's *Bottom* and the yellow *Mr Bean* one was played relentlessly until the rudimentary plastic housing almost fell to pieces. Then when DVDs took over I bought all the *Def Comedy Jam* DVD box sets at a 25 per cent Virgin staff discount and watched them over and over until they were scratched like a restaurant chopping board. I used to quote all the routines, which thinking back were clearly racially insensitive for a middle-class white guy to be shouting on the shop floor of a Virgin Megastore. Then when the internet took over I became obsessed with downloading Dane Cook MP3s for free on Limewire. He was huge in America at the time and nobody knew him in the UK, which of course made me love him more. Any hint of 'I knew them before they were big' when you're that age is unbelievably exciting.

I had very little sense of what good or bad comedy really was, but these were the things that I'd stumbled on and found they somehow resonated with me and made me howl with laughter.

Now I was here at Laugh Factory about to see some real live comedy for the first time. The show started and the first comedian stepped onstage. I was nervous for him yet I didn't need to be. It was his. He thought of something, said it and then he dealt with the consequences.

The atmosphere of the club was like nowhere else I'd ever been. A perfect mix of the creative yet alienating feel of a theatre and the fun feel of a nightclub. I immediately felt more comfortable here than I'd ever felt in either of those places. The mixed bill of four comedians threw their hearts and souls from their mouths to entertain the hundred or so punters in front of them. It felt dangerous and utterly thrilling.

One comedian was great, two were fine and one was terrible. This is the perfect comedy night for an English punter. Americans like it when every act performs to their full potential. English people differ. We have an ingrained sense of enjoyment of failure. We love to laugh, but we also love to see someone squirm to silence until they cry so we have something to tell the office on Monday. I enjoyed it so much I went back the next day. Then the next day. Then the next. After a few weeks they started letting me in for free like a vagrant English child who needed shelter. I was the Oliver Twist of comedy, returning and politely asking, 'Please, sir, can I watch some more?'

I never fathomed doing it myself. I didn't really know that you could do it. I assumed there was some sort of comedian university or vetting process you had to undergo before you were allowed to step onstage, like a driving test.

There were two shows on the Tuesday so that afternoon I headed down the hill again, thinking I could stay, watch twice as much comedy and be alone for less of my day. I'd come over to LA with the idea that I was going to attend acting classes, go for meetings and become a proper thespian but so far I'd shot a gun, played golf, pretended it was my birthday and walked to a comedy club every day.

There were maybe thirty or so pacing performers, way more than usual. I was to discover that the early show on the Tuesday was the open mic afternoon.

Everyone got their names drawn out of a hat to decide the running order and, as evidenced by the fact that I was the only one not pacing, I was clearly the only one there who wasn't performing. The MC approached me. 'Have you put your name in the hat?' he asked.

'No,' I replied.

'Do you want to?'

'No,' I repeated quickly.

'We have an audience member, everyone!' he shouted.

Everyone snapped round to look at me like I was a tray of canapés coming out of the kitchen at a party.

Clearly I was the only one. Nobody who isn't performing comes to these shows. This was the training ground and I sat on the edge watching like a voyeur in a bush. I'd stumbled upon the vetting process, the comedian university. There was no driving test; you just did it. It was as easy as shooting a gun.

The support the would-be comedians showed each other was short-lived. They all left once they walked off stage. The people who were lucky enough to have their names pulled out of the hat first had a full audience but the bunch slowly depleted and the possible laughter ebbed away until it was just me and the 'headliner'.

It's an odd thing watching a stranger talk directly to you through a microphone. There's a fine line between stand-up comedy and a conversation and when there's only one audience member, I think that line is crossed. He'd prepared his material and waited all afternoon to try it, so he just ploughed on and played it like it was a full room. He also definitely didn't need the amplification device for me to hear him but him holding a microphone was the only thing that made this a performance instead of a chat.

He looked so alone but so did I. There was a mutual respect between us, like De Niro and Pacino in *Heat*.

I laughed at everything. Maybe even too much, to the point it may have started to sound sarcastic. Even though there was nobody watching he was technically having the best gig of the night. It was soul-destroying yet strangely inspiring. He was working on something. Honing a craft. This was him practising in the garden with his nunchucks.

Most actors sit at home waiting for someone to call them to tell them that they can work, but these guys can work all the time. There's something palpable to improve at and a ladder to move up. Technically it's not work because you don't get paid for years but it feels like you are working towards something instead of floating in an ether of luck and hope.

'I think I can be better than them,' I thought. This is the catalyst for most comedians to get up and try it themselves. It's like a drunk person at a circus thinking they can tame a lion.

I went back to my adopted apartment and searched for local open mic gigs on the internet. I really have no idea how people lived before the internet. I imagine you just had to find out information on 'the grapevine', whatever the fuck that is. I decided not to attend the Laugh Factory open mic because I didn't want it to go horrifically and be unable to go back to my only entertainment within a mile radius.

The Google grapevine said there was another open mic night close by. It was in the attic of the 'Rainbow Inn' on Sunset Boulevard and it was . . . tomorrow. Fuck. That's literally the day after today. Shall I do it? Can I do it? Fuck it, I'm gonna do it.

I practised the next day for hours, walking around my friend's flat holding a cordless phone as a pretend microphone. It was the most I'd talked since I had arrived in LA two weeks before.

The Rainbow Inn was a sweaty thirty-minute LA walk up Sunset Boulevard from my lodgings. I whispered my made-up routines to myself over and over like a terrified Christian praying before being thrown to the lions.

The pub stood alone on the street with a wooden facade and a rainbow flag hanging above the door. I walked in. There was wood everywhere; they were really hammering home the log-cabin vibe. People were scarce. It didn't have the warm atmospheric feel of the Laugh Factory that I had become so used to. For a venue with a rainbow emblazoned over the entrance it didn't have that fun homosexual ambience you'd expect. I asked at the bar if there was an open mic on tonight.

'Upstairs,' the barman snapped without looking up. He was clearly asked that question a lot by petrified performing people and hated it.

I went up the inevitably wooden staircase into a compact room hidden in the eves. There was a sheet draped over one of the beams (wooden, obviously) that made a makeshift backdrop and people dotted around the room tuning instruments or talking to themselves while looking frantically at scribbled notes.

I approached a man with a clipboard standing at a small, brushed-steel – oddly enough – bar. Usually due to an ingrained Pavlovian response I despise clipboard people because they automatically remind me of a PE teacher or a nightclub door person. I had spent my life trying and failing to impress both of these natural authorities. It's very similar to the importance conveyed by a lanyard, as I have discussed, but lanyards are used for good by legends and clipboards are used exclusively for evil by pricks. The lanyard is the Professor X to the clipboard's Magneto.*

'I'm here for the open mic?' I enquired like a scared kid at his first day at a new school.

'Hi!' he said energetically yet insincerely in that way Americans tend to do. 'It's $10,' he added, cutting straight to the chase unapologetically in that way Americans also tend to do.

I put the crumpled money from my pocket on the bar. In America, when you're new in comedy people don't pay to watch you, you pay to be watched. It's something the UK comedy circuit has somehow managed to avoid by the wonderful 'bring a friend' loophole. The friend pays, and you pay for that friend to pay, so it's basically the same thing. It means that there are more people in the gigs; however it quickly kills your social life as you lose all your friends by subjecting them one by one to your inexperienced, unfunny, onstage attention-seeking.

'What's your name, kid?' Clipboard Man said like we were in a saloon in the Wild West and I was the new guy in town.

I didn't want to give my real name in case it went badly and they got in touch with my family and friends and they all disowned me. When you start comedy you have normal levels of shame. Slowly you realise that nobody cares and your fear of humiliation ebbs away until you are left with the thin veil of shame I'm left with today.

'My name is . . .' I paused for too long. Nobody pauses

---

* If you're wearing a lanyard while holding a clipboard, they cancel each other out and I have no opinions about you.

that long for a question as simple as a thing you have known all of your human life. 'Michael Brown.' This is my stepdad's dad's name (step-grandad?). I assumed I plucked it from the family connection but now I think about it I was petrified of speaking into a microphone and shitting myself during my set. Those two fears had probably coalesced and manifested in my impromptu stage name 'Mike Brown'.

'Are you a comedian or a band?' he said while looking at his clipboard.

'Comedian?' I replied with an obvious question mark at the end of it. I was very uncomfortable saying I was part of something I had never done before. It would be like saying 'I'm a fireman' when you are not qualified, have never been paid for it and you're scared of fire. But I thought I should take this opportunity to find out more about what I was letting myself in for.

'Have you got any advice?' I asked innocently.

'Enjoy yourself and just try not to die!' He said in a light-hearted, scripted tone like he'd said it to hundreds of newbs before me.

I chuckled uncomfortably, not understanding the joke or hazard. 'Sorry, why would I die?' I asked in the clichéd Queen's English that Americans all assume we speak in.

He laughed at my sweet naïvety. 'If you die it means you're having a bad gig,' he said. I can imagine. There's surely no way of having a heart attack and a good gig at the same time. I knew that Tommy Cooper had died live on television at Her Majesty's Theatre and he was so funny the audience thought it was a joke. I didn't want to die a nobody in an attic while a band set up behind me and the audience were just glad it was over. Clipboard Man could see the confusion on my scared face and informed me that 'die' is an American comedic term (which us Brits have now adopted) that means 'to have a bad gig'. He then continued to offer more knowledge of comedy colloquialisms:

Die = Bad

Kill = Good

Kill and not be killed. It seems this is very much the comedy mentality you are supposed to adopt. However, there is a spanner in the works to make it more confusing for outsiders:

Bombing = Bad

It seems the metaphor of killing one person is considered good but multiple people is bad, which seems entirely contradictory to the American approach to international relations. I started to realise why people watched plays and just told everyone through gritted teeth that they were all incredible regardless of the obvious deficit of talent they'd just witnessed.

'What about slay, is that one?' I asked.

Slay = You are watching an amazing Beyoncé concert, not a comedy gig

This was complicated. But by now Clipboard Man had had enough of educating me.

'Lights go off after three minutes. You're the one before the last act: after Electric Umbrella, before Fur Purse,' he said then turned to the next performer who'd just arrived.

'He needs to write the word "penultimate" on that fucking clipboard,' I said under my breath.

I'd prepared five minutes. That was too long. I'd just have to cut the middle bit and speak quicker.

I hadn't felt fear like this since Knifey Knifey Crash Mat or kissing Big Chin. I kept telling myself that if I 'died' the news wouldn't travel across the Atlantic and if it did, people would find it very hard to believe my step-grandad had tried stand-up.

The night started. Clipboard Man introduced the first act. Band. Comedian. Band. Comedian. Band. Comedian. The room got more and more empty as the performers slowly departed.

The atmosphere was thinning. However, doing comedy between bands meant that compared to the Laugh Factory there were a few more people there.

A band, Fur Purse, was on after me so hopefully there would be a few people for me to play to. If I were unlucky, Fur Purse would be a lonely solo acoustic singer. If I were luckier, it'd be a classic band set-up so I'd have three or four members as my audience. If I were very lucky, Fur Purse would be a Slipknot tribute so I'd have nine audience members, although people who love Slipknot don't seem too chipper and ready for a chuckle and if they did, laughing through a mask is hard.

The night wore on, the small room became roomier. Electric Umbrella were called to the stage, which was actually more of a corner than a stage as it wasn't elevated from the rest of the floor. They were terrible, but I was about to go onstage afterwards for the very first time and this wasn't a moment to judge.

The MC approached the microphone for the 'one before the last one' time and looked at his bit of paper. 'Next up, a comedian . . . Michael Brown.'

I sat for a second thinking someone had stolen my space then realised I had given a fake name. IT'S ME. The barman, Clipboard Man and Fur Purse (which seemed like a classic band set-up) clapped.

I jumped up to the microphone, pulled it out of the mic stand and even though I clearly didn't need it as everyone was no more than three feet from my feet, I spoke into it. It felt so different to holding the cordless phone in the flat. I was so scared. I started to shake. I wished the guy from the gun range was there to hug me from behind.

My first 'bit' was to talk in an American accent in an annoying energetic manner then suddenly cease and say, 'I'm actually English.' Gold, I think you'll agree. It got a titter. Less than I expected yet more than I feared. My first taste. I honestly can't remember anything else. It was probably a mixture of my own ideas and stories stolen from Lily's far funnier life.

Then just as I was starting to get comfortable, it went dark. I thought for a second I'd had a stress-induced heart attack and actually died like I originally feared then I remembered the three-minute comedy curfew. The faint noise of lacklustre clapping slowly spread around the six or so 'audience'. The lights flicked back on and I winced with the brightness. I had survived. I returned to my seat at the bar. It was exhilarating. It was just like a rollercoaster – a long wait in line, petrified, then you do it and it's not so bad and you just want to do it again. Maybe I could join the list after the band and put down my real name so they wouldn't notice it was me again.

People had chuckled. I wouldn't say they laughed, but they

chuckled. It didn't feel like a resounding success but it was definitely not a loss.

I stayed and watched the last band because I wanted to change the unsupportive system. They were shit, but so was I, and at least we were trying. I didn't care what anyone else thought. I didn't care what anyone said. I slayed and Oliver Twist had found a hobby. It was perfect for me; I loved stories and I realised jokes were just little compact stories. Instead of a beginning, middle and end, they have a set-up and punchline. The best stories occur when two unlikely things come together, and it takes you on a ride you didn't expect. A joke is the same. It's putting two things together you didn't expect, often for a funny image or reveal.

I returned the next week and did the same gig. I couldn't wait to experience that feeling again. It was a drug and I wanted the feeling of that first hit again and again.

I was suddenly excited about my future as a human being on this planet. I had something to focus on, devote my time to and improve at. I signed up to some small-time open mic gigs in London via the online grapevine. All comedians, no bands. I was already moving up in the world. I didn't know if it would lead to anything but it would certainly help my confidence with other things, like dating or auditions. If I could talk through a microphone to a roomful of people proficiently then surely I could become better at talking to one stranger without a microphone?

At LA Airport on my way home I had a spring in my step due to my new pastime and generally just loving airports. I always arrive early to soak up the sweet atmos.

I'd passed through security successfully with a little pat-down and, after helping to stack the security trays to show non-stackers I'm a better person than them, I wandered into a bookshop to buy all of the autobiographies of stand-up comedians I could find.

If you're young and don't know what an autobiography is, it's like a selfie but of words. This is not an autobiography. I haven't lived a long or exciting enough life to deserve to write one of those. Although that doesn't stop people writing one, or worse, pretending to write one these days.

I was browsing the non-fiction section, walking my fingers from spine to spine looking for comedians I'd heard of. There were so many I hadn't heard of. I had so much watching and learning to do. I worked my way down to the bottom shelf, going down on one knee on the soft bookshop carpet. There's nothing more relaxing than a bookshop carpet. I really have no idea why, it just feels so safe and serene. They should think about doing bookshop yoga. Sitting on a bookshop floor is also completely acceptable; nobody bats an eyelid. For some reason it feels odd everywhere else. They sell books in Tesco but if you sat down in one of the aisles and started having a read while everyone weaved their trollies past you'd be thrown out and you wouldn't get your trolley pound back.

A long set of legs upon powerful high heels stood next to me as I knelt.

I tracked my eyes upwards, like a devoted servant to a queen. I couldn't see her face. It was blocked by the copy of *Twilight* that she was swiftly leafing through. Then she slid the book back on the shelf and I got the first glance of her face.

She was a serious, no-nonsense-looking older lady, with short blonde hair that rested neatly on the shoulders of her grey, pressed suit jacket.

I realised I was staring. She looked down at me on my knees. 'Will you marry me?' I joked playfully. It was a boldness that I hadn't had previously. The comedy confidence was already working. She smiled and laughed but not enough to open her lips. She gazed back at the bookcase.

'That's my favourite book,' I said, gesturing towards *Twilight*.

It was a lie, I hadn't read it. I now know that it's the book of choice for fourteen-year-old girls and it's about sexy vampires and shirtless man wolves. It had a great cover* and I wanted to start up a conversation so hedged my bets and went for it.

'Why?' she replied, in an intriguing, sexy accent that I was unable to pin down after just one three-letter word. I hadn't expected questions that delved into the favourite book lie. So I just lied further.

'It's just . . . beautiful.' How incredibly vague of me.

This is me talking about the book I once saw voted on a website as the worst book of all time. So many books have been written in all of time. This was voted the worst. Of all time. And I just called it 'beautiful'. I'm just glad she didn't pick up *Mein Kampf* as I hear the cover is quite fetching.

I couldn't be sure how old she was. Yoga and expensive

---

* We are always warned to not to make cover-based book decisions. If you're reading this because it has a good cover than you are very naughty indeed.

creams had made her age completely unidentifiable. Either way I had definitely started a conversation with a lady about ten years older than me by recommending a book targetted at girls about ten years younger than me.

'Where are you from?' I said, finally getting to my feet.

'Half German, a quarter Danish and a quarter Polish but I now live in London.'

It was a sexy yet utterly confusing pie chart of nations.

She handed over a business card. Her name was Violet and she had a high-flying job in London that had at least three words in the title that I didn't understand.

I wrote my email with Biro on a crumpled napkin I found stuffed in my pocket. That was my business card. The sharp Biro kept piercing the soft tissue, making the process agonising and producing an end product that looked like a blue sneeze. I came away with an embossed finely printed card; she left with some of my doodled litter.

'I have to go, my flight is in thirty minutes,' she said in the now distinguishable, yet still sexy voice.

I kissed her left cheek then the right, going in and out of the range of her exotic perfume atmosphere.

'*Au revoir*,' I said smugly, immediately realising French wasn't in her pie chart and regretting it. My flight was in four hours so I went back and helped stack some more trays.

I arrived home a tired mess but excited by the glimmer of new horizons. I couldn't stop thinking about Violet and stand-up comedy in no particular order. After a week of hovering over the keys of my computer wanting to send her an email but unsure what to say I simply sent her a copy of

Twilight in the post instead. 'Books full of loads of words speak louder than words,' I thought. I still hadn't read it. I was unaware I was sending her a 'beautiful' book about a sexy teenage vampire who glistens in the sun.

I'll be honest, after I sent the book I devoted all of my thought to stand-up and I forgot about Violet. But then an email arrived in my inbox a few weeks later.

'Thank you! I loved the book. Violet.'

I imagined her saying it in her odd accent. I also imagined her trying to decipher my email address from the scribbled rag that I had passed her.

We slowly emailed back and forth, with the conversations growing steadily longer and more familiar. Every time she referenced the book I would say 'I love that bit' or brush over it as I still hadn't read it.

Meanwhile, I started on the open mic comedy circuit, picking up mostly horrific gigs wherever and whenever I could. It seems stupid to say now but I honestly didn't know comedians repeated the same jokes onstage on different nights. I spent the first twenty-five gigs or so doing new material at every single one. Never working on one bit, crafting it gig by gig into something solid, but just starting with a new bunch of shitty ideas every time. I couldn't understand why everyone was so much better than me.

As I started to gig with the same people, my generation of newbies, I slowly began to realise that the other comedians would be repeating themselves. It would be like a carpenter spending five minutes making an owl sculpture, not completing it but then abandoning it and starting a fresh owl the next day. After ten days the carpenter is left with ten shit sculptures that look like wooden World Cup trophies instead of one that slightly resembles a wise bird.

Violet and I met for our first non-airport encounter at a swanky restaurant. It was a little too up its own butt for me but I wanted to impress her and show her I wasn't a child.

We both looked so different, so un-airport-ish. Most people in airports are basically in their bedclothes, post- or pre-nap, sometimes with a pillow strapped around their neck like a dog who's just had their nuts snipped off.

By contrast, Violet was wearing powerful red lipstick, serious black-rimmed glasses and stilettos which made her slightly taller than me when I greeted her at the table.

'Hello,' she said in her strong Germanic tone as she sat down.

'I love your dress,' I said politely.

'I hate your shoes,' she replied directly with a hint of a tiny grin. She was so damn . . . *German*. So stern and unapologetic. I loved it. I always spent so much time and effort keeping people happy with little white lies that it felt refreshing to meet someone who just said what they thought, regardless of the lack of tact.

My shoes were horrific; she was right. I don't really wear shoes and it was almost like she could sense that they made me uncomfortable. I was trying to dress like an adult but they didn't fit the rest of my outfit so made me look younger, like a teenager who has been forced by his mum to wear shoes at a wedding.

'And so small,' she added, smiling slightly. Damn it. She had noticed my size six and a half feet.

'Women in a nightclub must assume you have a small

penis,' she continued. It was true they did but what she didn't know is I can fit into Heelys. I can round up women in a nightclub like a sheepdog.

I needed to change the subject. 'What year were you born?' I asked slyly, thinking it was a question easier on the ear than 'How old are you?' To which she of course replied, 'I am thirty-six.' Again with a slight smirk.

She had a PHD in some science thing; I had a GNVQ in art and design. She had a cool job I didn't understand; I had no job to try and understand. She had an exciting accent; I sounded normal. She had money, I had none and I was twenty-one and she was thirty-six.

We were so wonderfully mismatched, like the Lady and the Tramp or Kristoff and Elsa in *Frozen* and we just let it go and enjoyed it.*

It was incredible to meet someone who was so damn sorted. She knew exactly what she was doing with her life, friends, career and men. She already had all the lottery numbers and I was the bonus balls. I'd never dated anyone who wasn't my age before and so far it was proving excellent. I told her about my new exciting foray into the world of stand-up comedy while we ate oysters. I ordered them entirely to impress her. I think they're disgusting – they taste like drowning – but I thought it was worth it for the conversation about whether to chew or swallow them.

'But you are not funny,' she said while pushing her

---

* I love that song so much. Like everyone else I had it in my head for about a year and a half. However it becomes a completely different song if you imagine it's about fighting constipation.

thick-rimmed glasses back up her nose. She loved tearing me down with her cutting remarks and it was frustratingly sexy.

'I have a joke for you,' she added. I didn't realise it at this point but that's what most people reply with when you tell them you're a stand-up comedian.

'How many bananas can you eat on an empty stomach?' she said with no hint of humour in her voice.

'I don't know, how many bananas *can* you eat on an empty stomach?' I replied, excited for the reveal.

'One, because after that it is not empty,' she said, straight-faced. I chuckled out of politeness. Technically that's not a joke – it's a fact. She might as well have said, 'To know when to mate, a male giraffe will continuously headbutt the female in the bladder until she urinates. The male then tastes the pee and that helps it determine whether the female is ovulating.' Feel free to repeat that in the office on Monday; it's true, I read it on the internet.

I attempted to pay the bill but she heavily insisted on taking care of it herself. I really would have been happy to pay although it would have definitely taken me past my overdraft limit so I was even happier she stepped in. It feels silly being past your overdraft and ordering oysters. I think this officially meant I was a toy boy. And you know what?! I was quite content with that.

We walked to the taxi rank and I opened the leading car door for her.

'I'll get into the next one,' I said politely. We were both fully aware that I was not going to get in a taxi. I was clearly going to walk around the corner and get the bus home. If I'd worn my Heelys I could have used them.

She leaned in and kissed me firmly with the fearlessness of someone who knew what they wanted and how they were going to get it. The kiss was ill-matched. She had a technique and wasn't willing to mould it to fit mine or at least meet halfway. Different generations kiss differently just like we dress differently and listen to different music. I had more of a fluid slightly open-mouth policy and listened to Linkin Park, whereas she sort of pecked in and out like a woodpecker and probably listened to the Corrs.

She initiated the end of the face embrace and smoothly sat in her carriage.

'Goodbye, hoof boy,' she said, gesturing towards my tiny feet as the taxi door closed. I think I liked her. It was odd but utterly exciting.

I saw her again the week after at a similar-vibed restaurant. I started to relax more around her now that I understood her playful harshness a little better. I didn't feel like I was pretending as much this time and nor was she. I didn't feel the need to swallow sea jizz to impress her and she allowed herself to smile more. I went to pay the bill and again she insisted on taking care of it, slapping her black card on the table to trump my bright Natwest basic current account.

She invited me back to her hotel and I obliged. I remember thinking, 'Oh my God, she stays in hotels!' I was excited because I felt like Julia Roberts in *Pretty Woman*.

That night I put my trowel in her plant pot. That one was a euphemism. The sex was much like the kiss; we were very much on different vibes but it kinda worked. We were opposites attracted. I was in a hotel, with an older lady who owned a suit: that shit's exciting. Afterwards it felt a little awkward and she was very quiet. I blamed it on the fact she probably wanted to smoke because that's what people of her generation did after sex but the hotel rules wouldn't allow it.

I had so much to tell Lily. Last time I saw her I hadn't done stand-up comedy and wasn't dating a lady fifteen years my senior. I couldn't wait to tell the tomboy about being a toy boy. So much had changed. Apart from the cheese shop, obviously.

I was due to meet Lily in London as she was driving up to attend a very special gig, or 'concert' as Violet probably calls them. When we were fifteen we were obsessed with a band called Crazy Town. They were a band that did a frustratingly catchy song called 'Butterfly' in 2001. They were part of a movement in music called nu metal and Lily and I loved it. It was a mixture of metal, emo and rap and it was the newest and fleetingly coolest sub-genre of metal music. Not many people knew but 'nu' was the new word for new. Included in this sub-genre were bands like Korn, Slipknot, Crazy Town, System of a Down and Queens of the Stone Age. My mum once accidentally combined the last two and said, 'Joel, what's that band you like? Is it Queens of the Down Syndrome?' My mum had actually stumbled upon a great name for a band made up entirely of transsexuals with Down syndrome.

Crazy Town had reformed after years apart and Lily and I were to finally, after six years, see them live.* We were beyond excited.

---

* 'Live' not 'live'. It's so strange that 'live' and 'live' are spelled the same. I mean 'live' like in the flesh at a gig not watch them live as in watch them through a window from the bushes just existing in their dwelling.

The gig was at the Garage in Islington and we met at the Italian restaurant across the road to carb load before we attempted to mosh. When we sat down to our bread and olives we couldn't believe our eyes: Shifty Shellshock, the lead singer of Crazy Town, was eating at a nearby table! We couldn't contain our excitement. We didn't want to ask for a photo as he was eating and that seemed rude; nobody wants a mid-spaghetti selfie. Interestingly, one would expect a rapper to be sloppy with his manners but I can inform you that Shifty eats with his mouth firmly shut. Not entirely shut, obviously; he opens it to get the fuel in but once the food is inside the chamber and is being chomped his manners are impeccable.

I told Lily the news; I was seeing a 36-year-old German scientist and I was now a stand-up comedian.

'I have some news too,' she said, not reacting to what I said at all. She clearly wasn't listening to my news because she was thinking about her own.

She then started to regale me with a lengthy story which started with her and Peter walking past a ring shop – she described a ring they'd seen and liked – before going on to talk about their trip to 'Madrid, in Spain' a few weeks later, telling me of the turbulence on the flight, the weather every day and the horrific paella they had on the first night. Then on the Thursday, Peter got down on one knee and offered her the very same ring in a restaurant – the decor, patrons and food of which she of course described in minute detail.

'To cut a long story short – he asked me to marry him.'

I was happy for her but that happiness was blighted by

her classic terrible use of that phrase. I couldn't imagine any details that she'd left out. She said 'Madrid in Spain'. We all know Madrid is in Spain. If she wanted to cut it short she could have finished the story at the ring shop.

This blew my German scientist stand-up news out of the water. 'We're getting married in six months,' she said while doing tiny claps. Six months?! That was so soon.

I really don't like weddings. I'm up for people loving each other, that's great, but is there really any need for them to spend a year's earnings telling everyone they know? And people then pretend it's the best day of their life because they spent so much money on it. Was it really better than the day you went to Alton Towers and there were no queues? I doubt it. Even if it is the best day of your lives, it's really not for your guests. It's just a day of waiting for food – a festival with one shit band on. I think the thing I hate the most is waiting for the happy couple to get back from having a full photoshoot together with all the combinations of family members. I understand that formal photos were a thing in 1899 but now we all have cameras so why not just let everyone enjoy themselves and capture it naturally instead of forcing us to have our first photoshoot since school photo day? The only reason brides and grooms have all the formalities is due to the history of a religion that they most likely don't believe in anyway. Why don't people just have a party without the formalities?

And then there're the stag dos, which I hate even more than weddings. It's a licence for men to huddle together and act like gorillas on MDMA, a clusterfuck of masculine adrenaline in fancy dress. They're all away from their own unhappy marriages for the weekend and can't wait for their friend to join them in disappointing matrimony. It really shouldn't be called a 'do'. A 'do' is a civilised event where your mum might invite some villagers round and put on a nice spread with some blinis. There is nothing 'do-ish' about a stag do. It should be called a cock huddle or a stag don't. We're all expected to take a weekend off for the stag, then another weekend off for the wedding and, on top of all that, pay for a fucking toaster.

I really don't think my parents' divorce has had any effect on me at all. I don't know what you're talking about.

'The wedding's in Thailand,' Lily added.

Oh for fuck's sake.

'Flights are cheap if you book them now and I would love you to be there.'

She was going to have a small wedding in Thailand with the important inner circle people then a big party at home with the less important outer circle.

'The party is at Rockhampton Cricket Pavilion!' she squealed. I really had never seen her squeal. It was so wonderful how happy she was.

RCP holds a lot of history for Lily and me because it was where our band played our first gig. She couldn't play an instrument but she didn't let that stop her wanting to set up a band. She asked me to be the singer one day in maths class.

'I can't sing,' I said.

'It doesn't matter, you don't put that face on drums,' she replied. I grudgingly agreed, thinking we would probably never perform in public anyway.

The guitarist was Steve Dunne. He was my friend from blue group. I've known since Year 8 that I've been stupid, when our class was split into two 'random' groups, red and blue. All the pupils in the red group were like, 'We're clearly the intelligent group.' All the people in the blue group were like, 'I'm hungry.'

Steve was a tall and thin Irish boy with huge curly hair and terrible posture from a life of trying to look smaller to blend in. He looked like a leaning palm tree. He was a great guitarist. His fingers were as wiry as he was, being able to reach all the frets that other teenagers could only dream of. He was also wonderfully silly. Once, Jon Snow (the newsreader not the King of the North from *Game of Thrones*) came to our school and gave a wonderful speech in assembly about the importance of having an interest in news and politics.

'Has anyone got any questions?' Jon Snow asked at the end of his impassioned address. Steve was the only pupil to raise his hand.

'Do you like U2?' he asked proudly. The whole school laughed.

'Not really,' Jon answered.

I used to go for tea at Steve's house regularly. His whole family were Irish musical savants. At Christmas I would go round for carols and they would all pick up instruments and sing harmonies while I sang quietly and didn't know what to do with my instrumentless hands.

His mum used to always shout 'Peopleeeeeee! Dinnnnnner!' to rouse the troops for food. Once when ready to call down the family she accidentally shouted 'Paedophiiiilles! Dinnnnner!'

instead. Of course we all ran down much quicker than usual.

When Steve finally stopped laughing he asked her what had happened and she simply answered, 'I'm sorry, I was thinking about paedophiles and just got mixed up.' Fair enough.

Steve and I were real pranksters. We would prank each other constantly then shout our phrase 'You've been done-d!' at the top of our tiny teenage lungs.

'Hey, Joel, you know the phrase we've been using the entire term when we prank each other?' Steve said one day, his tall frame swaying in the playground wind.

'You've been dooooonnne-d!' I shrieked, cupping my hands around my mouth as amplification.

'I've actually been saying "Dunned". As in my surname,' he said, sniggering into his hand, barely containing his excitement.

'What? Why didn't you tell me?!' I pleaded.

'You've been DUUUUNNNNNNNED!'

Our prank phrase had been a prank the entire time. God damn you, Steve.

The final piece of the puzzle was a drummer named Brian. He was in the year above and he was friends with the bully bunch.* We didn't really enjoy Brian's company but he was an OK drummer and his cousin had a PA system.

Brian had glasses, long straight hair and was unbelievably

---

* Yes, I called them the 'bully bunch'. It's really not surprising I was bullied in school with a vernacular like that. I also got bullied because I used words like 'vernacular'.

negative. He sapped the energy out of any room by constantly saying 'That's shit' about everything. He would perpetually eat chocolate which resulted in him having a large round belly and no neck. In his green school jumper he looked like *Thunderbird 2*.

Due to Lily's brain being completely devoid of musical awareness she learned the instrument for people who can't play other instruments – the bass. By that I mean the bass guitar not the double bass or the sea bass (this will really not work in the audio book). I always feel sorry for people who play huge instruments like the double bass. The violin gets all the credit; they can play right up the front and it's easy to transport, while double bass players are hidden in the back and sign themselves up to a lifetime of ordering Uber XLs.

So, we had a band. Lily, Brian, Steve and me. Now all we needed was a name. We all threw plenty in the mix, Queens of the Down Syndrome being one of the first on the list. Steve, Lily and I would all agree on something then Brian would of course disagree with it saying 'It's shit', and we would be back to the band name drawing board

Nu metal really embraced a silent letter or a spelling mistake in their band names. 'Korn' is a perfect example. 'Corn' with a C would be a terrible name for a cool band due to it just being a common grain. 'Quorn' would of course be worse. That would be a band that sounds like metal but contains no instruments. 'Sw1tched' is another great example. 'Switched' would be too boring so why not throw a 1 in there? Great nu metal band names also make great WiFi passwords.

I checked with my mum to see what her current elaborate high-security password was for inspiration. I don't know why she always needs to make it so complex, given that she lives in the countryside. If someone was stealing her WiFi they would also have to be trespassing. Nobody wants to steal her unbelievably slow internet anyway, as it's quicker to send a letter or run to the nearest library.

'Mum, what's the WiFi password?' I asked.

'It's "Dommetts" but instead of O it's 0 and instead of S it's 5 and instead of the e it's an @ sign. All lower case apart from the Ms.'

'OK, so it's d0MM@tt5.'

'Yes.'

'It's not working.'

'Try it with an underscore before it.'

In the end no WiFi inspiration was needed: Brian declared at band practice that he had democratically decided on a name all by himself. 'Psirus with a silent P,' he said. We all just nodded and agreed because we had no better ideas, we were slightly afraid of Brian and we didn't know psoriasis was a thing.

We started practising in a damp farm barn with questionable electricity safety down the road from my house. We would lug amps and drum kits into a dusty corner and play constant noise for hours and write 'songs'. Every villager within a one-mile radius with working ears complained. Luckily in the village I grew up in there weren't many.

'You need to start writing lyrics,' Lily demanded. Apparently that was my duty as the lead singer.

What was I going to write about? My toughest life experience to date was being put in the blue group at school. I decided I would sneakily just pretend that things were worse than they actually were and see if anyone noticed, something I still continue to do in my comedy career.

Lily organised a gig half a mile from where we practised, at Rockhampton Cricket Pavilion. Don't let the Rock in Rockhampton distract you from the fact we were playing a gig in a village sport shed.

The RCP is the only thing in Rockhampton. No shop, no pub, just one cricket pavilion. For a kid like me who didn't like cricket it made my options there very limited. Although there was one classic red telephone box. Our saving grace. Lily, Steve and I would go after band practice and make prank phone calls because that's what kids did before high-speed internet happened. We could never remember any good numbers so 'prank' is a strong word. The only number we could remember was 0800 282820 because it sounded like an owl. It was for an insurance company and we just used to call up and get quotes.

The person on the phone didn't even think it was odd and would give us a competitive rate while we laughed to ourselves then put the phone down and shouted, 'You've been Duuuuuuuunnnneed!'

Lily thought instead of finding gigs elsewhere she would hire a venue and charge for tickets herself, thinking we would make a fortune. I don't know where this sudden entrepreneurial spirit had come from. A few weeks previously she was happy just listening to music, now she was a bassist and a promoter.

We ramped up our band practices to four nights a week.

'How was rehearsal?' my mum would ask when I got home.

'It's called band practice, Mum!' I'd shout then immediately run into my room to sulk and write lyrics about how lost and ignored that made me feel.

Finally, the day arrived. Brian's cousin came to set up the PA. We billed ourselves as the headliners even though it was our first gig. We had another school band supporting us. They were called 'Womb Bomb'. I thought it was pronounced 'Wom Bomb' because I didn't know the word 'womb'. I thought it was another nu metal spelling error. Turns out it was a horrific reference to abortion. It's funny now to think of such a violently named band playing in a venue made to watch cricket.

Lily arrived late in a panic and pulled me into the changing room. Usually at gig venues you have a dressing room. We had a changing room filled with cricket pads, helmets and penis protectors.

'I don't know any of the bass lines,' Lily whispered.

'It's fine, it's just nerves,' I reassured her.

'No seriously . . . I don't know any of the bass lines,' she repeated.

It turned out Lily, during our two months of practice time, had just turned herself down and been pretending to play the bass. For at least three nights a week for two months she'd basically been dancing. Through the incredible racket none of us at any point realised there wasn't the noise of a bass happening.

We called in Steve and he quickly and valiantly taught Lily the relevant bass lines amongst the grass-stained whites.

My mum had let me dye my hair red for the occasion. You

can't sing about being in the blue group and pretending to be sad with your natural hair colour. I also applied black eye liner and nail polish. I went full emo. Later on I would find out I actually put on mascara as I didn't realise that eye liner and mascara were different things. Instead of looking sultry and angry I gave myself some beautiful accentuated lashes. By trying to look frightening I ended up looking fabulous. I was just one extra chromosome away from being perfect for Queens of the Down Syndrome. I wore a goth black fishnet top baring my fifteen-year-old nips. I always think my nipples are too far around the sides of my chest. Lily used to call me 'fish eyes' because my nipples were around the sides of my body like the peepers on a fish. With the fishnet top on my body I looked like a snagged albino tuna.

Steve didn't really didn't care about his onstage look. He came straight from football practice so was just in his kit. He didn't even take off his shin pads. It felt strangely sacrilegious that he was in a football kit in a cricket pavilion. In hindsight he should have changed into full cricket gear. Lily wore baggy jeans and a crop top showing her belly button. She looked great. Dare I say it, I maybe found her a little bit sexy.

Brian wore his normal sweaty chocolate-stained jeans and a T-shirt and was pacing frantically. He was clearly more nervous than anyone else but wouldn't admit to it.

We peeked out of the changing room door as the crowd started arriving. They then almost immediately stopped arriving. Our final audience number was seven people. It was more of a cluster than a crowd really. That's fewer friends than Jesus had at the Last Supper and I hear he was quite unpopular at the time.

I'm not including our mums in that seven. So in total there were probably eleven but they weren't technically in the gig, they were just watching from the back next to the trophy cabinet, still insisting on calling it a concert.

I was frustrated about the turnout because I wanted to crowd surf. You can't crowd surf when there are only seven people to hold you. It would just feel like you're at your own funeral being carried into a church. We clearly should have spent our time calling around our friends to spread the word instead of calling an insurance company.

I felt sorry for Lily. It was her dream to be in a band performing to a full room who loved her and today it wasn't to be realised.

Nonetheless, the show had to go on. Womb Bomb went on and scared the seven people into the corners of the cricket club like the bullied bunch in the playground when Chris the bully would arrive at lunchtime.

The lead singer didn't seem to care about the lack of numbers and really got into it. He kept on licking the drummer's back while doing the devil horn fingers. The drummer would squirm and show his distaste for being cleaned like a cat while being unable to stop him because his instrument involved using both hands simultaneously.

They finished to a smatter of applause. They would have smashed up their instruments if they hadn't spent all of their allowances on them.*

---

* It must feel so cool to smash up instruments at the end of a set. I want to do it as a stand-up comedian but microphones are remarkably tough and it would really piss off the sound technicians

It was Psirus time. I looked around at the band we had created as we huddled by the door. Steve was ready. Lily was ready. Brian was . . . wearing a balaclava? I assumed it was Brian and someone wasn't robbing us for the £28 we made on the door.

'Brian, why are you wearing a balaclava?' I asked.

'It's my thing,' he snapped.

Basically he wanted to look like Slipknot but couldn't afford a good mask so instead he settled on looking like a member of the IRA who was ten years too late. He kept his glasses on underneath which immediately diminished any intimidating edge the mask had. There's nothing scary about someone who's had an eye exam.

We walked out. The drag act, the robber, the footballer and the token girl. We took our positions and I looked out at the parents and punters. Even though there were only eleven or so people it was still pretty cool.

We opened with a Korn song. We had a few covers littered through the set to keep the crowd entertained. Nobody wants to hear a band's new songs. A new band's songs are all new so we did other band's old songs instead.

It was a song called 'Blind' which was ironic because Brian's balaclava had already started to slip around so the eyeholes didn't match up with his eyes. It just looked like he was always looking left. Much like the Womb Bomb drummer he was using his hands so he had to wait till the end of the song to pull it back round.

'Blind' was the first song on the first Korn album – argu-

---

and you do not want to piss off people who wear shorts in winter.

ably the first nu metal album – and has a really long intro. I stood there awkwardly while the song built slowly over the course of a few minutes. I should have just come onstage after everyone else. When that's done at a normal gig everyone would cheer as the lead singer finally revealed himself. At Rockhampton Cricket Pavilion I think I would've just looked late.

The lyrics start with 'Are you ready?!' and I was supposed to shout it just before the heavy riff drops but I got lost where we were because I'd been standing there for so long and came in after my cue. I clearly wasn't ready.

Steve was ready. He hit the distortion pedal at the right time and the cricket shed walls reverberated to the noise of Psirus. I didn't react accordingly with my body language and continued to just stand there. I was a shy goth and I'd never been on stage before. I was so nervous even though I'd sung in front of more people at karaoke and Steve's Christmas carol nights. Luckily, the rest of the band were getting into it. Lily had been taught the basslines but I think she'd just turned herself down again and was dancing happily while pretending. Brian clearly regretted the balaclava as he was sweating even more buckets than usual and the holes were now completely round the back of his head so he looked like the girl from *The Exorcist*. Steve just looked like he was doing PE.

We dipped in and out of our own songs, which included titles like 'As I Walk By', 'Sick', 'Think' and 'Albino Black Sheep'. The only lyrics I can remember were to a song called 'Think':

Think about it
Think about it
Think about it
Think about it before you move into, the state of mind
you never wanted to
Think about it before you lose despair, lose all hope
and I'll meet you there

We really wanted you to think about it. It's probably the reason why I have remembered it. I also love how the first and second line rhymes 'to' with 'to'. Such riveting song-writing.

Amazingly, the seven people present started to mosh, which due to lack of numbers looked like more of a fight. I remember looking at my mum cowering in the back corner.

'What are they doing?' she mouthed to me over the noise.

'Don't worry, Mum, they're dancing,' I said into the mic. At the time I remember thinking it was the coolest thing I'd ever said but in hindsight I was talking to my mum at the back of a gig and there is really nothing cool about that.

I'm not very good at moshing. I think you have to have an ingrained anger which spirals from some sort of hardship to excel at it. It's hard to mosh when you can't stop thinking about how darn good your mum's lasagne is with its many wonderful layers.

We approached the final song, and it was a belter: Papa Roach's 'Last Resort'.

It was mine and Lily's favourite song and we were beyond excited to play it, or at least pretend. I stood at the front, mascara running down my cheeks like a fresh divorcée.

'This is our last song. This is Papa Roach – "Last Resort",' I said proudly.

The magnificent seven cheered.

'No! My hands hurt!' Brian shouted while shaking his head atop his thick neck.

The cheering ebbed away. Lily and I looked at each other in disbelief. He had bloody ruined it. I wanted to just do it anyway but unfortunately without the noise of the drums you'd really hear that Lily wasn't playing anything.

Brian lifted his achey hands aloft and walked back into the changing room. That was the end of the gig.

'His hands hurt so GOODNIGHT!' I shouted into the microphone and Brian's cousin immediately stepped in and started unplugging the PA. It was terribly anticlimactic. We were forced by Brian to end on one of our shit songs that nobody knew.

I realised after the gig he was obviously wearing the balaclava because he was ashamed. He thought fewer people would recognise him and talk about it in school. It of course achieved the absolute opposite effect: the news of him playing drums in a balaclava with his glasses on underneath spread like wildfire.

We struggled on for a bit and played one or two more gigs, even finding a new drummer called Nick, who was cool, but it didn't work out. Psirus broke up shortly after and never played again.

Lily was pretty devastated. She always wanted to get us back together but it never happened, even though she promised to learn the bass lines. Unfortunately, it was fun but it wasn't for me, Brian went into hiding and Steve joined another band who became big in Taiwan.

The idea that Lily was going to have her wedding party in that same venue was actually pretty incredible. It was going to be lots of fun with lots of stupid memories. I actually really liked the way she was going to do the wedding malarky. The main event in Thailand and then a party at RCP meant minimal people waiting for food. The fact I had to buy a flight to Thailand was frustrating but at least it meant I could get some sun on my pasty pins. I told myself that I was going to buy the flights the next day.

Meanwhile we had a Crazy Town gig to go to. We walked over the road from the Italian restaurant to the venue, handed our overly handled tickets to the doorman and wandered in. The stench of vomit immediately smacked you in the face as you crossed the threshold. After years of late-night revellers, the stink of caught-short spewers had soaked into the carpet leaving a gift for anyone entering.

There were way fewer people there than I expected. More than Psirus but fewer than I thought would be there. We missed our chance to see them live in 2001 in front of thousands of people because we had our GCSEs so we would have to make do with seeing them in 2007 in front of fifty.

We were an odd bunch. We were all clearly uncool kids who were trying desperately to fix that in adulthood. You could tell everyone in that room spent ten long years really panicking about how to wear their bag.

Crazy Town bounded out onstage, immediately throwing their T-shirts into the audience. There weren't enough people there to catch them and those present were past the age of wanting a sweaty man's T-shirt so they just flopped to the floor and stayed there. How were they sweaty already? They looked like they came straight from Bikram yoga.

There may have only been fifty people there but they really played that gig like it was 2001 and there were thousands of people screaming their names and not dropping their T-shirts. The lead singer threw water on the audience like we needed cooling down. We really didn't. It was actually rather chilly. If my mum were there she would have told me to change otherwise I'd 'catch a cold'. Out of everyone in there the band were definitely the ones that looked like they needing a hosing down. They were all still in great shape. Most rock stars usually let themselves go as soon as they can't afford drugs but they looked incredible. The carbonara didn't show. Maybe it was the Bikram.

Lily and I were loving it, singing along far more than the others around us and happily nodding along.

My favourite part of any gig is the links between the songs. I think it's possibly why I became a comedian because stand-up comedy is all link and no song. At one point, Shifty Shellshock came out with an absolute blinder.

'This is a new song,' he said in a gravelly Californian accent, panting heavily from the last track.

The room collectively thought, 'Just play "Butterfly".'

'You know when people give you negativity? People spout negative shit to your face, or on the internet? Sometimes you've gotta take those negative feelings and just put them in your backpack and get on your way.' Shifty stopped as if he'd finished then added, 'This song is called "Backpack".' Of course it was. It was either that or 'Spout'.

The link was great, the song was fine.

The gig finished on the big hitter we had all been waiting

for: 'Butterfly'. The room came alive. Everyone went to crazy town. Lily and I rapped along to every word; it turned out not many people knew the second verse like we did but we didn't care. The band left the stage triumphantly, oddly less sweaty than they arrived but with the drummer's hands perfectly intact, and we left the venue hyperactive and still damp. Next time I'll take my log flume poncho, I thought.

The night really made me reflect on how much Lily and I had been through together. The band, the bullies, blue group and crash mats. I couldn't believe she was getting married. It felt like it was time for her to move on. We were all growed up.

I saw Violet again the next day. We had a very strict system. She would text me on Sunday, I would meet her at a restaurant, then we would go to her hotel. It was a highly efficient German machine. Vorsprung durch Technik.

It worked for me because there weren't many stand-up gigs on the day of the Lord due to everyone drinking the day before the day of the Lord.

I was slowly picking up more and more stage time across the city. Sometimes travelling to more exotic places such as Luton or Gravesend (sorry, Gravesend). I was becoming obsessed with gigging. I'd print off a Google map of London then go on the *Time Out* website, select 'comedy' and circle all the gigs that had more than ten people on the bill. The more people on the bill, the more likely someone would drop out and I could fill their space. I'd find them on the map and head to the first one waiting for a no-show. If the bill was full, I'd head to the next one, and so on and so on, until success. At maybe one in four gigs I would get handed a £5 note afterwards by the promoter. It meant so much to me. The fact that I was earning money for this blew my mind. When I wasn't doing comedy, I was watching it or pacing back and forth in my bedroom talking to myself in the mirror. On one of the few times I had a gig on a Sunday, Violet came to see me. She sat at the back and didn't laugh at all. She was such a weirdo. I assume she wanted me to do more facts.

Slowly I started to get booked for gigs so I didn't have to turn up and hope to jump in as a substitute.

On one occasion I got offered two gigs in one night and I couldn't make the transport work so had to say no. The next day I bought a bike from a charity shop so I could never say no again and started flying from gig to gig, slowly improving my set of jokes and legs.

I'd read in Jimmy Carr's book that he did almost 300 gigs in his first year of comedy. That gave me a goal and I became hellbent on beating it on my bicycle. My thought was that the more gigs I had in a night the more likely it would be that I'd have a good one. I would also feel so much more confident at the second one. My idea was that I would keep going until eventually I was that confident at the first.

I went on my weekly day of the Lord date with Violet. We'd been dating for around six months by this point. I mean I say dating but it had never really moved further from where we reached on our second rendezvous. Just like in my comedy set, we had a routine and we stuck to it. We were comfortable around each other now but it was clear that she didn't want anything more.

'Would you like another bottle of wine?' I asked mid-date while chewing on an expensive steak.

'I'm married,' she replied calmly as if she'd just said 'Chilean Malbec'. Of course she was. Shit. It suddenly all made sense why this rich businesswoman fifteen years my senior was interested in a poor weird fledgling comedian who wasn't a student yet still lived in the squalor expected from one. I honestly couldn't believe I hadn't seen it before. Like when you found out Ricky Martin was gay.

A Rolodex of emotion flicked through my face. I was annoyed, then turned on, then angry at myself for feeling turned on, then annoyed again.

'I'm happy for us to keep our arrangement if you are,' she said as if we were in a board room at her work making a deal. I suddenly understood why she was so successful in her business life. She was cutthroat, selfish yet strangely likeable. I thought about it. I really did. I was enjoying it but I'm really not into helping people ruin their marriages. I purposefully avoided asking if she had kids. Since then I've always slightly wanted to know but think it's best that I don't.

'I'd rather not. I'm sorry,' I said like I was turning down drugs from a pushy friend at a party. She was completely fine with it and after that meal we never spoke again. Another example of beautiful German efficiency. I was her toy boy and she just carefully dropped me out of her pram. I was actually a bit sad. It was a strange relationship but I kinda liked it. I cheered myself up by going to TGI Fridays alone and saying it was my birthday.

'She was married!' I said to Lily down the phone. It was several months after the Crazy Town gig. I hadn't been in touch for a while due to burying myself in nightly mirth and a married woman.

'I'm never going to cheat on my husband,' she said. My heart suddenly sank and a heavy feeling that I'd fucked up slapped me in the face.

'Shit,' I said, thinking I'd said it under my breath but I didn't. I looked at my digital watch for the date; the wedding was next week. 'Shit,' I said again aloud, not learning from the first time.

'Did you forget the wedding?' she said. I *had*. I'd been so involved in my own selfish exploits I'd forgotten the most important day of my best friend's life. I'd been so wrapped up in talking to strangers I'd forgotten about the person who was most important to me.

'No, of course not!' I replied in cheery way, clearly over-compensating for my mistake. The wedding that was in Thailand in seven days' time. The wedding that just the important inner circle was invited to. If the inner circle was a nipple I deserved to be removed from the areola, off the boob and into the armpit.

As soon as I hung up the phone I Googled flights. They were £2,000. I was assuming there would be an easyJet or something. I couldn't afford it. That was forty days in the cheese shop. Or 1,600 comedy gigs.

I had two choices here. Pay the £2,000 and go to my best friend's wedding. Or I could just . . . not do that. I could lie and not go. I decided on the latter and it was one of the worst choices I have ever made. To make things worse, I txtd her the day before her wedding to tell her.

Hey H. I'm really sorry. I'm not going to make the wedding due to family problems. I hope you understand.

I was trying to make it better by telling a little lie but it made it worse. Not helped by the fact that she knows my family and they were at the fucking wedding. My mum told me after I'd sent it that she was going.

'I thought you knew!' Mum said as she was on the way to the airport. Ah shit. I'd really fucked this one up.

Lily understandably didn't reply so I called and sent a million more txts to apologise. I'd been a real prick. To make things worse my mum was having a fabulous time in Thailand and kept on sending me pictures of her hot-dog legs, a new craze she'd seen on the internet.

Was there anything I could do to make it up to her? What wedding present do you get your broken best friend in an attempt to hold on to them and make them realise how much they mean to you? An idea came to me while I was riding my bike to a gig with my earphones in* (don't try that at home . . . it's genuinely dangerous and I was silly tinker) and Papa Roach came on my playlist. It was a wild idea but if I pulled it off it would be a lot of fun: I was going to get Psirus back together. She always wanted us to reform and I was going to make it happen for her wedding party. We would reform like Crazy Town and play Papa Roach's 'Last Resort', finishing the gig that we never finished. It was stupid but it was the kind of thing Lily would really appreciate and I thought I could pull it off.

I needed to find Brian and Steve and I had two weeks to do it.

---

* I had since got a new iPod and I kept much better care of this one. The pocket was zipped firmly shut.

I saw Steve a few times a year, usually around Christmas, so getting him on board the Psirus ship would hopefully be easy. He was still a wonderfully good human and he now had the most solid marriage of anyone I know. I hate weddings but the saving grace of them is watching Steve and Katie dance together at them. They just seem to really love each other, have fun and be on the same page.

I was amazed to find out he had a mobile phone now. He didn't get one for ages because it was what everyone was doing and Steve doesn't like to follow the crowd. He was the only person in school who didn't watch *Titanic*. He's also never had a haircut, he just shaves it himself when it gets long and I've tried giving him new clothes but he just loves the same five T-shirts and two jumpers.

'Do you want to get Psirus back together?' I said. There was a lengthy phone silence. I thought maybe the signal had gone on his old Nokia.

'No,' he said in a downbeat tone.

'Why not?!' I pleaded. Another silence followed.

'Joel, I have prostate cancer,' he said solemnly.

The third silence fell. I couldn't believe it. This was utterly devast—

'YOU'VE BEEN DUUUUNNNEEED!' Steve shouted down the phone into my ear. God damn you, Steve. Once a prankster, always a prick.

'Of course I'll be there. Sounds like great fun,' he said while laughing.

'Relearn Papa Roach's "Last Resort",' I told him.

'I've never forgotten it,' he replied as if he'd been waiting for this call since Psirus broke up.

Brian would be more tricky. Since Psirus parted ways I'd never really spoken to him. He was in the year above and ignored Lily and me for the rest of school. He blamed us for the balaclava story spreading around school when we really hadn't, the rumour spread itself.

He wasn't on Facebook. He was off the grid. Luckily I found his number through a friend otherwise I would have had to find a phone book and learn how to use it or check the Magna Carta. I gave him a call and after a bit of reminding he seemed to remember me. He lived in London which was handy and we arranged to meet up a few days later at 'end of play in the City' near his work. I think this was business speak but I wasn't sure. By 'the City' I assumed he meant the financial district of London around Canary Wharf but then again he could also have meant any one of the other sixty-eight cities in the UK. 'End of play' I think is an adult office term meaning the end of the working day but it sounds like you are meeting someone post-sandpit. He was clearly very businesslike in his transactions. I am very much the opposite. I still put kisses on my emails to my accountant and start them with 'Whagwan'.

I checked the details and it turned out he did mean Canary Wharf and he did mean the end of the day. I smashed it with my adult translations. I waited on the Wednesday in the Starbucks near the station.

'Joel?' A tall skinny man looked down at me with slicked gelled hair and a sharp suit.

'Brian?' I said with disbelief. My voice went so high. He looked so different without glasses, two thirds of his body weight and a balaclava.

I thought people in the year above just seemed tall because I hadn't grown yet but he was actually tall. He now looked like *Thunderbird 1*.

I shook his hand. It was all very official like we were politicians who'd met ages ago at a G20 summit or something.

'I haven't got long, I've got a couple of dates tonight,' he said confidently while pulling up his suit trousers and sitting down the way Parkinson used to do. He had strikingly bright matching socks, the only splash of colour in his otherwise formal attire. I cut straight to the chase.

'Lily is getting married,' I said, covering up my odd Primark socks.

'Who's Lily?' he replied while checking his phone for more pressing issues. I informed him that she was the bassist in Psirus.

'She's getting married? I thought she was a dyke,' he said with a grin. He knew he was pushing buttons. I hadn't heard anyone use that word in years and I knew it was on the list of offensive ones. I was starting to understand that Brian had lost lots of weight but had very much kept his bellend badge.

'Do you remember Psirus?' I asked.

'Yeah, we were shit!' he said predictably. Brian clearly didn't look back on it as fondly as Lily and I did. He didn't remember his hands hurting and not allowing us to play Papa Roach and firmly denied it. 'Doesn't sound like something I would do,' he said like he was being interviewed in court. It definitely happened and in the short amount of time that I knew him, to me it sounded just like something he would do. He was just as negative as he used to be, sucking every ounce of optimism from the situation. He couldn't even get excited about the Starbucks Christmas cups.

I was just about to ask him whether he wanted to play in Psirus with us . . . but I stopped myself. I didn't think Lily would want this guy at her wedding party. She didn't like me as it was, so I didn't think I would be making it better by inviting a plus-one prick to the occasion.

Before the coffee had a chance to cool he said he had to go to his first date. We'd met for three minutes and in that time he told me he had two dates four times. I said goodbye so he could go off and probably have sex with one of them then tell them they were shit to make himself feel good.

'Take care of those hands,' I said to him on his way out.

It was a shame that he'd turned out like this. I always have hope that the bad eggs in school will figure it out, have a change of heart and become decent dudes. However, with me and Steve we still had most of Psirus. It wasn't a full failure. Yet.

Lily got back from Thailand and she was still not answering my calls. Should I still do it? I managed to get hold of Peter. I needed to check if I was still invited to the RCP party. He said 'of course!' as if nothing had happened. I then checked if it was OK to play a little song at some point and told him the reason. He didn't really get it but was happy for us to do it anyway. He was so damn chilled. I also took the liberty of asking whether a band was already playing so we could steal their equipment for one song. Luckily there was which really made this whole operation much easier logistically.

The day arrived. Steve and I rocked up ready to rock at Rockhampton Cricket Pavilion. It was so surreal to be back.

I had been back since the Psirus gig for various cake sales and fêtes but not for years. It was . . . well, it was exactly the same. But this time it was rammed. The outer circle was huge. It was exactly the opposite of the Psirus gig eight years before. There were so many people I knew, from our life together, and so many I didn't. I must say, it was the best wedding vibe I'd ever experienced. No waiting for food, no waiting for them to get back from photographs, no religious law admin, just some short speeches and a sweet party. Lily looked incredible. Even though this was just a party she wore the wedding dress. It had a huge billowing white cumulo-nimbus skirt and she floated from guest to guest saying hellos. She eventually floated my way. I was so scared she was going to slap me and tell me to leave. But she smiled when she saw me. We hugged and she told me she was glad I came. 'I'm sorry I have been ignoring you but I was a little hurt,' she said honestly. I understood and apologised.

'Your mum said you've been gigging a lot. I'm so proud of you,' she said. I don't think she had ever said she was proud of me before and it really meant everything to me. I was so glad we figured it out. I was so, so glad. I breathed a huge sigh of relief and felt physically lighter as this huge tension left my body.

This whole wedding process had made me realise how much she meant to me. They say that you don't realise how much you need something until it's gone. I'd felt it with my Young Person's Rail Card but never with a person. I almost lost her due to my own stupid selfishness and it ripped my heart apart. Did I love her? I knew that I loved her . . . but did I LOVE her? It didn't matter. I wasn't about to make the mistake of being selfish again. This was about her and Peter and I was going to be there for them as a couple. She looked so damn happy and I really couldn't be more delighted for her. I remembered what was to come and smiled.

'What?' she said, sensing something was afoot.

'Nothing,' I said cheekily.

Eventually after the party warmed up the band came on, managing to rouse people up to dance. I thought it was odd that Peter and Lily didn't do a first slow-dance. I knew it meant a lot to her, it always had. It was the one formality of weddings that she enjoyed.

After the band had played for a while, the vibe was right. It was time. I went to the toilet to prepare. I applied mascara and a black fishnet top, baring my ageing nips. I looked in the mirror. It was ridiculous. It was perfect. We walked through the crowd just as the band stopped. I took to the microphone, a place I was way more comfortable with these days.

'When myself and Lily were fifteen we were in a band. We were called Psirus with a silent "P" and we played a gig in this very cricket pavilion. It was our dream to play to a packed room of people and play Papa Roach's "Last Resort". Unfortunately due to only seven people turning up to that gig and our balaclava-wearing drummer's hands hurting we never got to realise those dreams. Until now. Please welcome to the stage . . . Psirus guitarist Steve Dunne!'

I could see Lily at the back with her hands over her mouth. Steve walked to the stage to huge applause wearing full football kit including the shin pads.

'. . . Our drummer Brian!'

A tall man wandered onto the stage. It wasn't Brian. Our miserable drummer wearing a balaclava eight years ago worked wonderfully in our favour; I could just replace him with anyone and it still had the desired effect. The guy in the balaclava was the drummer from the wedding band and to say he was excited to be playing Papa Roach was an understatement. He was just so happy to not be playing 'Lean on Me' and 'Don't Stop Believin'.

'And last but by no means least . . . our bassist LILY!'

She walked slowly from the back of the room. She shook her head and grinned from ear to ear. She was wonderfully embarrassed but so excited at the idea of what was happening. Peter still didn't understand it but he seemed to be enjoying it nonetheless.

'I don't know how to play it,' she shouted over the cheers.

'Eight years ago, she didn't learn the bass lines and instead just turned herself down,' I said to the now attentive crowd. I went to her amp and turned it down. 'Tonight will be no different.' Everyone cheered. 'Just pretend like you always did,' I told her.

We were all in place. The bank robber, the footballer, the drag act and the bride.

'We're Psirus. This is our last song. It's Papa Roach "Last Resort".'

'Stop!' The anonymous drummer yelled out from behind us. Everyone swung to look at him.

'My hands feel incredible,' he said while raising devil horns with his right hand. Lily laughed and the crowd cheered, loving it despite not understanding any of the specific references at all.

The song began and if I say so myself, we actually sounded OK. In fact I dare to say I think we sounded better than eight years ago, without any rehearsals. People started to mosh. It was wonderful. I gestured to Lily that she should crowd surf, then offered a knee up. She didn't give it two thoughts: she put down her borrowed bass, stood on my knee and jumped atop her outer circle. I wanted to follow and jump up too but offered it to Peter instead. It was their moment. He jumped up and they held hands while they surfed on the hands of everyone they knew in Rockhampton Cricket Pavilion.

To cut a long story short – we're still friends.

I'd finally stepped into the proper adults' world. I'd dated one, started a proper career and my best friend had got properly married. Scary big adult stuff was coming my way but I believed you could still have fun even though it was changing. You can get your old band back together, your career can be stupid and not involve a spinning office chair and most importantly you can keep the friends that remind you of the fun you had before you were an adult. I should grow up but I could grow up without growing boring.

I had finally stepped into adult-dom but unbeknownst to me I was about to step into another strange world. A world filled with weird famous people.

20 June 2004

Hey JD
Just snogged in a car with Jenny. May seem mental but it just seemed right. I really love her right now. She drove me back to Surbiton. She seemed a bit

weird after tho, I don't know whether she's changed
her mind or what. If Iris replied to a txt every now
and again then things might be different but they are
how they are and I think I am just happy. Jenny loves
me for who I am and she supports me physically and
emotionally.
Sincerely, Joel

'You have size six feet?' Hannah asks. It is usually a detail
that I refrain from telling a lady because the classic ye olde
fable scares some stupid people off. I tell her that small shoes
look better. Just like tiny umbrellas and ramekins. We finish
the plates that are palatable. I think they asked us to order
so many because they knew a quarter of them were completely
inedible. Hannah puts her knife and fork parallel and I smile
to myself.

'Who's the oldest person you have had the pleasure of
being with?' I ask.

'It wasn't much of a pleasure,' she answers, then relays a
blissfully short story that is way less eventful than mine with
100 per cent fewer tangents. She is much better at giving the
abridged version of her experiences.

The Spanish guitarist starts going from table to table like
a shitty magician. He's attempting to be sensual but sounds
more like a homeless guy singing through a traffic cone. He
approaches our table and starts serenading Hannah. He's like
one of those X *Factor* contestants that make the terrible
decision to approach the judges' desk. He isn't going from
table to table to add to the romanticism, he's just preying on
couples and trying to flirt with them. I look over to the bar

and Rodrigo appears furious. He's jealous that another staff member is flirting with my date mid-date. What the hell is this place? I feel like I'm on a hidden camera show.

I don't want to be too bold and ask the guitarist to leave; Hannah can clearly do that herself and I don't have any right to do so. Hannah smiles politely as he sings directly at her while resting one knee on the floor. His chest hair is protruding heavily from his very open shirt. He finishes his un Shazam-able song, we both clap and let out a false 'yaaay'. It is clearly our way of making sure it's the end and he should move to another table. Instead he strums the guitar and starts another 'song'. I can't believe it. Hannah is dealing with it wonderfully, attempting to nod along to his non-existent timing. She is so polite, not in a boring false way like a PR person or a good waiter, but in a really open, optimistic way. She seems to think the best of people even if they are being horrific and I definitely count myself to be one of those horrific people.

Eventually she realises that her nodding is the reason he's staying and turns to face me. After a while he loses interest and wanders to the next couple who are trying to ignore him.

'I liked the German lady's banana joke,' Hannah says, slyly trying to get the conversation back on track. I shake my head in faux disappointment. 'Do you not want to ever get married?' she continues, straying from the date format we'd forged.

'No, I really don't,' I answer. I still really don't see the point. You can be happy with someone and not have to tell everyone about it. It feels like most people do it so they can change their Facebook status and get a few likes. She disagrees with me but nothing is going to change my mind. After an interval of marriage-based conversation it's my turn to ask a question. We are about to get back on track.

'What's the most spontaneous sex you've ever had?' I ask. I am looking forward to her stories more than telling my own.

Hannah thinks for a while then answers with another beautiful tapas-sized tale then asks me the same question in return.

'What's the most spontaneous sex you've ever had?'

#30 The Neon Hero

I got my first televisual job presenting *MTV News*, which is like the normal news but with all of the important world events taken out. We would talk about Ice-T not poverty and leave out the election to talk about One Direction. I was still gigging as much as I could and of course still worked at my dad's cheese shop on weekends. Getting the MTV job meant I could probably soon tell Dad that he would have to find a replacement son to help him but I held on to it a little longer in case I fucked it up and it all fell apart. I was also slowly starting to like cheese.

It was my job to interview musicians and actors, the results of which would be chopped into bitesize packages to sit comfortably between programmes like *Geordie Shore*, which is arguing and casual sex, and *Sixteen and*

Pregnant, which is arguing and the effects of casual sex.

It wasn't a huge show, it was one of those shows that was on in the background while you made your coffee between the things you actually wanted to watch. It meant I was on TV but utterly un-famous. Passers-by on the street started recognising me but would assume I went to school with them. Once a big builder man, one of those guys who are covered in dust like they just spend all day rolling in it like a naughty child, approached me in the fruit aisle in Tesco.

'Hey, are you . . . umm?' He pointed at me and squinted like that was going to help.

'Yeah, maybe?' I said.

'You were our babysitter, right?' he asked, completely sure of his answer.

'Yeah. That's it,' I conceded. It was best not to correct him to save him and me the embarrassment.

'Give me your number. Me and the wife were looking for someone the other day.' I just wanted this whole exchange to end. I gave the random builder my number. He shook my hand and a plume of dust burst out from our connecting hands like a gymnast's when he chalks up. The handshake was of course uncomfortably tight. He texted me a few times a couple of months later. I didn't reply but a part of me did think about looking after his kids for the night to make some sweet cash.

My favourite part of the MTV job was talking to actors who clearly hated the movie they were in but were contractually required to talk about how good it was to a cavalcade of journalists and presenters. You could see the slight twitch in their eye when they said, 'I am so proud of this movie.' It was amazing how some astonishing actors who could pretend to be in a war zone, holding a pretend friend who was pretend dying while they pretended to cry, were completely unable to pretend that their film was good.

I met some incredible people: Denzel Washington, Ewan McGregor, Will Ferrell, Rachel McAdams, The Muppets, Tom Hardy, Chris Hemsworth and many more, all while still smelling of cheese from the Saturday before. I even interviewed Sienna Miller. She didn't recognise me and I didn't want to remind her because basically saying 'I touched your boobies on a train and you clearly don't remember' felt a little rude. It was such a pleasure to meet so many inspiring humans, but there were a few really horrific ones. I understand that promoting a movie is probably the most frustrating part of an otherwise entirely cool job, but when the worst part of your life is talking to people for a day while you are handed free fruit, I'm sorry but your job is fucking easy.

After being there for a month or so I was starting to get to grips with the schedule and procedure. I knew which questions to ask to make the producers happy and which ones to ask to make the interview interesting for me and the interviewee. One morning when I arrived in the brightly coloured office, my producer was there to greet me. 'You have three interviews today,' he announced.

My first was with Sean William Scott from *American Pie* fame. He'd starred in a film called *Goon* which I genuinely enjoyed. It was simple, stupid funny. I went to a special screening of it in a tiny cinema in Soho. There was nobody else in there apart from Jonathan Ross. I wasn't sure whether to sit next to him or give him his space. What's the protocol?

I compromised and sat with a one-seat gap between, inspired by the male urinal rule. I think it means that technically Jonathan Ross and I have gone on a date.

SWS walked into the unbelievably claustrophobic, incredibly warm MTV studio. It was a cupboard that had ideas above its station. A basic black box with the occasional flash of neon colour to give it the youthful MTV edge. A sofa lay at the back where the interviews took place.

'Christ, it's hot in here,' Sean said in his upbeat American high school fraternity tone. He was taller than expected, contradicting the 'smaller in real life' cliché, and wore a tight T-shirt showing off his muscled physique. I'm known as a fairly smiley guy but he entirely outsmiled me. His cheeky brazen audacity brightened up the dark cupboard.

The televised conversation started, the chat flowed easily about the film with inevitable throwback questions to *American Pie*, which I'm sure he was bored of answering though you couldn't tell.

'Great T-shirt, man,' he said mid-question, distracting himself away from what he was saying and making it entirely unusable.

It was a black T-shirt with a picture of Mona Lisa on it except her face was swapped for that of an ape. Yep, I wore that on TV. I'm sure the T-shirt company had not paid the relevant money to the Leonardo da Vinci estate or the ape for use of the image but I loved it and it was new.

Receiving a compliment for a garment that you've just bought is one of life's great feelings. 'Someone else loves it,' I thought. I should have just said that aloud and moved on yet I didn't. Instead, due to a mixture of habit and me confusing his professional kindness for friendship, I leaned in for a kiss, gazing into his eyes, then pulled away, saying, 'Sorry, I completely misread the situation.'

I laughed, expecting him to reciprocate with a chuckle but he simply sat there in confusion. He said, 'Okaaay,' but in a way where people elongate the 'a' sound to fill an awkward silence. I nervously jumped on to the next question on my card to which he bounced back with a great answer and the interview was rolling again. I had momentarily tripped on a terribly laid paving slab (which I wouldn't have laid) but I styled it out into a metaphorical dance move and nobody noticed.

We were back at full bant speed in no time.

'Where did you get your sneakers from, bro?* They're sweet,' he said soon afterwards, smiling from ear to ear. Such a barrage of compliments may sound false but SWS's appreciation felt remarkably genuine.

I thought fast. SWS didn't get the lean in/pull away thing the first time. Maybe he would get it if I did it a second time? It also needs a better name than 'Lean In Pull Away', maybe

---

* In the UK we don't use the word 'sneaker'. We say 'trainer' or 'shoe'. Both are terrible options because a trainer is definitely a physical human being who trains someone and shoes are the rigid smart things that a bouncer forces you to wear to get into terrible nightclubs. 'Sneaker' on the other hand is a beautiful word. It's a shoe but with a soft rubber sole so it makes you better at sneaking. I mean it's definitely creepy but it's wonderful. Nobody can sneak around in a shoe, you will be heard, and if you are sneaking around inside a trainer then it sounds like you are simply having an affair.

LIPA? It was good but the problem is people might confuse it with the university Toby went to.

Post-second-compliment, I leaned in for a repeat Liverpool Institute of Performing Arts. He recoiled this time, anticipating my stupid fifteen-year-old in-joke. 'What are you doing?' he rightly asked. His smile was fading quickly. I jumped in to explain myself.

'It's a silly prank my friend Lily and I used to do in school,' I muttered nervously.

'Why are you doing it now?' he asked seriously. He had a point. The room was getting hotter, which I didn't think was possible. I moved on quickly again. I'd tripped up on another paving slab but this time I didn't dance it out, I fell to the floor onto my stupid face and a bunch of PR people, producers, cameramen, cameras and the Stiffmaester were looking.

Before I could get the bant mobile up and running again the interview time was up. Everyone couldn't wait to get out of the awkward cupboard hotter than the sun where I'd just ruined a perfectly good interview.

I sat deflated on my lonely stool as the door opened and everyone cleared out. Sean stood up and made to leave, turned back and shook my hand, grasping it with the might of a dusty builder in the fruit aisle. He then leaned in for a kiss, pulled away and said, 'Sorry, I completely misread that situation,' then walked out with his hands aloft. Classic Stifler.

The second interview of the day was with Dappy. You may know him from N-Dubz or your local magistrates' court. He was ridiculously late which was odd considering he had such a big shiny watch and so many entourage people around him to remind him of the time. After he and his staff finally arrived an hour after they were due, they went straight into their own room next door and started applying make-up and trying wardrobe options.

After thirty minutes the producer went in to check on them. 'He's having his hair cut,' he reported back.

An hour later the producer went back next door to check on them again. 'Apparently he's still having his hair cut,' he announced. This was getting ridiculous. Was he getting it plucked? Fifteen minutes later – by now nearly three hours late – Dappy and his bunch finally left their hair cave and walked into the dark, hot cupboard.

I am not kidding when I tell you this. Dappy – after an hour and forty-five minutes of hair care – was wearing a hat. It was his customary bright coloured beanie with the long ear flaps. He had one of the ear flaps raised up, I wasn't sure whether this was for fashion purposes or to be able to hear. The producer was secretly steaming but for the purposes of professionalism he was hiding it behind politeness. Dappy was also wearing a huge bright puffer coat like a warm sleeping bag. He looked prepped for a quick ski. Surely he wasn't going to keep it on in this room? He was. Dappy – slow haircuts and entirely impervious to heat.

He sat on the stool and we started chatting about N-Dubz, being a solo artist and his incredible head cover. I asked him about the rumours about him with another famous person, attempting to get some salacious gossip. 'We didn't have sex but we did everything but,' he said confidently.

What does that mean?! Everything but. Everything. Essentially, no we didn't have sex, but we went rock climbing? Unless of course he was saying 'everything butt'. As in they exclusively did anal. If that's the case he's very much over-sharing and we had all the salacious gossip we wanted. Rappers have a really incredible belief in themselves. Sometimes I wish I could just take a smidgin of their abundant confidence and pop it in my insecurity knapsack.

The interview went well; he surprisingly didn't take himself as seriously as his public persona suggests. Under the layer of bravado and bad tabloid stuff he is a really nice guy. Just like under the layer of his bad hat he presumably has a really great haircut.

The third interview was now due to start late. It was with DJ Ironik. He rapped, he didn't actually DJ, so does that make his name ironic? Not sure. Like many rappers he always wears sunglasses inside in an attempt to cover up his kind eyes. He also wore a huge winter puffer jacket like an even bigger sleeping bag, which completely contradicted his summer eye wear. He also didn't take it off. What ice planet did these rappers hail from? Apparently the in look for rappers then was outdoor bedding and some sort of head accessory. We clawed back some time due to him having his hair cut in out-of-work hours and it went seamlessly. Another polite rapper in the (sleeping) bag. I was happy to get out of the cupboard so I could breathe again.

'We have a last-minute request for an interview. Don't go home yet,' my producer said happily. The thought of going back into that furnace room was horrific. Three interviews in a day was rare, but four was insane.

'Who is it?' I asked, expecting it to be another rapper wearing a monocle and wrapped in a hammock.

'Trust me – you're gonna like it.'

I knew immediately. She was in the country promoting her single and the producers kept telling me she might pop in at some point for an interview if she could fit it into her busy schedule. For the purposes of this chapter we will call her 'Poppy'.

She was well known as being unbelievably talented and one of the most beautiful girls in the world. She'd graced the covers of magazines and her singles reached the top of the charts worldwide. While she was over here the famously vicious tabloids were fighting over stories of her newly single status. I was suddenly regretting my Mona Lisa Ape T-shirt, which at this point in the day was damp with cupboard sweat. Why hadn't I worn a shirt? I was dressed to impress Stifler not a number-one-record-selling sexy lady. Had I got time for Dappy's hair man to come back and give me a quick hour-and-a-half trim?

'It's happening now, Joel, she's already been waiting for fifteen minutes,' the producer crowed.

I was handed pages of notes which included a biography, details of her new album and the name of her dog – Roy. I was just looking at it to give the impression of professionalism but I already knew it all by heart from her Twitter account and my constant Googling. I returned into the heat-filled camera cave and sat on my high stool, sweating like a lifeguard at a holiday pool.

She walked in, greeting every one of the crew and shaking their hands. I was expecting a huge entourage with a make-up person, hair people, eyebrows, agent, manager, and – if Dappy was anything to go by – someone who's paid to exclusively place your hat at the right angle. But it was just her. She'd waited patiently while our previous interviews had overrun, hanging out alone downstairs. She sat down and introduced herself.

'I'm Poppy,' she said as if I didn't know. She knew I knew but the fact that she didn't assume that I knew was so polite.

I was in awe. Unlike internet dating these days she looked just like her pictures. I wanted to tell her that I knew her dog's name off by heart but I held it in. Remain cool, Joel. We shook hands while the make-up artist brushed our shiny faces with powder. She was wearing a bright white dress, Alice band and white high-heeled shoes, the kind of thing Sandy in *Grease* wore before she went all edgy.

'I like your T-shirt,' she uttered. Two compliments in one day for the new T-shirt. I was never going to take it off. Although the way she said it felt more like the way you tell a three-year-old that you like their hat, like she was just giving a compliment to a poor guy who clearly had absolutely zero sense of style.

The interview went surprisingly well. It was a great mix of fun, familiarity and good solid answers to questions. I gave her the dating question that the channel always wanted me to ask but tried to put my own spin on it.

'Have you snogged anyone recently?' I asked. She carefully deflected the question.

'I love the word "snog",' she said adorably. She loved it because Americans don't use it. In that case Americans should in theory love modesty and an inside voice.

I wasn't about to tell her my favourite word is 'ramekin'.

I could have been wrong (I usually was about these things) but I felt like we had something. A spark? No, it was ludicrous. The idea that she could be interested in me was absurd.

The previous week she'd been to the Oscars. The previous night I'd been doing comedy to twenty-eight people in a room above a shit pub in Gravesend (sorry, Gravesend).

It was hard to tell with Americans, though. They were all so polite and camera-trained. She knew how to flirt subtly and professionally to get the press to love her.

'What are you doing for your birthday next week?' I asked, pretending I'd read on the cards that it was her twenty-second birthday, when in reality I just knew.

'I'm having a party in Vegas,' she replied. Of course she was. Imagine how incredible it would be, the party capital of the world. I still celebrated my birthdays at my parents' house on my four-year-old trampoline.

'You should come!' she said. It was almost definitely a polite formality but before I had time to question it my mouth had already shouted 'I'll be there!' slightly too loud. The sound guy in the crew who was listening in on headphones winced and lifted the cans off his ears.

I think she assumed most TV presenters would know that she was just being polite and if they didn't they would probably be too busy to drop all plans at the drop of a Dappy hat to fly across the world in a week. However, I assumed it was her way testing me to see if I was worthy of her love, like a knight fighting for the hand of his maiden. I couldn't fight but one thing I had learned from Lily's wedding mistake was to say yes to expensive flight opportunities.

Post-interview, while everyone spilled out of the oven, I casually asked if she was serious about the birthday.

'I'm heading to the US anyway next week,' I said unspecifically, clearly lying as America is unbelievably huge and you can be heading there and still be a ten-hour flight from her birthday. God, I needed to stop lying.

'Yes, I would love you there – add me on Twitter and I'll give you the details,' she said before saying goodbye to all the crew members while impressively remembering all of their names.

'I will,' I said back as if I didn't obviously follow her on Twitter already.

Her previous suitors were crazy hot famous people. I couldn't match up to that. Would I fly thirteen hours just to be ignored? Maybe. Probably. Almost definitely. Either way I simply had to try. It was a gamble but where better to gamble then Vegas?

You know what they say: what happens in Vegas – write about it in your book five years later.

I was going to have to ask my dad for time off the cheese shop but I thought he would hopefully understand, considering he clearly didn't really need me and it was costing him a fortune for me to work there. I unfollowed Poppy on Twitter, then immediately added her again so I would come up on her feed as a new follow. She followed me back and messaged me that night.

Come party in Vegas! Ironik is coming too!

There was going to another English suitor there. DJ Ironik. It made it feel a little better knowing I wasn't the only one travelling over. I was excited that the Nevada sun would finally give him a need for his sunglasses. OK, I was definitely going. It was decided. Right. I checked one more time, replying

'Are you sure?!', then when she said 'yes' *then* I was decided.

The next issue – what do I get her as a present? I don't mean to blow my own trumpet but I'm pretty good at presents (Iris excepted) and I really wanted to get it right.

When I was sixteen I asked Lily, 'What's your wildest dream?' Mine was fairly simple. I wanted to sell out the Hammersmith Apollo. At that point it was as a musician.

'My wildest dream is to buy every seat . . .' Lily paused. I assumed she was going to say on a plane, or maybe at the Hammersmith Apollo, then we could both achieve our dreams together.

'. . . on a Megabus.'

Her wildest dream, *wildest*, WILDEST – was to buy every seat on the cheapest form of transport available in the world. That's a dream worth £30. She didn't even pick National Express.*

'Why?' I asked.

'There would be so much room!' she replied, as if it was obvious.

I never let her forget it.

'You getting the Dreamliner?' I would say every time she travelled to London.

Her twenty-first arrived. Six years after she dreamt that dream – and I knew exactly what I was going to get her. Six months in advance, I bought all the seats on a Megabus from Bristol to London just after her birthday. What a fucking cool present. It was a little more expensive than I thought because

---

* If you are unaware, Megabus is like National Express's cheaper little brother that went to prison for a bit.

they go up in price the less space they have left. To this day it's the best £130 I've ever spent.

I couldn't wait for the anniversary of her birth to arrive. I love that feeling, when you have a good gift and it feels like more of a present to you than it does to them.

Finally, when the Mega dream day arrived, I printed off all the sixty-five booking references separately and slotted them into a big brown envelope. It felt like I was passing over cash in a drug deal. It couldn't be further from the truth.

'I bought you every seat on a Megabus in a week's time!' I blurted out while she was prising the back of the envelope open. I got excited and spoiled the surprise but it was still a surprise nonetheless. She flicked through the dozens of pages like a mortgage application and looked up at me in amazement. I expected laughter but it never came.

If I thought she was capable of it, I think she would have cried. I don't know the science of what happens when humans cry but I just don't think she has any tears in there. Her tear sac is permanently empty. She sweats a lot so maybe it's wired wrong and she's perspiring all her emotion out of her armpits.

She really loved it and I couldn't have been happier that my plan had worked. We embraced and I jumped on my own packed Megabus back to London. A week later I was awaiting her arrival at Victoria bus station, the destination of her solo voyage. She disembarked and we hugged.

'How was it?' I asked.

'Terrible,' she replied angrily.

'What? Why?' I shouted.

'There was one other guy on the bus. Not the driver. Another guy. It ruined it.'

She was genuinely upset. He must have booked really early. Super keen Megabus bean. I tried to console her saying that two people on a big bus is still pretty cool.

'He sat next to me,' she said furiously. I laughed solidly for at least thirty minutes. It was the only time I can safely say 'ROFL' as I actually was rolling on the dirty bus station floor laughing.

Poppy's present was never going to match that. I didn't think a famous person would appreciate getting every seat on a bus. Although maybe celebrities *should* hire entire Megabuses instead of limos. No paparazzi would expect there to be a famous person inside. They would just assume it was full of students heading home to their parents to be fed and get their laundry done.

I'd read somewhere that Poppy loved neon lights. Why not get her a neon sign that said her favourite word 'snog' in my handwriting? I thought. What an inspired idea. I went to a neon sign shop in Mile End whose sign strangely wasn't neon. Although inside there were plenty; it was a large white room with hundreds of bright, coloured lights spelling various words and phrases on the walls. It was like an ADHD dictionary.

'That'll cost £400.' I nearly stumbled backwards onto what I now know was probably millions of pounds' worth of light-up signs. I really didn't expect it to be that much but I didn't have any other good options. I couldn't turn up to Vegas with nothing. I've never even spent that much on my mum and I've known her exactly all of my life. Why couldn't Poppy just love signs written on pieces of paper in black marker pen?

That plus the flights plus the money I would inevitably have to spend to fit in with the cool people in Vegas was starting to mount up. This was turning into an expensive gamble that I really could not afford but this sign would start me off on the right foot and I needed all the help I could get.

'I'll pick it up in a few days,' I said, frustrated and beaten. A week later I jumped on the plane. Economy, of course. I say jumped; there's nothing jumpy about getting a bus to the airport at four in the morning to save money and getting there four hours early because I'm over-cautious.

I should just enjoy this, I told myself. This was the part of the trip when I could be myself and travel within my price bracket without pretending to be a little bit cooler and a little bit richer than I really was. The flight was fine. I slept almost the entire time, clutching an expensive bespoke neon sign made for a stranger I had met once.

I say almost. At one point I needed to urinate. I'd picked the window seat because I still think like a twelve-year-old, so I would have to wake up my next-door neighbour in order to get out. I felt rude. It was a mid-flight nighttime vibe and we all know how hard it is to fall asleep on a plane. Maybe I could climb over the guy using the arm rests and my incredible athleticism? I crouched on my seat then stood on the first arm rest. He was right there . . . gently does it. I didn't want to wake the dragon. Was this a terrible idea? Maybe I should just sit back down and wake him up like a normal flying partner?

'No. I can make this,' I said to myself. I made the step to the next arm rest. I was now straddling him like a creepy Spiderman.

'No going back,' I muttered to myself while I was inches

from his floppy head. I stepped across with my trailing foot and . . . Success! I'd somehow parkoured to piss freedom.

I looked around and was livid nobody had witnessed it. Like when you throw something in a bin from far away and nobody's watching, or when you get silver in a nunchuck competition and your mum can't make it. I celebrated to a sleeping plane with my arms aloft. It amused me to imagine the guy waking up now, seeing the seat next to him free and assuming I'd evaporated.

Until that point I had not thought about the fact that I would have to do it again the opposite way when I returned. I went to the toilet and set about my reverse seat leap, this time with added confidence. First leg on the outer arm. Then the second leg on the outer arm. I squatted down and stepped the first leg across him to the other arm rest. The man remained asleep. I was almost there. I was facing him, straddled across the two arm rests, balancing myself with the seat behind him. Just as I was about to step across with my trailing leg he stirred. I froze. Then he opened his eyes. The dragon was awake! He understandably let out a high-pitched yelp. I screeched back, for some reason choosing to mimic him, perhaps to soften the shock. Our respective yelps woke up the surrounding passengers, who assumed we were having an engine failure and were shooting towards our deaths.

'Toilet!' I whispered. While still crouched above him.

'No!' he shouted. I think he thought I was going to piss on him. Nobody wants to wake up with Gollum in flight socks hunched over them. I sat down in my seat, apologised profusely and insisted I was toileting and wasn't giving him a nocturnal mid-flight lap dance.

I arrived in USA in the late evening. It was starting to become apparent how ridiculous this whole idea was and how far I had come. I had just flown thirteen hours for a person I met once for fifteen minutes.

After standing in line for immigration for what felt like fourteen days I jumped into a taxi (you can jump into those) to go to the hotel. She had a suite hired out and said there were plenty of rooms. I would hopefully find a corner to sleep in amongst the hundreds of guests and if there wasn't a bed I could always ask to borrow DJ Ironik's sleeping bag.

I arrived at the fancy hotel. The foyer was bigger than any room I'd ever been in. It was like an aircraft hangar with chandeliers. Everything was white apart from huge canvasses on the wall that had splashes and brushstrokes of bright paint across them. Utterly shit but probably very expensive art. Even the staff wore white. It felt like I was in a mental hospital of the future.

I approached the front desk, which had two people sitting behind it, entirely expressionless. I hadn't really thought this far forward. What did I say now? I didn't have a booking for me so I supposed I should just say her name? But then surely any crazy person could do that? This was a highly famous person, there must be a list or dare I say it – someone with a clipboard?

'I'm here for Poppy?' I said to the human robot.

'Room 352,' the lady said without even looking at a computer. It was that easy. No password, no list, no nothing.

It was easier to get into this famous person's party than my mum's WiFi.

I went to the elevator and struggled with the fancy button system until a mental-health nurse from the year 2049 helped me out and I was whizzed up to the room in the fast future elevator.

I'm not very good at socialising at parties. I usually pop my head in then leave but this party had a 5,217-mile walk/paddle home and I had spent £400 on a sign so I was going to stick this one out.

Room 352. I stood there still clutching the box with the sign inside. I hadn't let it out of my grasp for twenty hours.

I was expecting to hear music pumping behind the door but there was nothing. I double-checked the number. Triple-checked. Then double- and triple-checked my outfit and knocked. After a small wait, Poppy answered. 'Heeeeeeey!' she said with her arms wide open in her upbeat American accent. We hugged. Her hair smelt so damn clean. I'm sorry, that sounded horrifically creepy. It's something an unrepentant murderer would say in court with a smile on his face but it really did.

She unlocked the embrace and I glanced into the huge room. There were five people there.

'Where are the others?' I asked politely.

'This is it!' she replied excitedly.

There were four girls and one boy.

'These are my bestest, bestest friends,' Poppy said. They'd all been friends for fifteen years, since school, and then there was me who she had known for fifteen minutes. I honestly thought there were going to be hundreds of us. I felt like I was imposing hugely. I had somehow found myself at the close family gathering of my celebrity crush. This was incredible but I couldn't help but think I really shouldn't be there.

'Where's Ironik?' I asked.

'He couldn't make it because he got stabbed,' she said casually as if she'd said, 'He has a chesty cough.' I laughed, assuming it was a joke.

'Seriously,' she said with a straight face. I immediately stopped my laugh and pretended to be concerned. It was true. I later checked the news and he'd been mugged for his expensive watch on the way to his house. Luckily he was alive and well, I just really hoped this wouldn't affect his wonderful time-keeping. I decided to lighten the mood and unleash the pièce de resistance – the most expensive present I've ever bought, the thing that hadn't left my side for almost a full day.

'I brought this for you!' I said, more excited about it than her.

'You shouldn't have!' she replied, while ripping at the box like she clearly thought I should've.

She came to the layer of bubble wrap, which she was tearing through quite violently.

'Gently,' I said tentatively, knowing the fragility of the contents. She ripped off the last bit of masking tape and revealed the red neon letters.

'Ta daaaa!' I sang while outstretching my arms proudly.

I looked at her face, expecting to see pure delight which would hopefully be followed by a hug so I could get another whiff of that barnet. She looked confused. My eyes tracked down to the package.

What lay before me was a £400 neon light that was somehow

completely smashed. The joined-up letters had snapped and were lying detached from each other in their bubble-wrap bed. I was holding it so tenderly on the flight – how could this have happened? The only time I left it was when I went to the toilet mid-flight. Maybe my plane neighbour did it? Maybe it was Poppy's aggressive gift-opening? Maybe it was me. I shouldn't have brought it on the flight in the first place. Vegas has so many bright lights it can be seen from space. It's the home of neon. I should have bought it from here. It was like buying sushi in London and holding it on a thirteen-hour flight to Tokyo. She said a slightly hollow thank you and skipped off to the lounge to leave me to put £400 straight in the bin. I had no presents apart from my presence but that's a terrible present. My attempts to start off the night on the right foot had failed and I was left with no foots forward at all. I left the broken snog behind me and tried to get on with the task at hand. The unpopulated Poppy party.

'Let's hit the clubs!' Poppy shouted to the group with her arms aloft. Her friends cheered.

'Better than getting hit by clubs!' I said to an entirely muted response. A deathly silence followed.

'You're funny,' one of the girls said while not laughing – the usual response to finding someone funny.

'Thanks,' I replied, pretending to be comfortable with where I was and what we were doing. Poppy stood up and made for the door. Everyone followed in unison like a line of ducklings following their mother. They were club-ready; I was jet-lagged and still in my sweaty flight comfys.

'I haven't changed yet!' I pleaded.

'You look great, let's go!' Poppy said without really looking at me. The group let out some hype-man whoops to show they agreed and walked out the door. We went straight down into the hotel basement. It turns out the mental-health institute had a nightclub.

I'm not great in nightclubs. I try to avoid them at all costs and they usually cost a lot. Clubbing is a testosterone-fuelled musical mating competition with nowhere to sit. It's as if every detail is designed to give me anxiety. The lights, music, confident drunk people and those fucking clipboard people.

If I'm honest, once it went badly and I've never really forgotten it.

Lily and I were in Bristol after our A levels; she was celebrating and I was commiserating. Just as I was starting to enjoy myself a thin scrappy kid in a Ben Sherman polo shirt with his hair gelled to his forehead started punching me on the dancefloor. His skinny fists were not connecting and when they did they had no power to hurt. I didn't retaliate. I did what I do best and adopted my classic grab-and-hold technique. I really stretched the shit out of his top. His mum was gonna be so damn mad. The crowd formed into a circle and watched, just like the old days. Luckily, unlike in the playground, I knew the security would flock to the scene of a ruck immediately so I sat back and let the punches rain. I waited and nobody came. I waited longer and nobody came. The polo shirt really was stretched at this point.

Eventually the bouncers bounded in and split us up. Ben Sherman was immediately ejected.

'What took you so long?' I shouted at the security guard.

'I honestly thought you were dancing,' he replied, laughing to himself. He had somehow managed to insult my dancing *and* my fighting technique. I assume the people in the circle around us thought it was a dance battle too.

I tried not to think about this incident now. The Poppy party exited the elevator and waltzed straight past the clipboard woman. Being with a famous person bypasses the clipboard cunt. What a revelation! I gave the list lady a look as if to say, 'If you're so cool, why don't you have an iPad?'

We were ushered to the VIP (velvet in perimeter) area. I opened the rope clasp to let our entire group in and attached it after the last one in. I realised I'd been practising my entire life for this by attaching and detaching a dog lead.

I'd never been behind the velvet rope before and I'll be honest, it felt pretty darn cool. It was full of lots of confident rappers with their sunglasses on. I assumed it was just DJ Ironik but it turns out it's an absolute epidemic.

The Poppy people were on my right, grouped in the corner with their backs to me. The rappers were on my left facing me but with their sunglasses on so they might as well have been facing away. I stood there alone, wondering if the massive ice bucket full of drinks was for us. Everyone seemed to be just dipping in and taking stuff. Was it an honesty-box situation where you pay the amount you think you owe at the end? I asked a rapper how I paid for my drinks. 'It's free in the VIP!' he said. I don't think he meant to rhyme but it happened. A natural rapper.

The drink was free? It doesn't make sense. On the other side of the rope where the poor people are, they're paying £15 for a vodka lemonade, but the wealthy people inside the sacred boundary are pouring it down their faces from massive bottles that they've been given gratis. It's probably the perfect metaphor for our current government but I have very little idea about politics so can't be sure. To entertain myself I started smuggling tequila outside beyond the rope like a nightclub Robin Hood. I made some strong drinks and when the coast was clear I illegally exported them across the border.

In a bid to not look entirely alone I pretended to be on my phone for a bit so it looked like I had friends but they were just someplace else. It clearly looked fake because the music was so loud that nobody could hear anyone on the other end of the phone. I was standing by the edge of the velvet rope and people started to assume I worked there. Maybe if I hung around long enough someone would give me a walkie-talkie? I saw a big bunch of people arriving through the crowd, coming towards my velvet rope. You know what they say, the bigger the bunch, the bigger the prize grape. OK, nobody says that, but it looked like a big-deal dude at the centre. He stepped up to the rope. It was Usher.

'You want to come in?' I said nervously.

'Yeah,' he said. I couldn't believe he replied with the title of his most famous song. I opened the rope and ushered Usher into the area then immediately moved away from the rope so I didn't get in trouble for my poor border control.

I nudged one of Poppy's party people.

'Is that . . .?' I said.

'Yep,' she replied.

'That's ludicrous,' I said.

'No it's Usher, Ludacris couldn't make it.'

'Is that ironic?' I asked.

'No, Ironik was stabbed, he couldn't make it either.'

With the nudge and Usher convo I managed to penetrate the Poppy party people perimeter. I was inside the VIP and finally inside the circle. Slowly, as the night dragged on, I danced closer to Poppy. Every ten minutes or so I would slip one notch around the circle towards her, like a computer game when you beat all the baddies to get to the big final boss.

After an hour or so I reached Poppy. It was too loud to talk but we shared a few excited thumbs up, and sang along to R Kelly's 'Ignition' remix back to back like the Charlie's Angels. They'd accepted me into the core group and nobody seemed to mind. Usher wasn't dancing although I suppose he dances lots in his job. It would be like a bin man picking up litter on his day off or me being funny in real life.

Maybe, just maybe, I could fix the broken snog situation

with a real snog from Poppy? I'm horrific at making the first move, especially in such a high-stakes game. I decided while dancing to 'Kissed a Girl' by Katy Perry that I would leave it up to her to make the first move. Almost exactly the opposite of what the song tells you to do.

We danced close, but not close enough to know she was interested, and we chatted fairly intimately but not intimately enough. I wasn't used to making bold moves. I was more comfortable hilariously pulling away from a kiss than committing to it.

We drunkenly danced, fuelled by free tequila, till the early hours of the morning then the whole crew, as a tight slurring unit, waddled upstairs to our convenient suite and slept in our separate rooms.

I lay on my bed with my ears ringing and the room spinning, still not really understanding why I was there. But it was definitely becoming fun.

Due to the jet lag I woke up later than everyone else. The others were in the lounge recounting tales from the night before and, just like normal people, one person had lost their phone. I don't really understand how she lost it; we basically walked downstairs then back up again.

I was sure I looked horrific. I realised the real reason why rappers wore sunglasses all the time: it's due to their free VIP libations. Poppy looked frustratingly fresh. It was like she was ready for a photoshoot from the moment she opened her massive blue eyes. 'We're having a PJ party at five! Come with us!' Poppy screamed, punctuated by the now inevitable entourage whoops.

Pyjama party?! It seemed an odd thing to wait till five

o'clock to do considering we were sitting here in our pyjamas now but I was definitely up for it. I love parties where you don't have to wear shoes.

I assume they must have sensed my confusion as one of the members of the PP (poppy party) said, 'PJ stands for private jet,' to help me out. I was momentarily disappointed about the pyjama party not going ahead before the reality of the private jet scenario set in. Oh my God! I was going on a private jet! Shit! Speaking of shits, I wonder if there is a toilet on those things? Now isn't the time to ask, Joel.

Whenever I had thought of a private jet in the past I would think of the nineties Gladiator Jet in her normal clothes just chilling at home. But now I was going to think of a real one, with me inside it. I'd also not be turning up for my economy flight back to LA, which added to the excitement. I'd never booked a flight and not had the courtesy to turn up for it, it felt so damn lavish. The person that booked the seat next to me could pop up the arm rest, stretch out their limbs and not worry about anyone climbing over them while they were asleep.

Surely her inviting me on a private jet meant she was interested? No, it wasn't enough. Wait it out, Dommett, I thought to myself.

Five o'clock came: it was PJ party time. We arrived at the airport and jumped straight onto the plane. No security at all. No taking your shoes and belt off, patting down, laptop out of the bag stuff at all. We just got on the plane and took off. I suppose if you're spending this amount of money on a journey they assume you wouldn't waste it by blowing it up.

It was so tiny, like flying in a Pringles can. Once your ears pop you can't stop. It was just us. Just the seven of us and the two pilots. It was depressing to think you could have fitted the entire Psirus gig audience inside the plane.

We all drank vodka – apart from the pilots because they were complete squares – and just sang for the entire thirty-minute flight. I was really tired but fighting to stay awake so I could remember this incredible event that I might never experience again (I still haven't!). It was reassuring to see the other PP people on the plane were as excited as me to be flying this way; it would have been a real waste to be spending this trip pretending to be cool and not taking photos.

'Where are you staying in LA?' Poppy asked me while we were airbound.

'With a friend of a friend,' I replied.

'Why don't you stay with a friend! Meeeee! I have a spare room.' She elongated the 'eeee' out for quite a while. I think the altitude-induced vodka was starting to take effect. Was she wanting me to stay at her house? Surely that was a sign that she was interested? But on the other hand she quite clearly said 'friend', 'spare room' and she was hammered. Damn, this stuff was so confusing.

The last time I'd been to LA I'd been there alone, with no money, no friends and no car. Nothing had changed apart from the alone part but it was still exciting nonetheless.

We landed safely and of course without any security or customs, we jumped straight in a limo. I'd usually be excited about the limo but the private jet had ruined the poor limo's thrill. There's no sadder limo than the one picking up people on a private jet comedown.

Over the previous twenty-four hours I'd been in my first VIP area, met my first Usher, gone on my first private jet and now I was in my third limo if you count a return journey to my school Prom.

The PP were dropped home one at a time and for the first time, Poppy and I were left alone.

It felt so quiet. It was like that silence when the fire alarm finally stops after burning some toast. I'd never been in a limo with one other person. It felt odd. I'd only been in one with huge numbers of other teenagers sprouting out of every window in dresses and tuxes. I resisted the temptation and remained firmly in my seat. I relaxed a little and she did too. Poppy was less forced without her friends and seemed less insincere. I realised she had a party persona that she put on like a mask at a masquerade. It was something I could probably learn from. I was like David Attenborough with the gorillas. So close to something so many people would dream of seeing. Does the gorilla want to have sex with me? All the signals of her keeping me at her side seemed to suggest yes, but her body language and zero flirting suggested no.

We walked together into her huge, beautiful, Tony Stark-esque flat overlooking the LA skyline.

Everything was so neat and the interior design had clearly been considered in minute detail. It was the exact opposite of the flat I lived in. A tiny, coffee-coloured fluffy dog ran towards her and jumped up at her legs. I wanted to call out 'ROOOOYYYY!' as I knew its name already but I pretended I didn't and let Poppy introduce me. We threw down our suitcases and she lay on the bed.

'Can you help me?' she said sensually.

'With what?' I asked in a cool manner, dialling up the huskiness of my normal grating camp tone. It was finally going to happen. This was my time to move in. Do it, Dommett. Do it.

'Help me send this email to this boy I'm into,' she said coldly, immediately breaking the sensual vibe.

'Ah fuck,' I whispered inaudibly. I assumed the email wasn't for me.

'Yes of course!' I said, my voice swapping immediately back to the camp kid in class. It may sound strange but for the next hour or so I laid on her bed and honestly helped her compose an email to a guy she fancied. I wasn't just in the friend zone, I was helping her get other men. I was cock-blocking myself.

She knew I wasn't gay; I had learned from my earlier relationship with Violet that I needed to throw in some heterosexual references early. I also knew I wasn't gay because I'd only just recently had my biannual bi-anal and passed with flying non-rainbow colours. Part of me was slightly relieved as I now knew where I stood.

We sent the carefully constructed man email or 'hemail'. My work was quite simply magnificent. No man would not reply to this as it was an inside job. Of course he immediately replied, swapped numbers and agreed to meet the next evening in my favourite of places – another fucking nightclub.

For the rest of the evening and following day we did what everyone does in LA: went out for breakfast, lunch and dinner and filled the space in between with trips to Starbucks. I did my friend duties and helped her pick an outfit for her evening with Hemail Man (let's call him He-Man). I quite enjoyed it – I felt like I was in one of those classic fitting-room movie montages.

'Leave me here, you go out and have fun,' I said in the evening, genuinely excited about kicking back and watching some American television.

'No! You are coming with me. It's your last night!' she insisted. Having me there made it less of a date for her and took the pressure off. I'd somehow become her wingman. I was like Goose in *Top Gun* but in this scenario Goose secretly wanted to kiss Maverick.

'OK,' I agreed. It seems I was going to watch a date with my dream girl and He-Man.

We entered a hip celebrity LA club. I'd never been behind a VIP rope in my life before this trip and I was about to do it twice in a row. We wandered over the velvet divide. There were no rappers this time; it was instead filled with the opposite end of the music biz – the entire cast of the then huge musical feelgood show *Glee*. It turned out the recipient of my wonderfully constructed email was one of the cast. I imagined when he received my email he danced around the living room and sang into a hairbrush. What a prick.

Nobody had sunglasses on because they all had so much cheery metaphorical sun in their hearts. There was way less standing around looking cool this time. Everyone was dancing and singing beautifully, really early in the evening without the need for alcohol to get them going. I suppose the *Glee* cast had been doing that already at work all day so they were oiled up, orally stretched and ready to go clubbing.

Poppy and He-Man seemed to be getting on well. I

distracted myself from the pain in my heart by transferring free illegal vodkas and cranberry juice to the Muggles on the dancefloor. I didn't drink anything myself because I'd learned from drug movies and the cheese shop you don't get high on your own supply.

I should have charged a fee, undercutting the price at the bar. I could've paid back some of the money I'd spent on a flight across the world to woo an out-of-my-league lady.

On a return journey back to bottle base, Poppy and He-Man were kissing. Or snogging as she likes to call it but he probably didn't know that. I knew it was coming but I was still devastated. Like England being knocked out of any major tournament.

I went big and took the whole bottle for redistribution. The kissing worked beautifully as a distraction and I was fast becoming a legend of the People's Republic of Dancefloor. I actually had quite a lot of fun sneaking around. It was a small personal victory in the face of a huge defeat.

Time passed. I was forgotten by Poppy. The ice bucket got refilled with more alcohol.

Poppy slowly started to get more inebriated, clinging on to He-Man and looking lovingly into his eyes. I could tell his interest was starting to wane. He wasn't going to able to take this lady home with him and he was looking for other options. She was minutes away from telling him she loved him when He-Man lost interest altogether and wandered off amongst the doting normals in the PRD (People's Republic of Dancefloor). I realised that me and Poppy at that moment were not so different. People who are not interested in me have people who are not interested in them.

I felt it was my duty as the friend to step in and take her safely home before midnight, like a Cinderella who got so hammered she lost a shoe. I helped her into a taxi and promised the driver she would not be sick.

Poppy sobered up remarkably quickly and we started to have a real heart to heart. She told me how difficult she was finding dating within this ridiculous celebrity realm and how hard a past relationship was because they never saw each other. It was the candid answers I dreamt of to the questions I had asked in our little interview a week ago. I told her when I broke her neon sign it broke my heart and that my heart broke again when she kissed the *Glee* guy – oh, and I knew her dog's name.

She smiled at me sweetly. The taxi was so silent. She leaned slowly in to kiss me. Oh my God, it was happening. It would be sloppy *Glee* seconds but I didn't care.

We connected lips. She touched my face and pulled softly away, looking deep into my eyes. She looked happy. Just like that *Glee* song told me: 'Don't stop believin'.' I didn't and it happened.

Suddenly the happiness on Poppy's face turned to confusion.

Then she vomited EVERYWHERE. Into my lap, down my front, on the seat, on the floor. Everywhere. I could identify every meal we had shared mixed together in chunks on my lap.

The driver skidded to a halt and turfed us out.

'You promised,' he shouted. It was true, I had.

While Poppy sat on the grass verge, the taxi driver demanded I gave him $100 for the cleaning bill. I didn't argue.

It wasn't worth it. I handed over the remainder of my US cash then I held Poppy's hair and expensive long earrings as she vomited more in some poor person's front garden. We walked the last couple of blocks home and it reminded me of when I used to walk home from the Laugh Factory before I first tried stand-up.

It made me think of how far I had come. Even though this trip hadn't gone as planned, it was a story to tell. None of this would have happened to a landscape gardener.

I went to sleep in my room and woke up early the next morning to catch my flight. I didn't want to wake her. I also didn't want to kiss her on the forehead while she slept because she wasn't a) my girlfriend or b) dead.

While waiting at the airport I wrote her a poem and emailed it to her. A poem is like an a cappella rap. When Eminem in *8 Mile* on his final rap says, 'Fuck it, I'll go a cappella,' I always think it would have been wonderful if he'd said, 'Fuck it, I'll do a poem.' He wouldn't have won but what an incredible turn of events.

Again I can't express how real this is and again, the guy who wrote this ended up writing this book.

So here's a new fairytale, to read while alone, and this
    one I assure you is scribed on a phone.
It's a fable that's true, of a boy that loves shoes, who
    travelled the world and a friendship was fused.
I'll start from the top, so read and enjoy, and get excited
    like Roy for a toy.
Once upon time, for the sake of a rhyme, a girl named
    Lemon and a guy named Lime

Met over make-up, in a place named London. It was
　　rushed but remembered, saved and sudden.
Lemon was weary from full-flight fatigue, and Lime was
　　aware she was out of his league.
They sat on a sofa and questions were asked, then she
　　left in an instant so fleeting, so fast.
Lime wished for more time but he wasn't a quitter, so
　　he embraced the help of a friend named Twitter.
'Come party in Vegas,' Lemon said to the Lime.
　　Lime assumed it was a line; she was drunk at the
　　time.
He checked the next day and again and again, she still
　　said 'Yep, come' to her timid new friend.
The bags were bundled and the flights were flown,
　　Ironik was stabbed so Lime left alone.
The present smashed along with the dream that Lemon
　　and Lime could one day be a team.
Lime knew all along in his heart of heart, but what he
　　thought was the end was in fact just the start.
They danced and they drank and they soon became
　　friends, Lime growing in confidence as the chaos
　　descends.
Lime wasn't a drinker he went on to tell them, but
　　tequila tasted so much better with Lemon.
They left Las Vegas, leaving fights and lights, and away
　　to LA to visit the sights.
Lemon and Lime found more fun to find, though
　　mourning the sign that was left behind.
They lay on the bed writing mails to males, laughing
　　and compiling fairytales.

The final night before Lime departs, the amigos partied
and wore sleeves on their hearts.
Lime was happy with his new favourite pairing. So
happy in fact that he held ill Lemon's hair and
earrings.
I'll cut to the end, my flight's nearly done, embracing
Clapham cold over LA sun.
It's been an incredible week for little young Lime; thank
you so much for a beautiful time . . .

J xx

So I didn't manage to get with the woman of my dreams,
but we did dance with Usher, go on a private jet, get driven
in a limo, sing with the cast of *Glee*, and kiss in a taxi before
she vomited all over me.

You could say we did everything but.

I also realised everyone is faking it. I thought it was just
me. Cool people are just pretending to be cool. The cool ones
are actually the people who don't try and be cool in the first
place. It's OK to fake it but it's better if you just be yourself.
I'd spent the last few days pretending to be rich, cool and
famous to try and impress someone but it was never going
to work because I wasn't being me. I was done with pretending.
Although on the way home I did fake one last thing – an
orgasm. But we'll come to that later.

'So, wait, you didn't have sex with her?' Hannah asks after
sitting through a story which clearly pointed to me sleeping
with the famous person all along.

'We technically swapped bodily fluids because some vomit went in my mouth,' I reply, regretting saying it as soon as it leaves my lips. Hannah reacts as you would expect.

'I didn't,' I continue hurriedly, 'but that's not the end of the story . . .'

#30 The Neon Hero (Continued)

I boarded the packed unprivate plane. I shuffled slowly in line past the smug first-class flyers. I wanted desperately to shout at them, 'I was on a private jet two days ago!', as they looked condescendingly over their complimentary newspapers at the parade of poor people plodding past.

I found my designated petite long-haul pew. I had swapped back to economy on planes and in life.

The seat next to me remained empty as everyone trickled onto the flight and the doors were ready to close. I couldn't believe my luck. But just as I lifted the arm rest to spread myself thinly across both seats, one last passenger slipped in the door and hurried down the aisle towards my sweet stretch room. We did the customary nod to each other as she sweatily put her bags in the overhead lockers.

I was envious of her grey comfy plane clothes and matching plane pillow which she already had clasped around her neck. She had long straight blonde hair, which flowed down her front like a mermaid. There was something about her. She had a kind, expressive face that lay between her middle-parted locks like a pleasant play between two theatre curtains.

Wait. I recognised her. I stared at her familiar face, squinting like I was in an eye exam. Oh. My. God.

Big Chin.

What were the chances? My first kiss, who flicked me off her face and told the whole school I was frigid was going to be sitting right next to me for the next thirteen hours. I hadn't recognised her because the attribute she had become famous for had become far less obvious. Incredibly, Big Chin had grown into her chin. Dare I say it, the rest of her face had caught up. 'Big Chin' was now just 'Chin'.

I now had to remember her real name. It would be a very long, awkward flight if I opened the conversation by reminding her of her horrific nickname based on her misshapen childhood head. I wish there was a Shazam-style app that could tell you the name of someone if you take a picture of their face. Imagine how much awkward 'dude'-calling we could avoid. It really doesn't feel far away.

While the plane was still on the tarmac I broke the no-phone rule and txtd Lily.

'What's Big Chin's real name?' I kept it simple. It was four in the morning in the UK and I was sure I wouldn't get a reply.

Almost immediately after I'd pressed send, a ridiculously fast reply came through.

'Olive.'

Yes of course. Her name was Olive.

'Are you Olive?' I asked, knowing that you have to get conversation in early on a flight or not at all. Starting a chat halfway through a flight is considered completely unacceptable.

She looked up at me, startled, and studied my face. She didn't know who I was. Was I that different? Unlike her, my facial features all grew at the same rate, so surely I just look like an older version of younger me? I didn't even have a beard at this point to hide my unchanged chin. She continued to look at me, confused.

'It's Joel!' I said, expecting her to get it from my mentioning a fairly rare biblical first name.

'Joel Dommett.' I added the fairly rare surname to make a very rare full name. Still nothing.

'From school?' Surely the place of recognition would work? We'd touched mouths, for God's sake.

'Oh God, the penny's dropped! Joel!' she exclaimed.

Due to my mother being called Penny here are some phrases she's selfishly ruined and what they mean to me:

A bad penny: Mum in a mood

A bad penny always turns up: Mum in a mood embarrassing me at a nightclub in front of my friends

A penny for your thoughts: I'll give you my mum if you tell me what you're thinking

A penny saved is a penny earned: If I save my mum I still have a mum

A penny saved is a penny gained: If you save my mum you have an extra mum

Not short of a penny or two: Loads of people with the same name as my mum in here

Penny-wise: Mum telling me to not do *Celebrity Big Brother*

Cut off without a penny: Disowned by my mother

Have two pennies to rub together: Disgusting. Not going to think about it

I felt like a penny waiting for change: Mum trying on clothes in a shop

Mean enough to steal a penny off a dead man's eyes: I don't know why Mum was sitting on a dead man's face in the first place

Penny dreadful: Mum's driving

Penny pincher: Mum's kidnapper

Spend a penny: I'd trade my mum to have a piss

Two a penny: Mum's gloves, socks or shoes

A pretty penny: 'Joel, your mum is a Milf'

The penny dropped makes me think of the horrific image of my mum falling over. I secretly shuddered and Olive leaned across for hug, squashing my face against her comfy neck pillow.

If it's OK for the purposes of this story I'm going to keep calling her 'Big Chin'. It feels odd calling her anything else and now, due to the rest of her face wonderfully catching up, it feels like a cute ironic nickname, like when someone is called 'Tiny' and they are seven foot tall or when my friends call me 'Small Dick'.

'Joel! Joel Dommett! From school!' I wasn't entirely sure whether she really recognised me or if she was just repeating, word for word, what I had said.

'We used to be in poetry club together!' she said in a much more upbeat way than I remember her being capable of in school.

'YES!' I replied. The passengers around us were tutting and sighing at the prospect of sitting next to this loud familiarity for the whole flight. She leaned in to my ear and whispered apologetically, 'You will have to excuse me, I'm very high,' while grinning like Wallace from *Wallace and Gromit*. Together we were Wallace and Dommett. I thought she meant altitude-wise. It felt like a very odd thing to say considering we were still on the ground. Then the mummy dropped. She meant drugs! Shit! Being on a plane in the vicinity of someone mentioning drugs immediately made me want to run away but unfortunately I was strapped in and the door was closed. This felt like the start of a story that ends in me being arrested and searched in my everything butt.

She told me she had some drugs left over from her trip to California, so had decided to do them at the airport so she didn't have to smuggle them through security or waste them. She was either going to really enjoy this flight or really, really hate it. Either way she definitely wasn't going to sleep.

I had to explain to her that I wasn't really a drugs person. I don't mind people who are, it's part of our generation and society and as long as it's done in moderation I think it's OK. It's just not my vibe mainly due to the comedown. I just prefer not to cry while watching *Cash in the Attic* on a Tuesday.

Those tiny see-through ziplock bags that drugs come in are officially the smallest bags that exist. They are exclusively used for spare buttons and drugs. I honestly didn't know they were used for drugs until very recently. I used to go to festivals and would see the empty little bags all over the floor and think, 'Wow, a lot of people have fixed their shirts at this festival!'

The conversation and the plane took flight. Lots of 'Do you remember this?', 'What happened to her?!' and 'Mr Barney was a dick!' It kept us happy for hours. Big Chin may have been high but she was a whole ziplock bag of fun.

'Do you remember us going out?' I said after my sixth gin and tonic (to try and level the stakes a little). She looked confused.

'We were boyfriend and girlfriend?' I was actually relieved that our fleeting romance was so short and terrible it had been removed from her memory. That meant she wouldn't remember the horrific kiss.

'Oh my God! You were the terrible kisser!' Damn it. The passengers around us who were attempting to sleep all peeked open one eye to look at me and shuffled loudly, subtly protesting our noise levels.

The fact that she said 'THE terrible kisser' made it infinitely worse. That kiss had happened around thirteen years previously and in all that time she hadn't experienced another one as bad for it to be named more terrible. 'A terrible kisser' would be fine, 'one of the terrible kissers' would be acceptable but 'THE terrible kisser' is just depressing.

She didn't know it was my first kiss and apologised for telling everyone I was frigid. I was later than everyone with everything in our school. I always felt like I was catching up but maybe that's how everyone feels.

'I thought I invented masturbation,' I told her, starting to slur.

I really did. I went to a party at the local rugby club then went home and thought about Big Boobs. I'm not talking about some random faceless large breasts, 'Big Boobs' was another nickname of someone in school due to the fact she . . . well, you know. It wasn't an ironic nickname.

You can say what you like about our school but we distributed simple nicknames. In fact they were less nicknames, more characteristics in 'Guess Who?' Big Boobs was on my school bus every day and she was quite lovely. She developed a healthy chest before everyone else in our year. She didn't know what to do with it and the boys didn't know what to do with the feelings they had about it. While thinking about Big Boobs in bed post-party, I just decided to have sex with my hand, because there was nothing on the TV and why the hell not? My first masturbation unexpectedly coincided with an incredible surge of happiness that I had never come close to feeling before (pun intended). It was the best feeling ever – and it was free of charge.

I honestly thought I'd stumbled upon the greatest human ability ever known to mankind. At that point I could only assume it was limited to men but I would have to do some research. I couldn't believe that until now nobody had thought to do it alone. I would reveal it to my friends at school tomorrow as a courtesy and then inform the tabloids and accept my inevitable Nobel Prize.

'Guys . . .' I looked over my shoulder like racists do when they are about to do one of their favourite 'funny' jokes.

'You can have sex with your hand!' They all looked at me blankly as if I was joking. Then replied unanimously with, 'Yeah, that's wanking, Joel, we've all been doing it for at least a year.'

Big Chin and I watched movies while giggling next to each other. It was almost an insight into what our life would have been like as a married couple if I hadn't been 'the terrible kisser'. I don't know whether she had changed as an adult or whether it was just the drugs but she was much easier to talk to nowadays. Gone were the days of a lunchtime of silence followed by a cutting remark before she left.

Halfway through the flight the arm rest came up and we shared her neck pillow and we put our combined blankets over us. I was really quite drunk by this point (there's a reason 'gin' autocorrects to 'fun') and she was clearly still high as she was subtly dancing to the movie soundtracks.

In the middle of the flight night, while everyone else was twisted into horrific positions trying to sleep, we sat wrapped around each other watching *The Fast and the Furious* 6. Inspired by Vin Diesel and Michelle Rodriguez kissing aggressively I moved my head up to hers and two miles above the world we kissed.

It was incredible to think that she was my very first and last kiss. She had bookended my smooch career. I felt like I was back in school and subconsciously snapped back to a teenage technique.

'Have I improved?' I asked quietly while pulling away from the intense snog. It was so much easier now I wasn't having to manoeuvre around her massive bobsled chin.

'No,' she said, smiling. There was that barbed tongue I was used to as a youth. I think she was joking but judging by the amount of alcohol I'd consumed she could have been telling the truth. My tongue was slopping all over the place like a wet fish desperately searching for water on a boat deck.

'Meet you in the toilet in five minutes,' she muttered into my ear, then got up silently and walked past the sleeping bodies to the lavatory. I wasn't sure whether she meant for drugs or sex. Which mile-high club did she mean? I assumed it was the latter. Having sex on a plane takes confidence but doing drugs on a plane takes fearlessness and stupidity to an entirely new level.

What an incredible weekend for me and aircraft.

I would usually think twice about doing such a prohibited act with a druggie but I was under the influence of gin and nostalgia so I thought – fuck it. Literally. I waited five minutes watching the huge not-to-scale computer plane on my screen pass slowly over a vast blue of nothing. Then I walked to the toilet, checking nobody was watching me while looking blatantly suspicious. I opened the unlocked door, jumped in quickly and immediately slid it shut behind me.

The lack of space was instantly obvious. 'This is going to be a logistical nightmare,' I said in a sexy voice.

We snogged erratically while we rushed through the air at 600 miles per hour and wasted no time getting to the nitty gritty. We didn't beat around her bush, so to speak.

I know airborne humping is supposed to be the epitome of rock and roll sexiness but I just hated it. I was tired and drunk, in an unbelievably tight, bright, plastic cupboard with a massive mirror to help us see how disgusting we looked.

I sat on the loo seat and she sat on top of me. We had sex where people had shat. It was clumsy and horrible and I just wanted it to end. Apparently so did my rapidly declining appendage. I was in the mile-high club but my penis was anything but high. It was like a wet fish that had given up searching for water on a boat deck. I was devastated. Is this what happens now? Have I reached that age already? It had happened before a few times with Rose due to inexperience and nerves, I guess, but never since. We both realised that it wasn't ending well, collected ourselves and our clothes and she left the toilet, leaving me to sit on the closed lid alone looking at myself in the bright mirror.

What a strange weekend.

I sheepishly went back to my seat and strapped myself in. It was like we'd pressed a factory reset button and started again. We smiled at each other politely and basically ignored each other. I soon fell into a contorted gin-induced plane sleep. Whatever I dreamt I'm sure it was less fantastical than what I had actually experienced in the last ridiculous forty-eight hours.

I woke up to an air stewardess nudging me politely then handing me a slip of paper. It was a warning that I had abused the rules of the airline and as a result I may not be able to fly with them in the future. Fuck.

Big Chin and I said a polite goodbye at the baggage claim and I never saw her again.

I called Lily a few days later once the gin lag had subsided.

'I had sex on a plane with Big Chin!' I said proudly.

'I know,' she replied.

'How?!'

'I heard it on Facebook from old school friends. She's telling everyone you couldn't get it up and that you're frigid.'

Goddamn you, Big Chin.

I learned two things that day. Don't have sex on a plane and don't have sex with Big Chin. Although I wouldn't have to deal with these things any more as very soon I would jump into the longest relationship of my life so far.

12 July 2004

Hey JD
 Last night I just couldn't get it up for Iris. It's so weird. I HATE MY WILLY.
Sincerely, Joel

'You swapped more bodily fluids with the famous girl than you did with her!' Hannah says, smiling. She's right, I did. That was two meaty main-meal tales for a tiny bit of vomit in my mouth and a non-ejaculative toilet fumble.

Rodrigo returns and asks Hannah if she wants some dessert while completely blanking me. 'Does that come in a normal size or do you have to get little ones?' I ask, trying to muscle in on their conversation.

I reach for the menu on the other side of the table packed with empty ramekins and plates that Rodrigo hasn't collected because apparently you can't clear the dishes while looking dishy. I grab it and while bringing it back to have a gander at the desserts I knock my sangria all over myself. Rodrigo laughs. The exact opposite of the response expected from a waiter. Hannah laughs too but she's allowed, she isn't on the Spanish payroll. I ask Rodrigo to fetch me some of that paper towel and he tuts and walks off with no haste whatsoever. Spilling sangria on yourself is like spilling red wine but you have the added indignity of the fruit chunks. This is the worst night ever. If only I hadn't reworn my favourite T-shirt I wouldn't be smelling of an un-Lynxed teenager and wouldn't have stained it with the most stainable drink.

'Why can we still spill drinks? We put humans on the moon fifty years ago, surely we can make an un-spillable wine glass?' I say, thinking I'm on to something. 'Because we're adults and we're trusted with more than sippy cups,' Hannah replies. She has a point. Maybe that's why people who drink wine are so smug. They're constantly thinking, 'I can't believe that I'm so grown up that I'm not spilling this.'

I understand how bad a restaurant this is when Rodrigo returns with white kitchen towels instead of the massive blue roll that only restaurants and bars have. This place is still working the single-sheet shit that you use when your house runs out of loo roll. He tears off and throws sheets at me like a rapper making it rain. If he were a rapper he'd be called 3-Ply. Once I've dabbed myself we order dessert. We know it isn't going to be good but at this point the date has become a masochistic endeavour to see how much more ridiculous it can become. Hannah thankfully doesn't choose the cheeseboard. Personally I think only a serial killer would choose cheese as a dessert. Its only saving grace is the tiny pile of grapes that are sometimes supplied to help you get the taste of cheese out of your mouth when you've immediately regretted your cheese dessert decision.

'It's my turn to ask, right?' I enquire.

'I've lost track, but go on,' she says, leaning forward to receive the question excitedly.

'What's your longest relationship?' I ask. It's a little deeper than the other ones, holding more significance than simply sex. I want to find out more about Hannah. This clearly isn't going any further – there will be no 'date two' – but that's strangely liberating. I can ask and answer questions without the pressure of failure.

Hannah proceeds to tell a story about dating a professional MMA fighter. That's exactly what you want to hear when you are on a date with someone, isn't it? That they used to be romantically involved with a person who hurts people professionally. I glance at the window and start plotting my potential weapons for if he suddenly arrives through it. I could use the ramekins as tiny terracotta frisbees then smash the acoustic guitar over his head. It would daze the MMA man and also stop the music, killing two birds with one stone.

A good while after ordering it, dessert arrives. They took ages to pretend it took time to make it individually when they obviously just cut it from a bigger cake in the kitchen.

I know Hannah is going to fire the same question back to me and I don't really have anything funny to say but I think it's a story worth telling anyway.

'So,' she says, settling back into her chair. 'What was *your* longest relationship?'

#37 The Relationship

One morning I was asked to come into the boss producer's office at MTV. I'd never been asked into the big office before. It felt serious. I had been there for nine months and I was starting to find my feet but if I'm honest I wasn't great at it. I look back at it now and shudder to think of the things I wore and the questions I asked.

The seriousness was confirmed when the producer said, 'Close the door behind you.' Seriousness always follows that phrase, whether it's ensuring privacy at work or tightening the airlock door on a spaceship. She had her suit jacket on to add businesslike severity to her normal bubbly persona.

'We're not going to renew your contract,' she said bluntly.

'Ah no! Why?' I said, feigning surprise. I knew it was going to happen. I just wasn't good enough at it.

'I'll be honest. You are a bit too old,' she said. She knew I knew it was true. I was twenty-seven.

'We are replacing you with two eighteen-year-olds,' she continued. I told her that two eighteen-year-olds technically added up to thirty-six. That was way older than me. I was clutching at straws. Do young people still use that phrase?

'Why am I too old?' I pleaded.

'Joel, when you interviewed One Direction you mentioned *Fun House*,' she said. Apparently if you're interviewing the most famous, sought-after teenagers on the planet for three minutes, you can't spend two of those minutes trying to explain to them in detail who Pat Sharp and the Twins are. I should have been asking about their new single but instead I was singing the theme tune.

Fun houuuusee, whole lotta fun prizes to be won . . .
Use your body and your brain
if you wanna play the game!

Harry and the boys stood there completely unimpressed.

I'd been pretending to love Katy Perry for nine months and it was probably time they got someone who genuinely loved her music. Although her lyrics had never felt more apt. I really did feel like a plastic bag, drifting through the wind, wanting to start again.

I was a little annoyed because I'd just quit the fucking cheese shop. Although you don't really quit when you work for your dad. You just sort of ask and he says yes.

Bless my dad, I knew I wasn't really needed; we didn't really have enough customers. He would pay my train fare from London to Haslemere and a decent day's wage, and then on top of that give me an unbelievable amount of food for the week. He couldn't possibly have made that back in cheese money. It's such a classic Dad thing to do. See your son weekly under the guise of employment and let him know he loves you by the amount of money he's losing on you. It was such a wonderful thing for him to do and really helped me, but finally I knew it was time to leave the warm cheesy bosom of my father's shop and attempt to survive on comedy alone.

I never thought I was going to be able to make it a job. It was incredible. I was being paid for something I loved doing. It was like being paid for jumping as a kid or paying a dog to fetch.

Soon after, I had a gig at the Top Secret Comedy Club in Covent Garden. It's an excellent name for a club. Just like with the Sienna Miller script, the words 'Top Secret' immediately make you desperate to find out more. It's always packed out every night, full of people who didn't keep the secret. It's so fun and the warmest club in town. Atmosphere and temperature-wise.

Every time I do stand-up I write down bullet points of what I am going to say in a little book with the title of the gig at the top. While on my way in on the train I wrote this:

<u>TOP SECRET</u>
SHOES
BISCUITS
CATS
PROSECCO
RUSSIAN
FINGERING

The suited man sitting next to me was looking over my notes, clearly thinking, 'That's the worst list of top-secret things I've ever seen. What's top secret about shoes?' To be fair, 'Russian' could be construed as something top secret. It's actually a bit about Russian dolls but luckily I think the observer wouldn't have seen that because the eye is distracted from 'Russian' and immediately drawn to 'fingering'.

After several previous gigs at this venue, I had made it onto the photo wall of the Top Secret Comedy Club, and not photobombing Eddie Izzard; it's a real photo of actual me on a wall and it's not a mistake. That's the dream, to have your photo on the wall of a comedy club, an Indian restaurant or a barber shop. I'd only achieved one of those so far but there was still time.

Onstage that night I talked about the Top Secret man on the train which went wonderfully. 'Cats' was also a particular highlight and 'Prosecco' was utterly disappointing.

Afterwards, I stood at the bar at the back watching the brilliant headline act after me. If you don't know, then a normal, non-open mic comedy night is usually ordered as follows:

Great Act.

Less Great Act.

Really Great Act.

This is so the less great act is protected between two better acts and fewer people notice how less great they are. I was still very much at the point where I was the less great act.

As I stood there, a lady with long, dark hair and swaying hips walked past me and prolonged her eye contact with me for slightly longer than the average looking-at-another-human stare.

I thought nothing of it. I'm not the kind of comedian to pick up women after gigs. It's not a great vibe. I'm different to my stage persona so I feel like I've misrepresented myself as a human being. I'm funnier and more confident onstage. Me onstage is the person that I would love to be in real life but, alas, I'm a scaled-down version. A less confident, less talented twin of my stage self. A Joel Dommett Lite. Diet Dommett.

She passed again. The prolonged eyes happened again. I said nothing – again. Talking to a stranger in a bar or in the street is like trying to jump on a moving roundabout in a playground. The longer you hesitate the worse it gets and when you finally make that leap you realise it wasn't that bad and you should have done it earlier. Some people jump on it without even looking. These people are almost always pricks.

The fourth time she passed she made eyes at me but those eyes momentarily rolled into the back of her head like she couldn't believe I hadn't got the point yet. She couldn't want the toilet that much. She either liked me or had cystitis.

I'll say something when she comes back from the toilet, I thought. I waited. She never came back. The roundabout had stopped.

I wandered outside and she was waiting outside with her friends. I wish I smoked. I would've had a reason to be there apart from following her. I stood in the cold doorway and lifted my hand in a coy wave. Big twin, full-fat Joel would have said hello thirty minutes ago, the sly dog.

She sauntered away from her friends and said hello to the non-smoking guy outside in his T-shirt for no reason.

Her name was Fern. She was a lawyer who lived in London and was mindblowingly smart, yet she was also delicate, like a scared cat that had been hurt by its trusted owner. The thing that struck me most about Fern was how she was not at all aware of how beautiful she was.

We covered all the polite chat bases within five minutes, swapped numbers then she left for the tube. That meeting would change the course of my life for the next two years.

We went to the OXO Tower for our first date. I had my first audition for the panel show *8 Out of 10 Cats* the next day so didn't drink and was carrying a huge holdall because I'd been shopping for an outfit. I looked like I'd just robbed a bank.

We talked until the restaurant was entirely empty and I got the bill and immediately wished I had robbed a bank.

We walked to Waterloo station and when our separate trains arrived both clearly felt the clichéd pressure of the romcom first-date kiss. We both went in for a kiss then veered at the last minute to the cheek.

'Do you want a T-shirt?' I said. I had no idea what my brain was playing at. I was panicking.

'Ummm, no, I'm OK.'

'Take a T-shirt,' I said, reaching into my bank-robber bag, grabbing a new T-shirt out and handing it over. Awkwardness really shows itself in incredible ways.

'Thanks,' she said, subtly shaking her head and smiling at how odd I was.

Over the course of the next few months we grew closer and closer and eventually became official boyfriend and girlfriend. My first for a long while. I hadn't been this far up the companionship scale for years.

Slowly, over time, I felt her moods swing drastically from one end of the scale to another. It was never with anger – she didn't have an angry bone in her body – it was always from utter joy to deep, deep sadness. It felt like the happier she got the further I knew she was going to fall. If we had a fun day together I knew the next day she would panic, thinking the happiness was all going to fall apart, then she would hate herself into a deep destructive hole until she would self-harm. Then she would immediately snap back to happiness and start the process over again.

I had no idea that this was depression. I had no idea what that word meant and I definitely didn't know how to deal with it.

My instinct was to save her, to ride in on my steed in full armour, holding a happy flag. But I just didn't have the tools. I didn't know how to ride a horse or even have the right flag. Saying, 'It's going to be OK! Just be happy!' wasn't helping anybody.

It was taking its toll on the relationship and I decided to do something I'd never done before. We talked about it.

The past she revealed to me was horrific. The things she'd gone through to become the incredible person she is today were astounding. It's not my tale to tell. I can't do it justice and it feels wrong for me to write it but all you need to know is it wasn't her fault. Not that depression is ever anyone's fault but what's frustrating was that her anxiety was caused by the people she should have been able to trust most at an age when she was most vulnerable.

It feels strange for me to write this chapter. I'm sure it feels odd reading it too. I know it doesn't quite fit with the tone of the other stories but Fern was such an important part of my life and it would have felt wrong leaving our story out.

So after checking with her first it felt important for me to share it. I hope you agree.

We moved through it the best we could. Enjoying the good times and fearing the worst.

We moved in together after a year or so, thinking the security of a mutual home would help ease the situation and create a stable environment for our relationship to flourish. I'd finally moved out of Toby's house and we slowly made moves towards Fern's life being a less scary roller coaster.

She started to see a therapist and I began reading about the issues to pick apart and understand the chunky knit of a problem we were trying to tackle. Slowly, we began to enjoy life. In an attempt to make this chapter a little more chipper I'll also tell you about Spanish John.

Opposite our new house there was a cemetery and a barber shop. I knew it was a barber shop because it had 'BARBER SHOP' scrawled aggressively on the wall in black paint with no care or attention to detail.

I'd never seen anyone there apart from one solitary old man with a moustache. He was always sitting in the same chair staring out the same window, thinking about the good old days and wondering why everyone else suddenly has moustaches in November. I became strangely fascinated by him, peeking through my blinds like a paranoid criminal to watch him sit.

One day while Fern was away at work I decided to satisfy my curiosity and wandered in.

The man stood quickly like he had been caught offguard even though he had watched me cross the road. He looked at me sternly like in a Western saloon stand-off. Obviously we were missing the cool saloon doors, cool noisy stirrups, cool guns, cool hats, cool toothpicks and cool modes of transport, but apart from that it was very Western-ish.

'Hi,' I said politely, lifting my hand a little in an apologetic tiny wave. His stare was so intense.

'Sit down,' he said seriously, offering me a seat in front of a mirror.

Barber chairs haven't been updated since they were invented. They're like obese office chairs and they always have been. Nobody's felt the need to make them smaller or less cumbersome; everyone seems perfectly happy with the fact that you can only move them with a forklift.

Moustache Man sat me down in what felt like a chair from *The Voice*, then started pumping me up higher. We've had electric windows in cars for twenty years yet nobody's seen the need to make this massive lump electronic.

'I do not do spikes,' he spat in a foreign accent. I was unsure whether he was talking about the type of hairstyle he refuses to do or if 'spikes' was an old racial slur I hadn't heard of.

'I only do proper haircut,' he added. Then he pointed to a signed photo on his wall of Chris Tarrant. If you don't know Chris Tarrant he's a TV presenter and has the cuddly voice of a teddy bear.

'Do you cut Chris Tarrant's hair?' I asked brightly, while being aggressively hoisted to an unescapable height.

'Yes,' he replied. Wow. The plot thickened (unfortunately the same can't be said for Chris's hair). This explained so much. Chris has had the same hairstyle for the last thirty years, never changing it with the times, because he was petrified of his barber.

There were two other photo frames either side of CT. The one to his left was a classic photo of Jesus Christ in his alive pose. This wasn't signed. They are hard to come by these days. If you don't know Jesus, he's the original celeb. The Kim Kardashian of his day and everyone loved his show *Keeping up with the Corinthians*. Dying on a cross at thirty-three was the best PR move ever and gave him and his dad a great book deal.

The photo to the right of Tarrant was a black and white photo of three people that I would assume was taken in the 1960s. The middle person in the photo was currently standing behind me holding scissors and I could have been wrong but the other two seemed to be the notorious Kray twins. If you do not know the Krays they were the legendary East End gangsters of the sixties that everyone feared.

If I was slightly scared before, now I was terrified. Murderers, saviours and *Who Wants to Be a Millionaire?* dude.

'Is that the Kray twins?' I asked, as casually as possible.

'Yes. I am a legend,' he replied in his thick somewhere accent.

'I am Joel,' I said, feeling like an introduction was expected.

'I am Spanish John,' he said flatly. What a magnificent gangster name that also helped me finally pinpoint his accent.

'Are you from Spain?' What a stupid question, Joel. Why are you asking Spanish John if he's from Spain? Of course he's from Spain, it's obvious.

'No,' he said, without giving any more information. OK, maybe it wasn't as obvious as I thought. It made sense: a gangster name that immediately throws you off the scent of finding out someone's real identity. The police had been looking for a Spanish man all this time. I would like to put forward my gangster name as 'French Joel 8/5/91 HSBC'.

Spanish John had already started cutting my hair by this point. He didn't ask what I wanted, he just started chopping. I can only assume he was making me look like Chris Tarrant.

'Who did this?' he said, pointing at my head like it was a crime scene.

'I cut it myself,' I said sheepishly. It was so unfathomably expensive to get your hair cut in London that I used to just use clippers to shave the sides and cut the top every now and then with huge office scissors. I'd done that since Janet used to come to my mum's house when I lived in Bristol and cut it in the kitchen. I don't think people go to houses to cut hair any more. It used to be a thing and they were almost always called Janet.

I stayed in the fat chair for thirty minutes and I slowly turned into a man with absolutely no 'spikes'.

We both slowly started to loosen up. I assume he realised I wasn't from a rival gang or one of the 'rozzers' and I realised he wasn't as scary as he first made out.

My favourite thing about Spanish John was the fact that when he asked a question he always said 'Do not lie' after it.

'What do you do for a living – do not lie,' he said in his no-nonsense tone. I'd usually lie to that question because no good comes from telling strangers you're a comedian. They either want you to tell a joke or they tell you a joke and neither ends well. I'm so glad that I can now say 'I'm an author' because they surely won't say 'read me an extract'.

'I'm a comedian,' I said begrudgingly.

'You are comedian?' he replied, as if he was unaware that it could be a job. I understood: until a few years ago I didn't know either.

I confirmed I was and waited for the inevitable ask/tell-joke scenario but instead he said without an ounce of humour, 'I know Jim Davidson, but I hate him now because he owe me £5.' Out of all the reasons to hate Jim Davidson, he disliked him because of the price of a London pint.

'What is your full name? Do not lie,' he then asked. I told him and I did not lie. He picked up his non-smartphone (do we call that a stupid phone?) and called someone. He waited for them to answer then without even saying hello said, 'Do you know a Joelle Dommert? He is comedian.'

There was a silence while he listened to the response of the person on the end of the phone. I waited in my pumpable throne with four-fifths of a Tarrant.

He didn't say 'goodbye' or 'thanks' or 'toodleoo', just hung up and threw the phone down on the side like we used to in the days when we were not petrified of a cracked screen.

'Am I about to be kidnapped, fifteen metres from my front door?' I thought. Was he just seeing how valuable I was? He must have found out I was very low level with some brief MTV experience because he just finished the hair.

It actually wasn't that bad – it wasn't what I wanted, but

it wasn't bad. He of course showed me the back of the hair with that little mirror.

'It's great,' I said. I've never, nor has anyone in the world, ever said, 'No, I don't like the back.' It's like when you are asked to taste wine before they pour you a glass. Surely nobody's ever said, 'I want a different one,' and if you have, you're a real arsehole.

Spanish John took off my gown, placed his hand on my shoulder and leaned in to my freshly trimmed ear.

'You do me favour,' he whispered. Oh God, I thought. He's going to ask me to kill someone and I'll probably say yes because I'm too fucking polite.

'I not charge you for haircut,' he murmured. This is clearly how Jim Davidson got into his bad books. 'You take photo with me. You go home. You develop it, twice. You put one in frame. Sign them. Bring back,' he said, listing it slowly so I wouldn't forget.

'You have one hour,' he added, then started sweeping up my dead hair. That was so much to do in an hour. I would have loved to just say 'yes' and never return but it was right opposite my new house. I'd be a prisoner in my own abode.

I have to do this or move house, I thought. We took a selfie on my phone. The fact you could see yourself in the phone blew his moustached mind.

'Cheese,' he said sincerely with a frown. He didn't widen his grin at all which of course makes saying cheese completely redundant. The photo was taken with our heads strangely close to one another. He was stone-faced like people in all photos prior to 1920 (before cheese was invented?) and I look like a petrified young Chris Tarrant.

I immediately went about my task. I printed the photos off because I didn't have a darkroom then signed them both with a thick black marker. I'm not proud of this next part: I took a lovely framed photo of mum and me off the wall and replaced the picture with Spanish John.

I got my mobster homework done in a cool forty-five minutes and popped back across the road. He unexpectedly hugged me.

'Thank you, Joel,' he uttered softly in my ear. I assumed I was in the Firm now. That was my initiation and I had passed. Turns out the initiation into the Krays was easier than an initiation into a rugby team. I was never going to drink a pint that John-boy had put his balls in just to sit on the subs bench for a season ever again.

From then on, Spanish John would wave and smile at me politely when I walked in and out of my house. It felt like I had tamed a wild dog as a friend. He was the ultimate neighbourhood watch.

'Come in for cut,' he shouted one day while I was locking my front door. It was a few weeks since I'd looked at the back of my head so I thought 'why not?' and popped in.

I sat in the hot seat and looked up at the photos.

Krays. Jesus. Tarrant. Dommett.

I had no idea what he did with the second photo. I assumed he just needed a back-up. Now I just needed to get my photo on the wall of an Indian restaurant to complete the dream trio.

After going on several breaks and getting back together, eventually after two years together Fern handed me back the

T-shirt and we ended things fairly amicably. We kept in touch to make sure everything was OK and although it was incredibly hard for both of us I think we knew it was for the best.

We really were just not right for each other, wanting completely different things. She wanted to settle down and have stability and at that point in my life I couldn't give that to her. All I wanted to do was gig, gig, gig. I was moving at a snail's pace up this strange comedy ladder and I couldn't focus on anything else. I was too selfish with my time. She needed more than most and it was more than I could give.

Things fell apart with Spanish John too. I made the mistake of going to a different hairdresser.

'Joel. JOEL! You come here please,' he shouted angrily one afternoon as I entered my house. I walked over and went in for our normal embrace. He didn't reciprocate; instead he grabbed my shoulders and stared at my scalp.

'Did you go elsewhere, Joel? Do not lie,' he said, now with an edge of sadness.

'Yes,' I replied guiltily, as if I'd been caught having an affair. It was a hair affair. A 'hairffair'.

'This is shit,' he explained plainly while pointing at my head. I apologised profusely and told him I had no choice due to me being away. The truth was I knew if I didn't go elsewhere now I'd be stuck and go there forever just like Chris Tarrant.

I think he wanted different things too. He wanted a son and I wanted a haircut.

Fern seemed happy; she got a new boyfriend and remained friends with me and my family, chatting to my mum and stepdad often. It's testament to how great my Mother Hen is that she was happy to take her under her little wing to keep her warm while she figured things out.

I'm still in touch with her and I'm unbelievably proud of what she's achieved since we were a couple. It's a constant battle but she's working hard to understand what triggers her difficult spells and learning to deal with it better all the time. It helped to finally get a more specific diagnosis for her condition – complex post-traumatic stress disorder – which made her start to understand what was happening instead of constantly blaming herself. She's also being honest with her friends and employers about the problems that she faces on a daily basis and this openness helps dramatically. Communication is key. If you feel like you experience any anxiety or depression issues, talking openly about it and understanding you're not alone is so important.

I'd like to say I also continued to stay close to Spanish John, but sadly it was not to be. However, it was not the end of our story.

About a year or so after the break up I bumped into wonderfully funny comedian Dara Ó Briain at the Edinburgh Festival in a small pub called the Brass Monkey. He was sitting with author, TV presenter and Joel Dommett impersonator Rick Edwards. Rick is everything I want to be in a body that looks just like mine. It's utterly humiliating. He is my *Sliding Doors* double. He went to Cambridge and I did a week-long course in cheese. He wrote a book about voting in an election and I wrote one mostly about bonking. To really rub it all in he is about four inches taller than me. I dread to think what size his feet are.

'I have a great story about you,' Dara said in his wonder-fully lyrical Irish voice.

'Me?' I'd never met him before and I really couldn't think why he would have a story about little old me.

I sat down with them, and Dara proceeded to tell Rick and me that his wife, who was a neurologist, had recently operated on someone. A month or so later that patient returned to the hospital for a check-up and thanked Dara's wife for essentially saving his life. Rick and I leaned in as Dara started to grin.

'Then, before the patient left the hospital he put his hand into his jacket pocket . . .'

He paused for effect. Rick and I leaned in further.

'. . . And pulled out a photo that had "To Spanish John from Joel Dommett" written in black marker pen across it!'

I couldn't believe my ears. Spanish John gave his other photo to Dara Ó Briain's wife when she saved his life? This was incredible.

Apparently when the patient handed over the photo he said in a thick accent, 'This is going to be big comedian one day.'

Dara said he assumed the accent Spanish John had was Spanish. I was about to blow his mind.

'Spanish John isn't Spanish!' I said.

'What?!' Dara and Rick exclaimed together. The story was growing wildly from all sides. I can only assume Spanish John had no idea that his neurologist's husband was one of the finest and most famous comedians on television.

Then Dara added that when Spanish John handed over the photo he said, 'Do you like it? *Do not lie.*' It was the most incredible turn of events and they hadn't even heard my side of the story. I quickly filled them in about no spikes, Chris Tarrant, and being on his wall next to Jesus. Dara now had my half of the story and Rick had a whole new one.

13 July 2004

Hey JD
Just had an erection on a bus. So think its just cos
I'm over thinking it (with Iris).
Sincerely Joel

'I'm glad you told me about Fern, she seems like good person,' Hannah says. The date has taken an odd turn but it has been a necessary break from the manic humping stories that have preceded it. Rodrigo arrives in perfect time to push the serious mood into overdrive. He always has a knack of arriving just when I have forgotten about him from his last visit.

'Would you like coffee?' he says, still not looking at me. Hannah orders an Americano.

'Do you do almond milk?' I ask, immediately regretting it: if they didn't have blue paper towels they almost certainly won't have almond milk.

'*Sí*,' he replies. If I'm not mistaken that means yes. 'Can I get a flat white with almond milk please?' I ask. Roddy looks confused then nods and wanders off. That's my order and it always has been for the last few years. I started with that and never deviated just like everyone does with their Nando's order. I was ordering flat whites before it was cool. I used to say the same thing about Green Day in school.

A flat white is a hard order at the best of times; surely he isn't going to get this right? It's supposed to be a double shot of coffee and half the milk. I think; I've never made it. I have no intention of ever being able to make my own coffee as I feel like other people will always be better at it than me and a coffee machine costs the same as four years' worth of coffees. I know that's a terrible way to live my life but in the time I could have been learning how to make a flat white and draw a little heart on top I've written a book.

Rodrigo the returner returns. He gives Hannah her Americano, and puts a tiny mug of something in front of me that definitely isn't a flat white.

'A flat white without milk,' Rodrigo says as he places it on the table. I'm about to correct him and say 'with *almond* milk' but it's not worth it. Just imagining him trying to figure out what a flat white without milk is makes me laugh. A flat white without the white? It's like asking for an orange juice without the juice, getting a musician to play a G minor major or finding an honest politician (am I riiighhhhttt?).

While my piping-hot double espresso is cooling, I excuse myself and go to the loo/toilet/restroom/potty place. The toilets are as bad as I'd imagined. They are bad enough that I want to write a TripAdvisor review about them. I'm not going to but I want to and that's what matters. I wee very quickly as my doctor says I have wide urethra. I think he was a doctor anyway. It shoots out all at once like a quick burst on the Bellagio fountain. I wee so quickly I often urinate then wash my hands and then just hang out a bit in the bathroom. Otherwise I guarantee I will get the 'that was quick' return conversation which involves the other person touching my wet hands as evidence of washing. It is a fine line because you want to make sure they don't think you are taking a MDS (mid-date shit), which is a stupidly brave and frankly disgusting move. I wait what I think is a perfect piss amount of time then return to the table. She says nothing so I clearly smashed it.

'OK, what's next?' I ask.

'I thought of a good one while you were shitting,' she says. 'What was your worst date ever?'

#38 The Tinder Girl

Even though I knew the breakup was right, I couldn't help but feel utterly alone. You get used to someone being there, having someone to call and lean on.

Ninety per cent of people at the gym start going after a breakup. That's a fact I just made up but it's probably true. It was definitely true for me. I wanted to be a sexier version of myself to embark on the dating circuit again. My mum designs gardens for a living and says redesigning your front garden can increase your house price by 20 per cent (I just checked and this is another made-up fact. I've clearly inherited this talent from her).

I was going to the gym to improve my front garden and increase my house price by 20 per cent. That felt like I was talking about sculpting my pubes and confuses the metaphor but I think you know what I mean.

Since I had been in my relationship I'd moved up the comedy chain considerably. As a result of this and my newfound gym regime I was asked to do a shirtless photoshoot for the *Gay Times*. The publication not the era. Although if we haven't yet named the epoch in which we are currently residing I would love to throw 'gay times' into the mix.

'Going for the pink pound are you, Joel?' Lily asked me on the phone. I didn't realise but apparently 'pink pound' means appealing to the gay market so they buy your tour tickets. I genuinely thought it was another term for gay-bashing and assumed Lily was inferring I was heading out to punch a harmless homosexual.

I had a month's notice so contacted a friend of a friend (a different one) who's a body builder called Dan to help me out with some nutrition plans.

Dan is the muscliest, veiny-est vainest man I've ever met. He looks like a map of motorways drawn on a tanned bag of footballs with perfect side-parted hair. He had the meanest body but the sweetest little Essex voice, like a Ferrari that sounds like a Ford Ka.

He drew me up a strict plan of exactly what to eat at every meal and recommended a huge list of supplements. After three weeks of mostly sticking to it I was looking leaner and getting stronger. I say mostly because I'm really sorry but I just fucking love a flapjack – please don't tell Dan. Although the last week before the photoshoot is when shit starts to get real in the body-building world.

'Drink five litres of mineral water and take 5000mg of

Vitamin C. EVERY DAY,' Dan squeaked. That grew to six litres and 6000mg for the last three days.

On show day (that's what Dan kept calling it), I'd drink nothing but you keep weeing at the same rate so your body dries out and you get that muscly motorway look. You look like a huge veiny penis and that's apparently what the gays like.

It's unbelievably difficult to consume that much water. You spend your entire day drinking and urinating. You basically pour it in and it comes straight out. You might as well just pour the Evian straight down the toilet.

'Ooh, I need the toilet,' I'd think to myself and by the time I'd finished the word 'toilet' I was in a blind panic, desperate to find porcelain.

Two days before the photoshoot I was driving to a car garage near Gatwick to get my car fixed on a rare beautiful hot summer's day. Clearly as I could drive there the problem wasn't that bad, like if someone can jog to a hospital.

'Ooh, I need the toilet,' I suddenly thought halfway through the journey. I looked at the satnav: I had twenty minutes left. 'It's OK, I can hold it,' I murmured to myself while picking up the pace. I'm an optimist. Almost every day I think to myself, 'I don't need to take my phone charger with me, I have 90 per cent battery!' then run out at 3 p.m.

Five minutes away from my garage it became clear I wasn't going to make it to my destination without relieving myself first. I saw a pub, pulled over, got out and ran to the door.

I was at the point of no return, running while holding my pee pipe at the end to seal the foreskin with my fingers. The urine was already in the chamber and that chamber was slowly expanding like a birthday balloon. I pushed on the door.

The pub was locked.

I looked around with the panic of a prison escapee to the other side of the car park where I spotted a secluded corner between a house and a hedge. I ran to it – still pinching my growing zeppelin between my thumb and index finger – reached the house, unfastened my belt, got my pinched appendage out then glanced up. There was a lady in the window looking out while doing the dishes. I didn't have time to move to a different spot.

Urine started spraying through my clasped fingers, like when you put your thumb over the end of a hosepipe to make a mist like rain, while an old lady watched me. The most incredible part is the sun shone through the piss mist and made a tiny urine rainbow.

It was beautiful. I was making a rainbow with my penis – and that's about the gayest thing possible.

I got back in my car covered in urine. A month ago I was in a relationship, happily eating burgers and driving my girl-friend to work. Now I was single, eating tins of tuna and sitting alone in my car in Crawley covered in piss. Then my phone battery ran out.

Breakups are difficult. Fern and I were together two years and it was hard but it was all put into perspective when my grandad died. He and Granny had been together for almost seventy years. Seventy. I really can't imagine how that must have felt.

He was always so strong, tall and healthy, not afraid to get his hands dirty from a life in the fields. He had many names: Grandad, Patrick, Grandad Dommett, Poppa Dom. My favourite place as a child was his workshop.

The blinking strip light would turn on and reveal an Aladdin's cave of carpentry. He kept everything. Every scrap of wood he would see in a gateway or skip he would pick up and put proudly in his pile. Our non-wartime generation has lost that hoarding mentality. He used to open all his Christmas and birthday presents slowly, picking off every little bit of Sellotape, carefully making sure the wrapping wouldn't rip, then fold it neatly and use it to wrap one of our presents the year after. We've become so wasteful. If something breaks we don't fix it, we just go on Amazon Prime and get a new one delivered in four hours.

He fixed and made anything and everything from his dusty machines that I was fascinated with but not allowed to touch. My brother and I were made huge rocking horses that rocked back and forth, rocking tractors that rocked back and forth, a crane that rocked – now that I think of it, he mainly made rocking things but to be fair he was really good at it. To this day the smell of sawn wood reminds me of him. Smell is such a powerful, emotional sense.

If he wasn't in his workshop he was in his office sitting in his spinning green office chair, which was so big he may well have stolen it from a barber shop. He was always writing and plotting. I never knew what but he was always lost in something.

A year after he died, Granny and the family finally got round to the unbelievably tough job of sorting through a lifetime of his collected possessions and paperwork. A huge cupboard full of folders, books and documents loomed over the office. It wasn't unorganised; it was clearly in some sort of order but none of us knew what that order was. Slowly, page by page, folder by folder, we pieced together an incredible life of a secretly creative farmer.

I found his diaries, written from 1949. It wasn't a personal 'thoughts and problems' sort of diary but more of a planning-type diary full of simple farming and food details.

March 6 1949
Ham and pigeon for dinner.
Rolling.

Literally that would be it. It was the Snapchat of 1949. The diary of a dairy farmer. It would be like someone reading my iCal in sixty years' time.

'Wow, in 2017 my Grandpa Joel missed his book deadline by a month!' my descendants will say.

March 30 1949
Liberty Hall Yeovil. YFC Public Speaking Dance.
Danced with Bridget Denning.

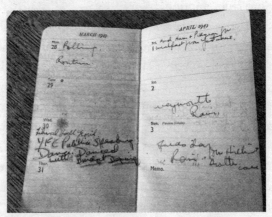

That was it. The day they met fixed in time in a line of Biro. Did they have Biros then? Quill? It was probably quill.

They met seventy years ago when they were sixteen, so to beat them I'd have to meet someone right now and live to a hundred. Due to my clumsiness, looking the wrong way when I cross roads abroad and a diet of mostly red meat and Tangfastics, I find it highly unlikely that I will make it that far.

On their first date they went to 'the pictures' in Yeovil and saw the movie *The Paradine Case* with Gregory Peck in it.

He used to ride seven miles to her house on his bicycle every day, then over time bought a motorbike, then a car, then they bought a farm in Gloucester together, then had three children, then those children had children, one of them became a stand-up comedian and wrote a book. I decided to get a little tattoo of Gregory Peck on my arm to commemorate their first date. I found the photo I wanted, then checked he was never a paedophile and headed to the tattoo studio.

My problem with getting tattoos is that I find tattoo artists quite intimidating, mainly because I think they are super cool but also because of the tattoos on their face. I just find it hard to disagree with them and compromise is really important when deciding something to put on your arm for the rest of your life. Basically I went in for a small one and ended up coming out with a massive, almost life-size tattoo of Gregory Peck's face on my forearm. It's kinda cool. You can stretch the skin and move his eyebrows into different emotions and draw glasses on him. It has 'Paradine Case' written below it. I still haven't seen it but apparently it's really bad. Rotten Tomatoes calls it 'Alfred Hitchcock's worst'. That's just what I do. I get average movies of the past tattooed on my body. I can't wait to be seventy-five and get 'The Fast and the Furious: Tokyo Drift' tattooed on my back. I got it for Granny but as soon as I got it my mum said, 'Don't show it to Granny.' Ah well, the first date of my grandparents was now seared on my arm forever.

Dating these days is very different. While I was in my previous relationship, dating apps had become a huge phenomenon. The dating and mating world hadn't seen a shake-up like this since the invention of the marker pen and napkin. Internet courting used to hold such negative connotations. It used to be the last garrison before subscribing to a life of cats and whiskey – but now everything had changed. Young people were heading out on a huge number of dates with people they met online and it had apparently become cool. It was perfect for me. No longer did I need the confidence to approach someone in person; I just had to swipe their face, putting me on a level pegging with all the confident dudes in the nightclubs.

I joined Tinder, Bumble, Happn, Plenty of Fish, Raya and Loads of Gash. OK, the last one at point of publication was not a real dating app but I have no doubt it's already a website. I also joined Grindr. Not because I'd failed my biannual bi-anal but because I genuinely thought it wasn't just for gay people. After signing up and scanning through four pages of men I got the idea. So many people use their penis as their profile picture. I couldn't believe it. I was slightly frustrated that none of them thought to draw a little face on the end. It was a missed opportunity.

Tinder was the easiest app with the most users. I'd sit there all day swiping through hundreds of people, judging them entirely on face value, left for no, right for yes. If they share your interest then you get a match and can start messaging each other.

Picking photos is a nightmare. You have to try and give the sense that you are fun, approachable, have friends and have been on at least one gap year.

My first match was with a lady called Hazel. Her photos were all taken while she was at festivals covered with glitter, face paint and the customary cut-off denim shorts. She had black hair in a bob with a fringe hanging to her eyes and covering her eyebrows, making her facial expressions 50 per cent less readable.

'Where do you live?' she asked, getting straight to the point. It was a brave opening gambit, showing the difference between the new world and the old. Imagine if anyone approached you in the street and demanded, 'Where do you live?' You would lie and run a mile, the opposite way to your actual house.

'Nunhead,' I replied.

'No way! I'm at a party near your house, I'm going to come to your house in half an hour,' she typed quickly. All I could think was, 'I'm gonna clean my house.'

I didn't really understand whether this was a scandalous liaison or a date. Is that what people are doing these days? I felt so out of the loop. I'd heard people were squeezing in a lot of dates; maybe this is how it worked? She would come over then if it was not right she would move on to the next house. Like efficient Deliveroo dating.

I started a quick simultaneous clean of me and my flat, moving my discarded pants from the sofa (flat), changing my shirt (me) and cleaning the intimate areas (flat and me).

She didn't arrive thirty minutes later so I carried on cleaning. She didn't arrive an hour later so I carried on cleaning. After two hours, my flat and I were spotless. If I'm honest I was quite happy Hazel hadn't turned up. Having the deadline of someone seeing my flat turned me into a tidy overdrive. If I could have a non-starter scandal tease every week, my house and I would look wonderfully groomed. It's the inspiration I need to get me started on a domestic blowout. If people kept standing me up I could finally decorate the bedroom or put up that shelf I have been meaning to do for years.

I went to bed in my immaculate flat. I even changed my sheets and made the bed. I never make my bed. I never see the point as I'm only going to get back in it again. Although as I slipped under the flat, clean duvet with plumped pillows that night I started to understand what my mother had been shouting about each morning for all those years before I left for school. It was fresh, like lying in a field of buttercups, but comfier and not outside. I found myself spreading further across the bed instead of cowering in the corner in the foetal position under a crumpled, mismatched cover. I was going to get the best sleep ever.

I tucked myself up in my PJs (pyjamas this time, not private jets) ready to have nightmares about being alone forever. I closed my eyes and slowly drifted off.

'BUZZZZZZZZZ.' The doorbell rang out. When the doorbell rings I always get momentarily excited, thinking I've been woken by the postman and it's a parcel delivery. I looked over at my phone. It was 2 a.m. This was even outside the delivery hours of Amazon Prime.

Surely it couldn't be Tinder girl? That would make her three hours late. I slumped sleepily downstairs and looked through the peeping hole (is that what it's called?).

What stared back at me was a real-life slightly-worse-than-the-photos version of Hazel standing a wood's width away, and it really wasn't the type of wood's width I'd anticipated (I'm talking about sex).

She was royally hammered, with the customary glitter all over her face. She looked like a pixie who'd been in a car accident. As I looked through the miniature porthole (it's not that either is it?) I was over it and not the kind of over it I'd anticipated (I'm talking about sex again). The discovery of the newly washed, flat bed sheets was far better than a one-night stand with someone I didn't like.

I tiptoed away, pretending I wasn't in.

BANG BANG BANG.

She started aggressively banging on the door.

'I can hear your footsteps,' she slurred. Damn it. My neighbours were almost definitely going to complain. I had to let her in or get rid of her. What do I do?

BANG BANG BANG. 'Fuck,' I whispered to myself.

Maybe she'd lost her lift home and was stuck in Peckham. I didn't want to be responsible for a girl having to walk home to Gravesend. I wasn't sure where she lived but she had a Gravesend air about her (sorry, Gravesend). I should let her in. I silently took one last look through the glass eye (yep, that's definitely what it's called), hoping that she'd gone. Her fish-eye face was staring at me like we were at two ends of a very short telescope.

I turned the latch and due to her leaning all her weight on the door she stumbled past me into my house and stood in my hallway in a daze, trying to focus her eyes.

'Heeeeey,' she said, raising both her arms above her head. 'You have any beer?' She sat heavily on the sofa. Only an hour ago I was happily Hoovering down the cushion cracks and lining up the pillows all nicely and now I had a drunken stranger fucking it all up again.

'I think maybe you've had enough?' I said, feeling like a fifty-year-old party pooper.

She stumbled to my fridge and grabbed one out regardless. I really didn't know what to do. Should I call the police? 'Yes, Officer, a tipsy Tinder lady has taken me hostage in my own flat, bring everyone you have.' It sounded like more of a prank call than the actual prank calls I used to do as a kid.

'How are you going to get home?' I asked, shouting slowly and clearly like my dad talking to a foreign person on holiday. Silence.

She'd already fallen asleep. I started to think maybe she was homeless. Is this what she did every night? If it was, I take my hat off to her. So she can collect money in it, obviously.

I carried her upstairs to my bedroom. Perhaps in hindsight I should have just left her there but the sofa was new and I'd just cleaned between the cracks. It was a bespoke blue suede J-shaped sofa that I'd waited six months for.* It's my dream to be rich enough to spell my name with furniture.

I picked her up and attempted to carry her up the stairs. She was either heavier than I anticipated or I was weaker. Either way it was a hell of a struggle. I kept hitting her limp head against the bannister. It was like the movie *The Bodyguard* if Whitney Houston had filmed it later in her career.

I tried to place her on the sheets gently but it ended up being more of a Highland Games toss and she fell to the mattress with a thump. I inflated my blow-up camp bed with an electric pump. I was hoping the Hoover-esque noise would wake Sleeping Brutey and she would offer to kip on the floor herself or, better still, fuck off – but alas, I had no such luck. I slept on my own floor while she snored in my bed just like that prick Goldilocks.

I had a terrible night's sleep. The blow-up mattress deflated quicker than it went up and it was cold too. I wished DJ Ironik was there so I could borrow his sleeping bag.

I was woken at 6.30 a.m. by her knocking my scented candle off my bedside table. I looked over.

---

* Everything else these days you can order and it arrives almost immediately. Apart from sofas. I can only assume they are made on Mars and sent in small space rockets down to Earth, thus taking an unbelievably long time from order to delivery.

'Sorry,' she said in a hushed voice as if she hadn't already woken up the only other person in the house.

Now, what happened next was unbelievable. I couldn't believe my tired eyes.

She stumbled off the mattress, then leaned on the bedside table, pulled down her skinny ripped jeans and just starting urinating next to the bed.

Surely this must be a nightmare? I rubbed my eyes, hoping I would wake up. Nope. I think it's definitely happening. This is happening. On my floor. That I'm sleeping on.

'Hey! Stop pissing on my floor!' I shouted. I couldn't believe that it was something I was having to actually say.

She looked over at me as if I'd disturbed her.

'Just . . . look away,' she replied casually, shooing me with her hand.

'Privacy is not the issue!' I said, trying to find my angry voice. She was sort of half awake and half asleep so I tried to wake her fully.

'Shhhh,' she spat, pressing her finger to her lips. She turned her head back round remarkably like the girl in *The Exorcist* and continued her heavy flow.

I felt powerless. She was ignoring me and I couldn't get near her because it was starting to splash. I couldn't rugby-tackle her or carry her out like a dog in the movies, it would go everywhere, so instead I just sat there and watched.

It usually takes months to get to the point in a relationship when you can comfortably urinate in front of each other and carry a girl to the bedroom. We'd done both and we were only five hours deep.

She really went on for ages. It kept on coming, like a

magician miraculously pulling a huge piece of fabric out of his ear. She honestly didn't seem like a big enough vessel for that much liquid. Goldilocks was not a shots girl; she was definitely a pints lady.

Eventually, the magican ran out of cloth. She dripped her last drips and crawled back into bed and immediately fell back to sleep. Not that I expected her to, but she didn't even wipe.

I can only assume she just got out of prison and that was where her toilet was located in her cell – either that or she was due to have a photoshoot for *Gay Times* in a few days.

On a night when I thought I was going to meet a fancy new lady in a fancy new way, I found myself at 6.45 a.m. Googling 'how to clean up human urine'. My Google history reads like this:

Best dating apps
Tinder Download
How to clean up human urine

My screen displayed a mixture of answers that mainly came from people asking about babies. Or people in my position pretending to ask about babies.

After blotting up any excess fluid, sprinkle a generous amount of bicarbonate of soda over the soiled area. Pour a water-and-vinegar solution directly onto the baking soda to create a mini cleaning volcano that will actively eat away at the stain. Blot and rub gently dry with a soft cloth after letting it sit for five minutes.

The next thing in my Google history is now:

> What is bicarbonate of soda?
> Bicarbonate of soda, or baking soda, is an alkali which is used to raise soda breads and full-flavoured cakes such as gingerbread, fruit cake, chocolate cake and carrot cake.

Or soaking up piss, apparently. Such a diverse product.

I went down to the kitchen while Hazel snored gloriously upstairs. Fern loved baking cakes so I went to her cake cupboard that out of pure laziness I'd left untouched and grabbed everything I needed.

It was a horrific evening, although I have to admit, some enjoyment was experienced while cleaning up the urine as it felt like I was making a *Blue Peter* model volcano. I applied the bicarbonate of soda while the post-piss princess snored beside me. She and the bicarbonate of soda were both taking the piss in different ways.

'My ex girlfriend used this for baking my birthday cake,' I said to myself. Times had changed. I was now using it to soak up a stranger's bodily fluids.

I went back to sleep on the sofa. I wasn't going to sleep next to the yellow volcano.

I woke her up in the morning and reminded her of what she had done. 'Please don't talk about this onstage,' she said huskily.

'I won't, Hazel Fowler,' I said. To be fair she said nothing about putting it in a book.

My bedroom had gone from the cleanest it had ever been

to a service-station toilet in a matter of hours. There was white powder, glitter and splashes on my wall. It looked like I'd had sex with a fairy with a cocaine and incontinence problem.

It was the date to end all dates. A lovely World War One reference there . . . but, just like World War Two, unbelievably we did another one. She apologised profusely and asked if she could take me out to make it up to me. Every part of me wanted to go to her flat and shit on her carpet but I didn't. I agreed and we went on a second date – far away from my house.

We went bowling. I lost the first game even though she could only just lift the lightest ball. It had holes the size of pencil sharpeners and it would roll down the alley at a snail's pace yet frustratingly push all the pins over. I was trying to use the heaviest ball and hoof it down the lane to show off but it went in the gutter every time.

'We are all in the gutter, but some of us are looking at the stars,' I said. I told her it was an Oscar Wilde quote about bowling and she believed me. I won the second game because I conceded and squeezed my farmer fingers into a pencil-sharpener ball.

Incredibly, after our horrific false start we dated for a month. I ended it before it could get serious as I was now utterly petrified of relationships and whenever I smelled urine, I would think of her. It's such a powerful sense.

After we had cleared out my grandfather's stuff, I continued leafing through his farming admin. In his last few years he had become wonderfully obsessed with our family lineage.

Something that caught my eye was my great-great-great-grandmother Emily Willis who was buried in south-east London. It was our family's only connection to the capital.

As I live in south-east London I went looking for more details in the stuffed ring binders. I found it. She was buried in Nunhead Cemetery, which I had bought a house right next door to *after* Grandad died. To save money she was buried in the same plot as the rest of her family. There were five of them in there in total. It got stranger. I turned the page and Grandad had written a poem about Nunhead in 2010. The place I now lived. He didn't write lots of poems about lots of different places; this was the only one I could find. What were the chances? This is it.

NUNHEAD

Nunhead Cemetery, Peckham,
Where bushes and trees abound.
There are families to be found there,
Resting, deep below ground.

There's poor baby Charles Harvey,
For his memory we may weep.
The first of the grave's occupiers,
They slumber, twelve feet deep.

From August Eighteen Fifty-Six,
And for the next four decades,
Four more times could be seen and heard,
Gravediggers and their spades.

The next to fill the gaping void,
Seeking Charles, was his mum.
Young Emily, with typhoid fever,
At twenty-three, the fever won.

Richard and Mary Harvey,
Charles's grandparents, joined them there.
We presume old age despatched them
To the family vault, to share.

Their son, George Hounsom Harvey,
Charles's father, topped the bill.
He was by no means an old man,
When sent to that grave to fill.

An engraved headstone, stood erect,
A grave tended with loving care.
Now, upheaval has taken place,
With tree roots, that grave must share.

Sadly overgrown, neglected,
Full of memories and history.
But with the diligence of descendants,
They've uncovered a mystery.

PBD. Dec 2010

Turns out I wasn't the only Dommett who liked a poem.

It was so incredible reading Grandpa's diaries. It was an amazing yet simple snapshot in time to what he was doing over seventy years ago and it was utterly fascinating.

'You should read yours and compare them!' my mum told me on the phone.

'Mine?' I said sceptically.

'Yeah. Do you not remember your diary?' she said. I had absolutely no idea what she was talking about. It was a detail of my life I had forgotten. Like putting your chair on the table at the end of a school day or glue guns.

'It's still in your room,' Mum said. Of course it was. All my belongings were untouched, like the room of a missing child that the parent thinks might come back one day.

'I'm on my way,' I said immediately, jumping in the car which still smelled of urine and reminded me of Hazel.

I went back to the room I grew up in and there it lay, between the *Bottom* VHS and *Def Comedy Jam* DVDs like a dusty wizard spell book. The memories came flooding back. I wrote it for about five months after I was dating Rose. I was eighteen and I hadn't thought about it since I put it down after my last entry.

My writing only fills around one tenth of the book. I obviously massively overestimated how much I was going to share. I called over Lily immediately and we screamed at the entries written shortly after Rose and I broke up and when I first moved to London.

Lily and I were particularly fascinated by the entry about not wanting to have sex with more than forty people because it's slutty. What a strange young adult I was.

'What number are you on now?' Lily asked.

'I really don't know.' I stopped counting at ten because it felt laddish to tally it like the drinks count after a stag do.

For the next hour we sat and plotted my sexual history just like my grandad before me worked out his family tree. Pissy Hazel was number thirty-eight. I had two more chances not to disappoint teenage me. I had to literally stop fucking about.

'I'm going to find the one,' I told Lily boldly, standing aloft like a superhero deciding to save the world. I love a good story and this was going to be my perfect love-life romcom ending. I was serious and I wasn't going to fail.

'You're so weird,' Lily said plainly.

There were plenty of good fish in the sea but unfortunately the next fish I would find was a catfish.

'Oh and by the way, Peter is having an affair,' Lily said casually.

15 September 2004

Hey JD,
Kissed Vince today. A man. Wasn't as weird as I
thought.
Sincerely, Joel

'I needed the toilet throughout that whole story,' Hannah says.

'If you go in your chair I know how to clean it up,' I reply wittily.* Hannah gets up and heads to the bathroom and lets me sit and think about the date of devastation that has occurred.

---

* When I write 'wittily' feel free to assume that at the time I said nothing and I have made myself funnier when I wrote this book.

I am still soaked in deep red Sangria, while the table is filled with a mountain of uncleared glasses, plates and ramekins.

We are among the last few stragglers in the loosely named 'restaurant' and it is now time for the terrifying part – the bill (in my head I sang *The Bill* theme tune when I wrote this, please feel free to do the same). While Hannah is away I give the castanets a click. I can't resist. It was always the last-choice instrument in the box at primary school and I haven't touched one since then. Rodrigo looks over, called by the instrument of his homeland. If I knew it was going to work this well I would have used it before. I do the universal sign for the bill payment, the writing on paper mime, while mouthing 'bill'. Rod nods. A few minutes later he brings over a piece of paper and a pen. He misunderstood the universal sign for paying the bill for me wanting to write something down. It's the first time I've actually liked Rodrigo. It's quite a sweet mistake to make. I politely tell him that I want the bill, not paper.

'Oh for fuck's sake,' he says under his breath. I immediately go back to hating him. Hannah arrives back just in time to see Rodrigo throw down the bill on a tiny silver tray with three mints on it harder than bullets. He wants to go home so much he's finally given up on flirting with her. Of course the tip is already added on and branded as 'optional'. Nobody would ask them to take it off and they know it. I couldn't ask for tap water so clearly I can't ask for the additional tip to be removed.

We have a few obvious choices for the paying of the bill:

I pay.
She pays.
We split it.

Do I pay it and be a traditional man? I feel like offering to pay is noble but patronising these days. I don't want to infer that she's not an independent woman with her own funds. I kinda believe men should continue to pay for everything until the gender pay gap is non-existent so it speeds up the process to abolish it. It's a good idea but would be an utterly wanky thing to suggest at bill time on a debut date. Bill time is all OK if we're on the same page. If she's a non-payer and I'm a payer, then it's fine, but if we're both splitters then that's wonderful too.

'Do you want to go Dutch?' Hannah says. I look at her, confused. I don't know what that means. If I remember rightly she is Dutch – is she flirting with me? Is that her end-of-date catchphrase like 'no lighty no likey'? She can clearly see my facial struggle. 'It means split the bill,' she explains helpfully. SHE'S A SPLITTER! We are totally on the same page.

We place our cards on the tiny metal tray (why don't they just use a ramekin?) and wait for the waiter. I really hate the back-and-forth bill process. You ask for it, then they eventually bring it, then they leave again while you put your cards on the tray, then they return, see your cards then leave again to get the card machine then they return and you finally pay. It's utterly stupid. It's why everyone loves Nando's so much: it's slightly to do with the chicken but mostly because you can eat and leave without having to watch the waiter do sprints back and forth from the bar like a cricketer who's hit a ball to the boundary.

'So you've slept with thirty-eight people?' Hannah asks while we wait for the waiter.

'I had when I found the diary six months ago,' I reply. For a moment I'd forgotten about what happened last night but the numbers remind me.

'Who was number thirty-nine?'

#39 The Catfish

Lily had told me about Peter having an affair so calmly, like a professional doctor giving bad news to a patient.

'WHAT?!' I'd replied, like a patient receiving bad news. It turned out Lily had found sexy emails on Peter's computer from a girl called Nancy.

'Where is he now?' I asked. I had so many questions but this was for some reason the first one that escaped.

'He's with her in Paris,' she replied.

'WHAT?!' I repeated. Along with the dirty email she found two return easyJet boarding passes. Peter had lied to her saying he was away with friends for the weekend but he was actually on a Parisian weekend of infidelity. Lily decided to check his emails because frankly, who goes to Paris with friends?

'Does he know that you know?' I asked. I wanted to console her, but I seemed even more upset than she was. I tapped her on the back like my dad used to say goodbye to me before he bought my affection with a cool computer. I was also desperately trying to suppress the urge to say that her marriage to Peter had clearly 'petered out'.

'No,' she said, again sounding completely composed.

In this scenario I would be a blubbering wreck but she remained a sturdy ship or at least a sturdy dinghy that had strayed from a sinking relation-ship.

'Is he still in Paris?' I asked, my voice rising to a higher pitch with every question. Lily nodded and looked at the floor. What could I do to repair this? I felt powerless. Then it occurred to me.

'Do you know when their flight's getting in?' I asked. Lily nodded, looking up suspiciously. After years of hanging out with me she knew where this was going.

'Let's meet them at the airport!' I said, trying to remain sincere while hiding the fact that this was potentially one of the most exciting ideas I'd ever conceived.

'Yeah. Why not?' she said with a hint of a smile.

I wanted to make signs that said 'WELCOME HOME TO A DIVORCE' and 'CHEAP AIRFARE (AFFAIR)' but she wouldn't let me even though I told her I was good at bubble writing. So, sans sign, the next day we headed to Bristol Airport. I love airports more than most but utterly despise them when I'm not travelling anywhere. It feels like you're outside a party and your name isn't on the clipboard list.

I couldn't wait to film Peter's reaction; surely this would

go viral. It was the exact opposite to the end of *Love, Actually*.

We got there early and parked the car in the extortionate short stay car park. I had confetti just in case it was necessary for a bit of extra pizzazz. Lily was understandably quiet although she remained composed, like an athlete before a big race or someone who'd just discovered her husband was having sex with someone else.

'Would you mind if we didn't do this?' she suddenly said as we sat in the car. I saw it coming and of course I didn't mind. I felt bad that I wasn't the one to suggest it. I can't say I wasn't disappointed but I obviously knew it was for the best. I was just trying to cheer her up.

'I need to speak to him alone,' she said, nodding to give herself confidence. I'm really bad around sad people. I had got a little better at it during my previous relationship but I still found it hard. I gave her an awkward car hug across the gearstick and central console and she left. It was probably a good thing that I wasn't leaving the car because I almost always can't find it when I come back. I lose everything. Once Lily bought me a fob to put on my keys so I wouldn't lose them but before I could take it out of the box and activate it, I lost it.

I sat in the car, pockets full of confetti, listening to Magic FM because Radio 1 seemed a little too upbeat. Thirty minutes later Lily came out of the lift, striding purposefully. I got out of the car and we hugged for a long time in the short stay. Lily and I never really hugged so when we did we both knew it was needed. We held each other so long that it almost felt like the simple slow-dance that Peter had refused to give her at her wedding. If there was music then we probably would have started rotating but unfortunately there was nothing but the noise of an impatient man beeping, wanting to know if we were leaving our space.

We jumped into the car and as soon as Lily closed her door she burst into tears.

I'd never seen her cry before then and haven't since. I wished she had done it while we were hugging, as I now had to console her over the central console. It was horrible seeing her hurt. It affected me in a way I didn't expect. I felt myself welling up too. There we were. Two people who don't usually cry or hug, crying and hugging.

'Let's go, this car park is costing a fortune,' I said to break the embrace. I was going to try my best to be a best friend and nurse her back to the strong, happy person that Peter had dented. Fucking hell, happiness was hard.

Lily wasn't the only one with relationship problems. I was still searching in the dark ether of the internet for a girlfriend and trying to desperately find The One to end my romcom story.

After my terrible string of internet dates, my confidence in Tinder was starting to wane. A flicker of excitement came when a lady named Staci Ramsey added me on Twitter. She was unfathomably beautiful and had over 100,000 followers, so I immediately trusted her. That's trust these days. Instead of vicars we place faith in people with a blue tick. Her tweets were genuinely funny.

Just for once I want someone to look at me and say, 'That's her, that's the one' and not follow it with 'who ate cake out of the garbage'.

Just saw someone eat a Kit Kat bar without breaking off each individual piece and now I can't stop twitching.

Life gave me onions. Onionade sucks.

OK, they were mostly about food, but still funny tweets. She had a wonderful sense of humour, was stunningly beautiful, and she had a huge amount of followers so would hopefully be able to understand my ridiculous chosen profession.

I added her back.

Staci had long, straight bleached-blonde hair and dark huge doll-like eyes that you just couldn't stop staring at.

Then she messaged me. What was happening? She contacted me first?! This really was too good to be true. We exchanged messages back and forth in quick succession and seemed to get on marvellously. She said she was from America and worked in real estate. It sounded so much cooler than living in England and being an estate agent. In the short space of time that we talked, Staci really made me laugh and didn't seem to mind me being a little weird. She kept on calling me a 'dork' which I thought was cute, in the same way that Poppy loved the word 'snog'. We also seemed to have so much in common.

'I love nu metal,' I typed when she asked me about my music taste.

'Me too! We are such dorks!' she replied. I had somehow stumbled upon someone incredible here. It was a shame that she lived in the US but that could work in my favour. We could take things slower and really get to know each other. We agreed that we were both bored of dating apps – another thing we had in common. We even both had the same favourite Christmas carol. That's rare. It's especially rare when it's 'O Come All Ye Faithful'. It was around Christmas time, she wasn't crazy enough to ask in March. Although I listen to 'OCAYF' all year round: I don't let the seasons dictate when I can listen to my fave Ye Olde Tunes. It's the middle bit that we all love, the bit that goes quiet then builds up:

O come let us adore him
O come let us adore him
O COME LET US ADORE HIM CHRIST THE LORD!

It was the only time you could shout in assembly. Teachers can't tell you off because it's in the Bible. Probably.

'That's my favourite! I love it so much!' Staci said, following it up with multiple crying laughing emojis. She loved emojis so much. Almost too much. We've built up a complexity of language over 5,000 years since the Egyptians and in 2017 we have fully regressed back to hieroglyphs. It makes me so sad face.

We chatted back and forth for around fifteen mins (short for minutes, because mins is money).

'Do you want Skype sex?' she typed along with the gritted teeth emoji and a monkey covering his eyes.

'Yes,' I typed back, giving it zero mins' thought.

It would help me feel less lonely, I would see boobies and there was no danger of her pissing on my carpet. It was a win-win situation, instead of a wee-wee situation. I know I said her living in the US meant we could move slower but it couldn't hurt to get the long-distance relationship going. I was also fully aware that it didn't count towards the forty so why the hell not?

'Great!' she replied quickly. The aubergine emoji hadn't happened yet but surely it was going to happen at some point.

I suddenly realised I had no idea what Skype sex entailed. She definitely sounded like she'd done it before so, like with Sienna Miller before her, I would just follow her lead and play it by ear.

'My microphone is broken.' Maybe we won't be playing by ear after all. 'So you won't be able to chat to me, you'll just be able to see me. We can type to talk,' she said.

'That's fine,' I wrote, not seeing any problem with that at all.

'What's your Skype name?' she asked. I really had no idea. I hadn't used Skype since I was in Los Angeles when I first started stand-up comedy. The foreplay to Skype sex is apparently reinstalling the app on your computer, trying desperately to remember your username and password, having a few tries at it, giving up and getting them both emailed to you.

When a login page says 'forgotten your password?', it makes you feel a tiny bit stupid to click on it. When you have to click on 'forgotten your user name AND password?', it might as well say, 'Have you lost control of your life completely, you carefree, lazy sack of shit?'

Finally, after fifteen minutes of sex admin, the Skype log-in noise rang out. It's the sound of someone breathing in, like preparing to go under the water in the swimming pool or opening a bin you know you should have emptied three days ago.

I added Staci, a relative stranger, who I was probably about to see naked. She knew her Skype name off by heart. A blonde lady appeared in her bedroom in a grainy video communication. It was happening.

We typed to each other instead of talking. It got sexy quickly.

Lots of 'show me this' and 'do that' followed, although obviously being slightly more specific. We de-clothed quickly, returning to the keyboard periodically to type various instructions.

The aubergine emoji happened. Later than I imagined but better late then never.

We ramped swiftly up to what I assumed was 'Skype sex', which I swiftly discovered is not as good as the title suggests. It's got 'sex' in the name so you think it's going to be exciting like sex – it's really not. I would do the washing up all the time if it were called 'plate fucking', only to find out it's just scrubbing dishes and nothing like sex at all. It's like calling masturbation 'me sex'. Actually that's an incredible name for it and I think I might adopt it. We did it. It happened. We did 'Skype sex', which was basically two people, in different places, looking at each other doing me sex.

I regrettably wore a red beanie. Who wears winter headwear when they're masturbating?! Me apparently. I assume rappers keep on their summer headwear. (The image of someone keeping sunglasses on while having sex is one of the funniest things I've ever thought about, dare I say it, even funnier than a beanie.)

It would have been funny if I'd worn a similar smaller beanie on the end of my penis, maybe stealing one from an Innocent Smoothie bottle. Unfortunately I didn't think of it at the time. A frustrating missed opportunity.

There was a poster on the wall behind me of my first Edinburgh Fringe show in 2007. I can only assume Staci was hugely turned on by my four stars from unheard-of publications and made-up quotes from the *Guardian*.

As quickly as it began, it finished.

'That escalated quickly!' she said. Before I had time to reply she'd already written 'Bye!' and signed off. From her first hello to bye was probably an hour. 'What just happened?' I thought.

I messaged her the day after. She didn't reply.

I messaged her a few days later. She didn't reply.

I messaged her a week later. Staci Ramsey didn't reply.

It's OK. I understood. She wasn't into my casual use of woollen headwear as sexy lingerie. I didn't hear from her and I didn't think about it again until a year later in 2016.

I was at Melbourne Comedy Festival being driven in a taxi to a gig in some strange Melbourne suburb. I checked my Twitter and I was added by an account named @celebbustedUK.

'Oh my God, Busted are celebs again!' I thought excitedly. Then my eyes shifted to the bio.

'If we follow you we have naked pictures of you.'

What?! Why would anyone have nak—

'STTTAACCIIIIIIIIIIIIII!' I shouted. The blood drained from my face. What had I done? Who would do this?! Who would take a fleeting private moment and display it to the world? It was at that moment that I realised – I'd really fucked up.

This was apparently an internet phenomenon known as 'catfishing'. Catfishing is a type of deceptive activity involving a person creating a 'sock puppet' social networking presence for nefarious purposes. I'll be honest, it wasn't me who wrote that definition. It's a quote from Wikipedia. I just stole someone's identity while explaining the definition of someone who steals identities. I'm fairly sure you knew it was someone else due to the use of the word 'nefarious'. I still don't really know what it means.

Basically, catfishing is when someone pretends to be someone else on the internet for perverse reasons. I was not the only one to be caught out. The catfish scandal story broke in the newspapers the next day. The good ones like the *Daily Star* and the *Mirror*. The *Mirror* headline read:

CELEB SEX LEAK SHOCK
TWITTER ACCOUNT CLAIMS TO HAVE NAKED
PICS OF OVER 80 STARS
  A Twitter account has alleged to have gained access to naked pics of 84 stars including *Geordie Shore*'s Aaron Chalmers and rugby player Ben Cohen.

I hadn't heard of either of those people. This did not bode well for the eighty-two less famous names, which included me.

'Staci' had stolen photos from a genuinely beautiful

person's profile and created a fake profile. 'She' (or maybe he, who knows?) then bought fake followers and stole tweets from genuinely funny people to lure in low-level naïve 'celebrities' who couldn't believe how lucky there were that such an incredibly funny and beautiful person had got in touch. I was confused. 'How did we have Skype sex?' I thought. She must have been a real person! Then I remembered.

'My microphone is broken.'

It suddenly dawned on me and it all made sense. I connected the dots. One year too late.

It wasn't a two-way Skype conversation, the catfish just played a webcam video of someone slowly undressing then she would type something whenever the woman in the video returned to the keyboard to make it feel real. I thought I was having sex with someone but I wasn't; someone was basically watching me watching porn. Like a porno *Gogglebox*.

When I thought about it, the person in the webcam video was different to the person in the profile pictures. I remember thinking, 'She looks different,' and brushing it off (not a euphemism). She was a different person entirely who just looked slightly similar.

The catfish combined a beautiful person to lure you in, a funny person to lower your guard, and a porn star to capture you. She created a beautiful monster and I fell for it. Someone now had images of me brushing it off (that was a euphemism).

'Everyone is bored of Tinder,' she said. Of course I was going to agree with that, it's what everyone single thinks who is on Tinder. She preyed on me like a mind reader preys on the weak, using vague assumptions and throwing shit at a wall until it sticks.

'Email us if you want the pictures to disappear,' it said in bold in the bio with an email address below.

I felt horrific. How could I have been so stupid? I was so naïve. Should I just pretend it never happened? Ignore it and hope it goes away? My career was slowly moving up the ladder; the story would obviously appear at some point. No, I had to meet this head on and own up to it. I emailed the address.

Hi there,

I have reason to believe you have a photo of me with my penis out. Is this true?? I have a terrible recollection that I was wearing a beanie. Please don't tell me I was wearing a beanie. Seriously, who wears a beanie with their dick out?

You haven't released it so I can only assume you are waiting for my *Chase* episode to air.

Let me know if you have one. If I'm mistaken then this is very embarrassing indeed. Almost more embarrassing then the dick pic itself.

Sincerely, Joel Dommett

Dick out beanie on.

I signed it off 'Sincerely, Joel', making it feel like a diary entry. Incidentally, *The Chase* is a quiz show where the more questions the celebrity gets right the more money they win for a chosen charity. I did OK considering I was solidly in the blue group. Then Sinitta stepped up. She was a professional pop star in the eighties and since then has been a professional friend of Simon Cowell.

She got everything wrong. Everything. Even simple questions like 'What's your favourite colour?' she would panic and say, 'There's so many.' OK, that's an elaboration but honestly not too far from the truth.

It's fine to not be intelligent but don't go on a programme where your level of intelligence dictates how much money you win for a charity. Hers was a children's charity which is wonderful but I've checked, she has been on practically all of the celebrity quiz programmes – and there are so many of them, *Celebrity Pointless*, *Celebrity Mastermind* and so on – and she hardly EVER wins any money. If she were getting questions right she would have won hundreds of thousands for her charity but she takes away nothing. Essentially Sinitta is killing children and we really need to put a stop to it.

Anyway, back to the story. Celebbusted replied quickly.

This is not Joel.
Bye.

They didn't believe I was me. I was having to prove to someone who pretends to be someone else that I wasn't pretending to be someone else. They thought I was catfishing the catfish. I guess the people involved in such scandals usually get their lawyers involved immediately instead of just emailing them from their own Yahoo account.

I replied.

I can only assume you don't think this is me because who is lucky enough to have just 'theirname@yahoo.com' without having to add numbers or underscores? Here is a picture of me holding a sign saying this is me. If you want to request a photo of me doing something specific? Maybe a yoga pose. Please do and I'll send it back.

I sent it along with a selfie with me holding a piece of A4 with 'This is JOEL' in red Sharpie and awaited the reply.

You can add on Twitter and I will tell you what I have on Joel.

They still didn't believe it's me. It turns out when you are a massive lying piece of shit, you just assume everyone else is the same.

BUT I AM JOEL.

I'd resorted to capital letters. Internet shouting. It was getting serious. I added them on Twitter, sat back and let the blue tick of trust tell them it was the real me.

They sent me a direct message.

So it is you.
I told you! Who catfishes a catfish?
What do you want to know?
Is Jon Snow in *Game of Thrones* really dead?

I was keeping it light. I didn't want to scare them away by being too angry. Jon Snow had recently been killed and rumours were rife about him somehow coming back to life. We are talking about the King of the North in *Game of Thrones* not the newsreader that hates U2.

They replied with an emoji. Obviously.

2 x laughing crying face
   Just kidding, I want to know if you have a picture of my penis.
   I do. Give me £3,000 and I won't release the photo.

I was angry that I'd been taken advantage of. It was embarrassing. Not just the fact that someone had naked pictures of me but more so that I'd fallen for it. Although I'm not very good at getting angry. Later that night there were some people being very loud outside my house. They were being proper tinkers and I couldn't sleep. That plus the internet humiliation was too much. My anger simmered to the top and spilled out of the pan and I showed my rage to the world – by closing my curtains angrily. Although when you close curtains angrily, grabbing the fabric and pulling them quickly shut, the top half closes angrily and the bottom half just follows gracefully.

I decided I was not going to pay the catfish ransom for a few reasons.

1. I wasn't famous enough. Nobody knew who I was. I'd been on a few programmes but I was not well known. If they released a naked picture of me nobody would care, and if they did they had mistaken me for Rick Edwards. I was probably eighty-fourth on the list of the eighty-four celebrities and the eighty-three above me would surely eclipse my shame.

2. They said 'the photo' as if they had gone to Snappy Snaps and developed one picture of my dick. I was aware that's not how it works and if I paid them they would still have the images and they clearly would still release them. The best I could do was to ask them to give me 'their word' but unfortunately the 'their word' thing hasn't worked since medieval times.

3. That's so much money. If I had that kind of money I would have paid for the flights to Lily's wedding.

I didn't reply. I didn't pay it. I didn't hear from them and they didn't release the photo. It all worked out OK. Or that's what I thought.

Six months later I got a phone call from my agent, Rick. 'Alright bruvvvaa,' he shouted in his forced London accent as if I'm a regular at his market stall. Hearing his bubbly voice always makes me smile. 'I got a weird one for ya,' he said. These were always my favourite phone calls and are usually followed by a request to perform at a wedding or do *Celebrity Chase*.

'Do you want to go on *I'm a Celebrity Get Me Out of Here!*?'

Wow. I really didn't expect that. For those who are unaware, it's the genius idea of starving celebrities in a jungle while they throw bugs on them every few days for good measure. It's one of the highest-rated TV shows in Britain – and rightly so.

I wasn't sure. I hadn't watched it for a while and I didn't seem like that sort of 'celebrity'. I had been carving out a career on the comedy circuit for eight years now, slowly moving up the chain. I had been working so hard persuading the industry, audiences and other comics that I wasn't completely shit with my Edinburgh Fringe shows and TV choices. Would saying yes to this show put me right back to the beginning? Ironically, I wanted the comedy industry to take me seriously. It could be a disaster. On the other hand, it could be a triumph. The well-trodden route of selling out a tour because you got on *Live at the Apollo* didn't work any more. The panel shows like *Mock the Week* all had their favourites and I wasn't one of them. No other young(ish) up-and-coming comic had done it, only slightly grumpier older ones with less to lose. I would be a first. Maybe this would be my untrodden route to moving up the ladder. I said I would think about it.

'Yeah, why not!' I said an hour later while opening the curtains happily. It was a gamble but one that I surely wouldn't regret. If I didn't do it I would always wonder, 'What if?' There would be no what ifs if I said yes. So I went ahead and said yes.

This decision was to change my life forever.*

I was surely the least famous person that had ever set foot in the jungle. When I did *Celebrity Chase* I was inundated with angry tweets spitting 'Who the fuck is that guy!' This was going to be a hundred times worse.

I had other reservations, too. *I'm a Celeb* is a show about confronting your fears and it would prey on my three biggest ones: being in a confined space with celebrities, heights and wearing a fleece gilet.

I tried to reassure myself about the fear of heights (I couldn't do anything about the other two). How high can things in a jungle really be? It's not like it's in a city where there are lots of high-rise buildings and cranes. 'Keep my fear to myself,' I said to myself cleverly so nobody would find out my Achilles heel.

---

* It's only been a year since I made the decision so by 'forever' I mean 'the next year and potentially the remaining time in my life following that year so right now we are not sure but it's looking likely'.

I was under strict contractual instructions that I wasn't allowed to tell anybody outside of close family. I told Mum, Dad and finally – Lily. She was overly excited for me. She watched the show more than I did so she was an excellent person to ask the litany of questions I had about what was going to happen to me. It was an exciting time for both of us as she was sorting a divorce from Peter and seemed so much happier and more in control of her life. I was heading into *I'm a Celebrity Get Me Out of Here!* and she was heading into the divorce lawyers to say, 'I'm in a marriage, get me out of here.'

I was sent the flight details. It was the airline I had previously been banned from for attempting to 'thumb in a softie' in their onboard toilet. Embarrassingly I had to call customer services to make sure there wasn't a logged warning on their system.

'OK, what was the warning for?' the voice asked officiously.

'Sex?' I said for some reason with a questioning tone.

'There is nothing on the system, sir. You're free to fly with us, but I recommend not doing it again,' she said seriously. She had nothing to worry about. My flights of fancy days were over.

We were flying business class. I'd finally made it to the smug part of the plane. The link between economy and PJ. On the outward journey, I got on the plane and was immediately ushered to a huge reclinable hybrid seatbed. I assumed people would be wearing top hats and monocles in business class but it turns out everyone dresses like normal.

I realised something else: nobody does business in business class. It's comfier than economy but there's a reason why you don't work in bed – it's because you wouldn't get anything done. Prostitutes being the obvious exception to the rule.

When I fly I secretly want it to have a little crash – just a little one so nobody gets hurt – for one reason: we would get to use the slides. It looks such goddamn fun in the videos. Knowing my luck, if it did happen then a lady in front of me would spoil it for everyone by not removing her high heels.

I arrived at Brisbane Airport, unbelievably tired. Even though I had a bed comfier than a real bed, I couldn't sleep at all due to me spending the whole flight thinking, 'SHIT! I'M LYING DOWN ON A PLANE!'

Once we'd landed I wearily picked up my heavy luggage full of clothes that I might not need depending on how early I got voted off. I left the baggage claim area and entered the arrivals hall to a blinding array of unexpected flashes.

I had never been 'papped' before. I immediately assumed I'd done something wrong, like Hazel was dead and her DNA had been found all over my carpet.

Turns out I was just the first to be announced on that year's *I'm a Celebrity Get Me Out of Here!* It suddenly became so real. Before then it had just been a decision. Now this relatively unknown comedian was here, having his photo taken by strangers shouting at him after a sleepless twenty-five-hour flight, with dry-roasted peanut dust down his front.

In the car I was told I was allowed one phone call, just like a prison movie where they always recommend calling your lawyer. I went against the movie advice and called my mum. She didn't answer. Damn it, I should have called my lawyer. They then sealed my phone and laptop in an envelope, like a magic trick where they pretend to smash them up.

For the next week I was in 'holding' in a hotel somewhere north of Brisbane. This meant my phone was disconnected and I was told not to leave the hotel room without my minder. This turned out to be the most relaxing week of my whole life. I honestly don't think I'll have another one like it again. I had no phone and laptop so I couldn't do any work even if I'd wanted to, no social media to scan and no friends to contact. There was nobody else to think about but me. I went to the gym every day then went back and forth to the restaurant and sat by the pool. All with a skinny Australian lady following me around like a tiny bodyguard. I had no idea what I was walking into but it was edging closer day by day. I knew whatever happened it would be hectic so I just tried to enjoy the last few days of silence before the noise.

I watched Donald Trump become president the night before I went in. What had the world become? A reality star had become president and I was about to become a reality star. Did that mean I was going to be president one day? Perhaps I should take this one step at a time and not get ahead of myself.

The morning of the first day arrived. I was blindfolded and escorted onto a boat, like a very gentle kidnapping, and a few minutes later I was arriving at a 'garden party' where Ant and Dec were waiting. I'm pretty sure I know which one's which nowadays but I'm so scared of getting it wrong that I stick with the collective 'dudes' or 'guys'. I do the same on the comedy circuit with sketch groups.

It feels so odd saying it in reverse alphabetic order. Dec and Ant. It's utterly jarring. It's like saying 'Juliet and Romeo' or 'Dad and Mum'. I love mixing up a classic duo mid-conversation. It makes people utterly freak out.

Anyway, Dec and Ant welcomed us to the party and we were each handed an iced tonic and gin.

The rest of the camp mates arrived too. An incredible bunch of strangers who'd never met before but would be weirdly connected for the rest of their lives. It was as follows.

Carol Vorderman from *Countdown*.
Ola Jordan from *Strictly Come Dancing*.
Scarlett Moffat from *Gogglebox*.
Adam Thomas from *Emmerdale*.
Jordan Banjo from Diversity.
Danny Baker, the guy who made all the best television.
Martin Roberts from *Homes under the Hammer*.
Sam Quek from the Olympics.
Lisa Snowdon from my teenage dreams.
Larry Lamb from *EastEnders* and *Gavin and Stacey*.
Wayne Bridge from football.
And me from Bristol.

Some incredible people. Danny, Carol and Larry were legends of British television and I immediately liked the vibes of Adam and Jordan . . . but above all I couldn't believe I was in the vicinity of Lisa Snowdon. I was obsessed with her when I was a teenager. She was on my sexy hidden *FHM* calendar when I was fourteen. She was March and as far as I was concerned in my bedroom it was March all year round.

Scarlett walked up the stairs. 'Well, she is clearly going to win,' we all thought collectively. Her natural likeability and instinctive wit were incredible, all in this tiny Geordie package. As we lined up in the scorching hot Australian midday sun, Dec and Ant revealed the first trial.

'You must walk along a plank off the side of a skyscraper in the city,' Dec or possibly Ant said. THEY HAD IMMEDIATELY FOUND MY ACHILLES HEEL. It was like they'd read my mind.

I developed my fear of heights from my mother. Although luckily mine is a slight dread, hers is a debilitating anxiety that stops her from crossing footbridges and enjoying a sweet balcony view. Height is a valid fear. It's not like a fear of balloons, or putting out the recycling. It's your body's natural instinct saying, 'If you fall off this you will die so don't go near the edge, you stupid idiot.' It's the way our body has developed over millions of years to help keep us alive. It's for the same reason we find the sound of water soothing because it keeps us alive, and hate the smell of shit because not eating it keeps us alive.

Apparently the sound of a baby crying has developed over time to be a noise that adults hate so we help them and keep them from dying. Imagine how many more babies would die if their unhappy scream was akin to a relaxing classical opus. It would be horrific but imagine how much better we would sleep on flights.

By the way, if you're thinking, 'This sounds like something you heard on a podcast, Joel,' you are absolutely correct: one point for you, smarty pants. What I think I'm trying to say is, if you're not scared of heights you probably love eating shit and killing babies. OK, I'll be honest, I didn't listen to the end of the podcast.

My fear of heights, like most other people's, doesn't come from simply being high up. It comes from my fear that I'm going to suddenly lose my mind and leap off that height. I'm petrified that I'll fling myself off the edge shouting, 'That was a terrible split-second decision!' It was the same fear I'd come up against in the gun range in LA.

The rules of the first trial were to walk out along the plank, stand on the end, count for sixty seconds then walk back. The three camp mates that got the closest to one minute won the challenge. Basically, it was counting under pressure.

We walked out onto the roof. The warm coastal wind immediately hit me in my petrified face. Then I saw it. The plank that protruded from the top of the tall, slim building like a fascist's stiff arm. I couldn't believe someone wanted me to stand on that.

I got fitted into my harness and helmet, which was utterly necessary but made me look like a real prick early doors in the show. I've seen climbers look really cool but this wasn't cool stuff. It felt like when you go ice-skating and you're given the shit hire-skates. I just for once wanted to be one of the guys with their own cool pair who skate around backwards and get all the chicks.

Carol went first, slowly, yet utterly relaxed, while the plank swayed from side to side. I assumed she sang the *Countdown* clock song at the end to count her minute. Jordan went second, his huge feet dwarfing the tiny runway. He walked straight out, stood like he was waiting for a bus and wandered back without a care in the world.

Me next. I took one step on the plank. My feet immediately

started to shake, wobbling the metal frame. It was just like lighting Sienna's cigarette in the train all over again. The extremities I needed to be most stable shook like a seismic needle in an earthquake. Or anything in an earthquake really, I suppose.

I was fighting thousands of years of evolution and an entire childhood of my mum telling me, 'Don't go too high!'

I took one step at a time, cautiously making my way to the edge. Too slow if anything. It was a good thing it wasn't live or they'd have had to move the news. I made it to the end and waited. I looked across at the high-rise flats opposite, never looking down, trying my best to count. It turned out it's really hard to count under pressure. I got to what I thought was sixty seconds, turned and walked back like the worst catwalk model in history. I had never been that scared. And I really don't think anything will come that close again. It was worse than doing comedy for the first time, shooting a gun and Megaphobia all put together.

The good news was it meant I had got my worst fear out the way first and that helped immeasurably for the rest of the experience. It was like I had jumped off the biggest diving board first so now I could just enjoy the springy ones below. I tried to think of the rest of the experience just like the plank. Just take everything one step at a time.

However, I had no time to enjoy the adrenaline of conquering the fear on completion. We were thrust tightly into a helicopter and lifted off to the jungle.

After stepping off the side of a building, flying in a helicopter felt easy peasy lemon squeezey (I love that phrase. It's so joyous. I also enjoy the fact that ironically it's so much easier to just say 'easy'). Then, once we had landed, after a long walk we arrived safely in our jungle home. It felt so odd. You were inside an environment you'd seen so many people live in, over so many years. It was like being on the set of *Friends* or *Seinfeld*; you felt like you knew it so well yet you had never been there before. We'd be living here for at least a week and at most three. This was home. As with the paparazzi flashes, it suddenly felt real. It was happening. Up until that point the experience had been a bit of a whirlwind but now I had time to sit on my new hammock and think about the gravity of this decision while wearing a fucking gilet.

We tried to start a fire, which it turns out is hard lard lemon scarred (this is the less-loved brother of lemon squeezey that I'm trying to give a leg-up). Luckily, Larry Lamb jumped in and proved to everyone he was the father figure of the group, a title he deserved and wonderfully lived up to throughout the whole experience.

Slowly we all gelled as a group. I don't think I'd made this many friends so quickly since the cheese course. It felt like there was something missing. Where was the annoying one? In all these reality shows there's a frustrating trouble-making catalyst placed in the centre of the bunch to fuck things up and make it spicy viewing but nobody seemed to take up that mantle. Where was the prick? Martin Roberts arrived late and his presence was a little antagonistic but he wasn't a prick. He was just a sweet misunderstood weirdo who knows about property.

I assumed Carol would be hard work because of how incredibly long she has been famous but she was delightful.

If I'd been the first lady on Channel 4 and at one point the highest-paid woman in Britain, I'd definitely be a dick-head.

My favourite daily pick-me-up would be when Carol would say, 'I'm just going to the toilet,' and I would say, 'One from the bottom please, Carol!' She became my second favourite Carol. Behind 'O Come All Ye Faithful' obviously.

We all got on and it was wonderful. I think I would have really suffered if it had kicked off. I would have just hidden in the toilet, rocking in the foetal position, having flashbacks to Chris the bully and my parents' divorce.

That year, 2016, had been a hard year for everyone. The country was reeling from the bereavement of Prince, David Bowie, Gene Wilder, Mohammed Ali, Ronnie Corbett, Terry Wogan and Europe. We all felt like we were being monotonous to watch because we were so harmonious but it turned out it was exactly what the country needed. Due to Brexit the country had been arguing all year long. The serenity of the peaceful camp in a nightly reality show was exactly what the nation needed.

There was one problem: five days in I still hadn't shat. They warned us that constipation would be an issue but I didn't think it would last this long. It was due to the diet change, thinking about a whole crew of people listening in, and the fact my teenage calendar crush was standing on the other side of a hessian curtain washing her perfect face.

That was also the day I started to cry. I was so tired and hungry I began getting emotional in the bush telegraph. If you don't know the show, the bush telegraph is where you go to talk to the camera. Like the diary room in *Big Brother*, which is what I kept on calling it and they kept on having to remind me to stop calling it.

I was so full of emotion and faeces.

Eventually the bowel movement happened. It may sound strange but it really was one of the highlights of the whole experience. I would have eaten the poop because I was so hungry but luckily I'd listened to that podcast.

It was incredible what you started to miss. I missed routines, like going to the gym in Peckham, then going for breakfast and a flat white at my favourite café afterwards. I missed my family, Mum mostly, but Dad too. And I missed Lily.

I didn't miss my phone. I thought I would. I thought I would miss the internet but my life without it had become so simple. It was so tranquil not having death, racism, war, bigotry and *Geordie Shore* flashing in front of me on a screen throughout the day. Without the internet or television you concentrate on eating, conversation and sleeping. It was how I imagine it was in the eighties or still is in parts of Wales.

Due to not being able to eat to enjoy ourselves, we talked about eating to enjoy ourselves instead, every day for at least three hours. I began craving specific things I hadn't thought about for years. A breakfast Rose used to make for me, fifteen years ago. White Toblerone, the huge ones from airports that I hadn't eaten since I started going to the gym and stopped wanting to bruise the roof of my mouth with its stupid angry shape.

It took your appreciation of food to another level. You

really miss flavours like pepper and salt (feels so odd that way round). If we won a small treat you'd be gifted the prize of one square of chocolate or an eighth of a muffin but you would suck on that one tiny two-centimetre piece of chocolate for twenty minutes. The flavour was insane, immediately triggering that tiny sugar high. We all throw so many flavours and additives into our faces in our daily lives, not understanding how incredible every flavour is because of the sheer amount we consume these days.

I'll probably never get the opportunity to starve myself of food or communication like that for the rest of my life. I think I learned that the simple, important things matter and the peripheral noise that gets in the way of that simplicity doesn't. Maybe if you strip it all back you'll enjoy things more. I'm obviously talking metaphorically, not over Skype.

If you didn't gorge on an abundance of food, maybe you'd enjoy what you do have and similarly, not crowding your life with so many friends means you can enjoy the ones that really matter.

I thought about Mum, Dad and Lily every day. I didn't think once about my Twitter followers. I'd run moments over and over in my head when I'd be at home with Mum ignoring her while I was perusing nothing on social media. We spend so much time buried in our phones these days, talking to thousands of strangers who are far away, that we forget to talk to the important people who are right there.

I also learned that I don't want to go to prison. It's slightly similar to the jungle. You're stuck in a guarded environment with other inmates, with very little food, unable to escape.

The big difference with *I'm a Celebrity* is that you are stuck there with a man from *Homes Under the Hammer* instead of guys that have broken into homes with a hammer.

People slowly started leaving one by one and I have no idea how but I somehow stayed. Unfortunately I couldn't better my nunchuck silver medallist 2002 result and I came second. Although this time more than two people competed so I considered it a triumph. As we used to say in school, first the worst, second the best, third the one with the hairy chest. Though actually Scarlett is anything but the worst and Adam who came third is as hairless as one of those smooth cats that look like a ball bag.

I really couldn't have imagined getting that far and remaining longer than such an incredible, illustrious stable of people.

Unfortunately, coming second means you are the only camp mate who doesn't get to experience meeting the family member on the bridge. I was devastated but I'm sure my mum was happy she didn't have to show the nation her fear of heights by being the first family member in the show's sixteen-year history to crawl along the bridge on her hands and knees. Instead we met in a busy corridor of people and hugged briefly with a few tears before I was pulled from thing to thing for literally the next seven hours. After the immediate meal, they rush you into a room to consult a doctor and psychiatrist, weighing you and making sure you're fit for the outside world. I'd lost one stone. That's the equivalent of seven pineapples, a nineteen-inch flat-screen TV or one mysterious, vague-sized stone.

'Slowly introduce things into your diet and increase the volume gradually,' Doctor Bob said clearly, knowing that nobody heeds his advice. I nodded seriously then left and ate two whole cheesecakes. Whole cheesecakes. I'm not talking slices. I'm talking two full 100 per cent pie-chart cheesecakes.

I could taste every ingredient, every grain of sugar and every speck of cheese. It was wondrous. It was what I had dreamt of for three weeks. I hadn't however dreamt about throwing it all back up nine minutes later. Although it was so soon after I'd eaten the cheesecake, the vomit still tasted like cheesecake. It was delicious. Four for the price of two. I was like a dragon that breathes dessert.

My body desperately wanted food. Every crumb, chunk, piece or sliver of edible items I saw I threw in my mouth. When I was full I would keep piling it in until I felt ill. Then the ill feeling would subside, or I would be sick, then I would just eat some more. I was a human Henry the Hoover and my body was utterly confused.

Later that evening, we were thrust into an after-party with all the hundreds of incredible crew that are involved in such an event. It was insane to see how many cogs made the machine work and that I was part of what was being produced by this massive mechanism. I couldn't handle it. I had to leave after thirty minutes; there were too many people and too much noise. I had become used to the distant noise of frogs and Larry's snoring and this was too different. It was good to know that although lots of things were about to change my dislike of nightclubs firmly remained.

I didn't turn my phone on until after the party, trying my best to delay the inevitable slide back into the old internet-obsessed me.

The first person I rang was Rick.

'Alright bruvvvvaaaa!' he shouted down the delayed line from across the world. It was great to hear his familiar voice. 'We've put a date on at the Hammersmith Apollo,' he said proudly. I couldn't believe it. That was the moment when I realised the gravity of what had happened and how much things were about to change.

We all returned home on business class again. I had showered three times but I still smelled of BO and fire. On the way over all the seats were facing the same way, however on the return flight you sat beside another business-class person but *facing* each other. I was on the window side as per, so if I wanted to get out, I had to step over my fellow passenger's legs. However, I'd learned from previous experience not to try to climb without their knowledge. You have a divide between you that you can raise or drop, depending on your familiarity. Like the glass divide between the driver and the passenger in a limo. Or a more inclusive example: like an electric car window or the shutter that opens at Asda on Black Friday.

A businessy-looking stranger was sitting opposite me. He wore a tie which he only took off a few hours in. It was a complete contrast to my full bedclothes and neck pillow get-up. He of course was reading the *Financial Times* and had the clichéd spectacles of an intelligent man in finance.

I didn't put up the middle divide because it felt rude. I didn't want him to think I was offended by his face so I kept it down and reclined my seat.

After a while he did the same. It felt like we were having a sleepover and we were topping and tailing. I was the ying to the banker's yang. He fell asleep and I watched him nap for a bit then after a few hours he woke and he ate. I basically watched a man exist for twenty-four hours. It was like the old live stream of *Big Brother* where they would cut to the chickens when they would swear.

I ate twice. I smashed down a first meal but Henry the Hoover wanted more. I asked for another and the steward thought I was joking but I was deadly serious. In economy they would say no to such greed but in business class they facilitate your self-indulgence. I threw down the second meal triumphantly, like a rubbish bag down a chute, then almost immediately regretted it.

My stomach expanded to the size of a pregnant lady in her fourth trimester. The banker was looking at me as I squirmed. He knew something was wrong. When someone looks suspicious on a plane you immediately assume the obvious – that he is a terrorist, not the less obvious assumption that he is a bloated man who has been starved in a jungle for three weeks with Carol Vorderman.

I was trying to play it cool but I felt like a water balloon ready to burst. The businessman's watchful eye became more wary as my torso bloated to the size of your average bomb vest.

There's no way to put this prettily. Without any warning, I then violently shat myself in business class while looking another adult in the eye. I wish I'd had a few seconds' extra delay so I could have shouted some jihadi phrase aloud before my bowels exploded. There is something magical about the idea of someone shrieking 'Allahhhhhhhu Akbbbbaaarrr' before letting out a massive fart on a plane.

If I had been a balloon I would have flown around the plane darting from one direction to the next until I was a fully deflated version of my former pregnant self. Alas, I sat there empty and shrunken in my reclinable seat. He smiled at me politely. Then, twelve hours into a fourteen-hour flight, he raised the electric divide. We were so close to being divideless, having no boundaries between two strangers – but I ruined it by soiling my pants just before the end.

While I was in the jungle I was sure @celebbustedUK would release the naked photo. They didn't.

They released a video.

That's worse. Way worse. My mum used to have a Google alert on my name. We had to take that off swiftly.

Sex is something done in the moment and when you are out of that moment it looks frankly disgusting. I am not great at dancing but when everyone else is doing it and you are in the mood and the atmosphere is right, you blend in and nobody notices your dance moves. If you videoed me then showed it to me the next day when we were not on the dancefloor I'd be horrified and the distribution of that video would be a huge violation. The only way the leaked sex tape could have been worse was if I was also dancing.

I didn't want to watch it but people kept on tweeting it to me, so to understand the gravity of my situation I gave it a gander. I watched myself self-sex myself. It was horrible. I don't even like listening to a recording of my own voice, let alone this.

My internet was being slow so it kept on pausing, which made it worse. I was buffering in the buff.

I feel weird about calling it a 'sex tape'. I'm not having sex with anyone but myself. 'Self-sex tape?' Is that better? Although looking on the positive side, after my fumble with Sienna was cut I finally had my own filmed sex scene.

Penises should have a safety lock on them like guns. If we had an extra moment to think twice about using them then it would save the embarrassment of millions of men and the disappointment of millions of women.

The worst thing about it is the angle. My laptop was sitting on my low-set coffee table in my lounge which was actually a dining table that I hacked the legs off. God, I wish I left it taller. It's so unflattering. Everyone takes selfies from a high angle so it looks like they have no chins. I have a chinny dick. Nobody wants a chinny dick.

I don't have a beard in the video and it's quite bad quality so I thought about claiming it wasn't me and it was someone else. Unfortunately there's huge poster on the wall behind me with my name across it.

I laugh about it because I can and that's just how I deal with things but in all seriousness it was horrific. I'm lucky enough to be a comedian so I can joke about it. If I were a teacher I'd have lost my job.

Four teenagers committed suicide last year due to someone catfishing them and holding them ransom. That's insane and that's just the ones we know about. If you meet someone online, it sounds simple but please meet up with them and make sure they are a real human before you show them your genitals over the internet. I didn't realise it but some people are fucking arseholes. Literally and figuratively.

My problem is I treat everyone the way I would like to be treated. I assume the best of everyone and think that because I wouldn't entice someone to get their dick out over the internet and then show it to everyone, that everyone else is that courteous. It's unfortunately not true. Some people are dicks and their hard drive is full of videos of other people's dicks.

I decided the best way to deal with this ridiculous situation was the way that most people in the public eye deal with scandals: I 'released a statement'. Although I thought it would be funnier to release it from the perspective of my penis. Or 'my public eye' as I now call it.

I released it on my Facebook and linked to it on my Twitter, the place where all this began.

The following is a statement written by Joel's penis before it went, with Joel, into the jungle. His penis wrote this as damage limitation just in case pictures of it arose in the tabloids and on the internet while Joel was in there and Penis was unable to defend itself:

Recently, after being a relative recluse for Joel's entire life (with the exception of the odd drunken public appearance), after a stupid error on Joel's part there are now pictures of me, 'Joel's part' on the internet. I was quite happy being a completely unknown penis and this newfound fame is frankly horrific for me and

Joel, although we have both realised that it's better to laugh about it than cry about it (only Joel can laugh but we can both cry . . .).

Joel was catfished a long time ago by somebody pretending to be someone else on the internet and was lured into Skype sex. That Skype sex session turned out to be entirely fake and has come back to bite Joel in the ass (Joel's ass is a good friend of mine and also features in the video). It's a genuinely horrific thing for another human being to do, to take advantage of what is private in someone's life and make it public for everyone to see. He obviously chose to go into *I'm a Celebrity Get Me Out of Here!* and people may argue that you are forfeiting a life of privacy with that choice, which he agrees with to a degree – but there is a line. A cruelly obtained video of Joel 'jerking off' (you may prefer other terms such as 'jerking the chain', 'strangling the monkey', 'washing the carrot', 'humiliating the unicorn' or worst of all 'masturbating') in a beanie (seriously who wears a beanie when they 'polish the bath taps'?! I'm supposed to be the only one who wears a hat during sex. He is a hideous human being and I'm embarrassed to be attached to him) which he thought was private is crossing that line.

This is a new type of crime and it is not just happening to people of below-average levels of fame like Joel. Below is a link to an interesting article from the BBC about the problem and the number for the Samaritans which is a good place to start to sort it out if it has happened to you.

Thanks for listening.
Sincerely, Joel's Penis

I tried to go to the police but didn't really have enough information for them to proceed. I went to a geeky hacker friend and again didn't have enough info* to find them. All I had was a Twitter page which was brazenly, almost three years later, still fully active. The Skype call itself was so long ago I'd since lost all the Skype call information and obviously forgotten all my passwords.

I felt thoroughly wronged and they utterly had got away with it. How would I solve this? I couldn't leave it. I couldn't be beaten by me beating off in a video.

I contacted Twitter to inform them 'Staci Ramsey' wasn't the person she was pretending to be.

To shut down a false account the real person needs to
log a complaint and send proof of themselves.

Maybe that's something I could do. A small good deed to let the real woman in the Twitter photo know her identity was being used for tricksy purposes.

Finding her would be difficult. I'd have to traipse through thousands of blonde pretty girls on the internet to find a picture that matched that of the stolen Staci Ramsey face. Surely it would take me weeks, perhaps months? Years even.

It took me thirty seconds. It turns out you can just put

---

* Info is short for information. I'm sure you know that but I just wanted you to have all the info(rmation).

the image itself into Google, it'll find other similar images and her real Instagram will immediately pop up.

Her name was Jasmine.

Just like when I'd lustfully fallen for her the first time round, I couldn't help notice she was undeniably beautiful. Although this was the real woman. There were enough pictures to know that this wasn't fake and by some mad coincidence her profile said she lived a mile from my house. I talked to a fake person claiming she was from America and had Skype sex with her because she lived so far away when it turns out I could have bumped into the real girl if I'd gone to my local supermarket.

I could see the five or six photos that Staci had stolen for her own perverted use. It's a strange compliment, in a way. Her face was beautiful enough to entice men to give up their better judgement and get their bits out online for a stranger. Helen of Troy was the face that launched a thousand ships. Jasmine was the face that caught eighty-four dicks.

> Hi there, this is a strange message to receive but I was contacted on Twitter by a person called Staci Ramsey and I've since realised that she is a fake profile or a 'catfish'. She has stolen your photos and is pretending to be you. I thought I should let you know in case you wanted to try and shut it down. I hope you are well – and real.
> Joel Dommett

In the time from when I went into the jungle to the week after, I had gone from 7,000 Instagram followers to 450,000.

You could say I went into *I'm a Celebrity Get Me Out of Here!* and it wasn't until they got me out of there that I became a celebrity.

People started recognising me and shouting one of the following: 'You are that guy from that thing!', 'I loved you in the jungle!' or 'Hey, I've seen your dick!'

Of course as soon as I realised how many Instagram followers I'd gained I immediately went against what I'd learned inside the jungle and started ignoring my mum again in favour of social media – but now I ignored her while feeling guilty, which was a slight improvement. I helped her set up her own Instagram so she could talk to me through that instead.

I am fully aware that what I am experiencing is a fleeting fame, like Groupon or bird flu. Reality shows are not exactly known for giving people career longevity so I'm prepared for it to all ebb away. It does happen sometimes, I suppose. There are a few who were catapulted into people's homes by a reality show and they've remained there ever since, treading a new career path, but most are forgotten when the next shiny thing comes along.

The best thing about stand-up comedy is that I have a vocation. I have a palpable thing to do, get better at and sell. Luckily, if the reality TV fame is fleeting I can just continue gigging; I don't have to put on weight, get photographed in a bikini then lose it for a DVD deal. I can just keep touring and that makes me happy and hopefully I won't be forgotten like bird flu or, worse still, die from it.

Lily had now got the keys to her shiny new divorce and

moved to London a few miles from me. When I returned home I was able to exploit the best perk of my newfound known-ness. I could now get into VIP sections and redistribute the wealth of vodka myself, without having to be with a famous friend. As a celebration of our achievements, I decided we should have a night out to our old enemy the nightclub to experience life behind the velvet rope. I couldn't wait to show her the beauty of Robin Hooding.

It turned out she wasn't very good at it, distributing most of the vodka down her own throat, but aside from that, I was unbelievably proud of her that night. She looked . . . liberated. In personality and the way she looked. She had a new red Zara dress on and her hair was down, flicking back and forth as she danced wildly. It was like those high school movies when the geeky, goth girl takes off her glasses at the prom, everyone suddenly notices her and unexpectedly she wins prom queen.

I now started to realise how unhappy she had been in her marriage. I don't necessarily know if she knew she was unhappy at the time but now she definitely knew. They'd been together so long. It was her first real relationship and sometimes it's hard to know how stuck you are until you escape.

She was making conversation with everyone around us, something she wouldn't have done before she got married. It sounds horrible but I think his affair turned out to be a gift. I was celebrating coming out of the jungle, she was celebrating coming out of a marriage.

'I think it was a good thing that your marriage Petered

out,' I said, excited to be finally letting out a joke I'd held on to for three months.

Just as Lily got a number from a preppy man in the VIP, I got a reply from Jasmine.

> I am aware of Staci. She has been stealing my photo for two years now. I have had her profile taken down twice but she returns, buys followers and starts up again. It is very annoying.

I couldn't believe it. It was a real message from the real person behind the real fake face. I replied a little too quickly. I perhaps should have waited a few more minutes, at least pretending that I have my notifications turned off.

> This is going to sound mad. I have a gig in Greenwich tomorrow. Would you possibly want to meet up so I could take a photo with you and send it to Staci's profile saying, 'Look, I'm with you!'?

It was worth a shot. It would be a great end to a horrific story. I thought the fact that I was 'working' made it a little less creepy and slightly more official.

> Haha! Yes. Why not?

I was going to meet the real fake person and she didn't overuse emojis.

Bill's restaurant stood across the road from the venue. We arranged to meet there first as comedy clubs are not conducive to chatter and I had a lot to explain. God, I love the restaurant Bill's. Destiny's Child loved it too apparently.

I arrived after her as she basically lived upstairs. I saw her eyes from across the restaurant, like huge swirling galaxies in her face. They really were massive. Her make-up accentuated them too so they appeared even larger. I know how this works from wearing mascara in Psirus.

In real life her personality was softer than the filters of Instagram had given her credit for. She smiled, whereas on Instagram she never did.

I introduced myself and kissed her cheek. Like the juice glasses at a hotel breakfast, she was smaller than I imagined. She had the kind of face that went with a tall person but Instagram had hidden her tininess.

'I'm Jasmine,' she said in an unbelievably strong Eastern European accent.

'Where are you from?' I asked.

'I grow up in Ukraine,' she said, sounding like an evil Bond villain who predictably would end up in James's bed.

'Then four years ago I move to Cardiff,' she added with her accent switching swiftly to Welsh when she said 'Cardiff'.

I told her the whole story, from beginning to Bill's and surprisingly she didn't seem disgusted by me.

'I have seen the video of you,' she said, smirking slightly. She had watched a video of me masturbating thinking I was watching her. Surely this couldn't get any weirder.

She seemed sympathetic to my naïvety and the harsh realities of the internet. We'd both been wronged by the same person and strangely it had brought us together. I paid for the meal because Destiny's Child had taught me the importance of paying my Bill's then we headed to Up the Creek, the comedy club across the road.

I had a fun yet rowdy gig, hopefully proving I wasn't completely inept at my chosen profession. I kept on looking over at her in the corner to see if she was still there, like a kid looking for their mum at the nativity. She seemed impressed. She wasn't laughing maniacally while stroking a cat like I imagined but she laughed nonetheless.

We hugged and said goodbye outside the club, both of us lit devilishly by the red neon sign above that spelt 'Comedy'.

'Goodbye, Joel Dommett,' she said, like she was about to put me in the tank with the sharks.

I suddenly remembered something.

'The photo!' I shouted, a little too close to her face.

We took a selfie on my phone, her knowing exactly how to angle her face for optimum beauty and me apparently knowing mine for optimum panic. We parted ways in the Greenwich night.

I sent the photo to Staci Ramsey along with the caption: 'You looked great today.'

She didn't reply but I didn't expect her to. I thought of sending the same message to Jasmine but instead I left it. I set out to get the photo and that's what I got.

I kept telling and retelling the story of meeting the face of the fake to friends, ending in the reveal of the photo.

'Did you meet her again?' people would ask.

'No,' I would always answer, to a chorus of 'why not?'

and 'you idiot!' Maybe they were right. Maybe a photo isn't the end of the story. It was almost like she knew too much and we had started on the wrong naked Skypey foot. I felt like I'd been caught touching myself in the bushes outside her house so it would be weird to be let inside and go on a date.

I decided I would leave it.

Then a week later she liked a picture of mine on Instagram and I thought, 'Ah, why not.'

A like on Instagram is like a nudge on a pinball machine; it shows that they are potentially slightly interested. The further down the feed the photo is that they like, the more they like you. Although it's a fine line, apparently: if they like a photo too far down your feed they are weird and you should walk away. This internet stuff is complicated.

We went on a few more dates and they all went well and eventually on the fourth date we made the leap of not going to Bill's.

After the fifth date we had sex.

The face of the catfish was number thirty-nine. What a remarkably modern romcom fairytale. It isn't one you can tell the grandkids but it is a good story nonetheless.

We stopped dating after a few months because unfortunately her visa ran out and she moved back to Ukraine.

Then we had Skype sex.

The definition of someone who is smart is someone who has a big capacity to learn. I'd not put into practice anything I had learned from my past experiences with the catfish. I wasn't being romantic, patient, grown up or the best version of me. All I'd learned was that I needed to learn. Relationships were like pens. They were all so different; some you could write better with than others, some ran out quickly and some last a while.

I kept losing my pens and I suddenly realised there'd been one behind my ear all along.

25 September 2004

Hey JD,
Vince asked me if I wanted to be gay with him.
Kinda messed me up 'cos I didn't want to hurt him.
Is it weird that I'd rather be gay than rude?
Sincerely, Joel

'How long ago was that?' Hannah asks.

'A couple of weeks ago,' I reply. She is shocked. Our stories have caught up with ourselves. They are now no longer mistakes that happened way in the past.

Rodrigo still hasn't returned. There are no waiters in sight. It's like they are trying to be a terrible restaurant at this point. We sit with our cards on the tray, lying on each other with the receipt around them. I think about mentioning that our cards look like two people in a bed with a paper duvet but I realise that as the cards have our names on them it would look like I was insinuating that we would be doing the same soon. I know we almost certainly won't. After ten minutes of waiting, I realise there is another sneaky option on the bill list.

I pay.
She pays.
We split it.
We walk out without paying.

Option four is a real dream of mine but I've never had the confidence to do it. I've been waiting for a restaurant terrible enough to not feel bad about the loss in earnings. It's a bold move for a first date but I suggest it.

'Shall we just go?' I ask. Hannah smiles and I know she is up for it. We can now add stealing to the list of horrific things that have happened on this first and last encounter with Hannah. We wake up our little cards from their little card bed and casually make for the door.

As soon as we leave undetected, we run. We don't know where to but we both have mischief running through our veins. 'Feels like I'm stealing Daniel Bedingfield CDs from Virgin Megastore,' Hannah says as she runs. That story feels like an eternity of tapas ago. We reach the next corner and hide behind it like giddy children. Nobody has followed us, obviously. I don't think anybody cares but it momentarily feels like we are in a cop movie and it's exhilarating. We are hiding next to the grand, street-level doorway of the Duck and Waffle, a cocktail bar atop the Heron Tower, the tallest building in the City of London.

'Shall we go in?' I ask. Hannah nods and we approach the bouncer. He pulls aside the velvet rope and lets us in. It's not a specific VIP area, the rope is across the door of the entire venue. That makes the whole thing VIP. Although the drinks are not free in the entire bar as that would be a terrible business model. It immediately feels like I'm walking into the future, with glass, orange lights and minimalist modern art everywhere. Two lift doors lay open in the entrance lobby, awaiting humans to carry to the roof of London. We enter and I immediately panic. The glass lifts stick out from the side of the building, the way a catheter runs down a leg. I know how far this lift goes up and my fearful brain kicks in. It can't be as bad as stepping off the side of a building in *I'm a Celeb*, I keep telling myself silently.

The clear lift whizzes you upwards at an incredible speed; you think it's going to stop but it just keeps going and going and going. I grab on to the rail tightly, not wanting Hannah to know about my fear of heights. Ah fuck it, I've told her everything else tonight. 'I'm scared of heights,' I say, trying to make my gripping of the lift handrail look like a casual lean.

'I'm scared of tapas restaurants,' Hannah says, smiling. We reach the top in a matter of seconds. The lift door opens to the toilets which is somewhat underwhelming but past that the view really is incredible. I can see lights as far as the eye can see and it's mesmerising. The staff welcome us and take our jackets and sit us down with a drinks menu by the window. We've only been here thirty seconds and it's already better than the entire tapas experience.

'So were you hoping I would be number forty?' Hannah asks.

'No', I reply and I am telling the truth.

I'm really not used to this honesty malarky and it feels wonderfully cathartic. I might as well tell her. What have I got to lose? Ah well, here goes.

'I've already had sex with number forty. Last night I failed my goal and had sex with number forty. I literally fucked it,' I say seriously. Hannah laughs again. The fact I am taking it so seriously is clearly making it funnier. Forty may seem a lot to some people. I'm not sure by today's standards whether it is or not. But back in 2004, forty felt very high. I guess the rate of acceptable sexual partners rises year on year, like inflation. If you had a pound in 1938 you were practically a millionaire and if you'd slept with three people you were a massive floozy (or whatever the 1938 equivalent of a hoe bag is).

'So . . . tell me about number forty.'

#40 The One

Last Sunday I was on a sluggish train down to visit my dad in Crewkerne, Somerset. The grey concrete of outer London gradually faded into the luscious green of the Great British Countryside. It was one of those trains that stop everywhere along the way. No station was unturned.

Dad had recently sold the cheese shop after twenty years of trading and moved to set up a bed and breakfast in the countryside. He had now completely swapped career three times in his lifetime. A feat most people do not have the courage to achieve once. It's actually quite inspiring.

Now I was no longer his unnecessary assistant at the Fromagerie I tried to visit him as much as possible but due to my growing stand-up comedy commitments it would usually end up being twice a year or so. Essentially I would see my dad as regularly as I would watch gay porn.

We would talk every other Sunday on the phone like clockwork. It has been that way since I was about eleven. Never Saturday, never Monday. Always Sunday. I'm sure it's not true but it felt as if a fortnightly weekend call was written in the original divorce document and slowly over time it became habit. We would always, without fail, chat about the Grand Prix. I never know whether to call it the Grand Prix or Formula One. Both terrible names. Formula One sounds like milk you give to newborn babies and Grand Prix sounds like a collective noun for a group of massive pricks. I don't like the Grand Prix but I've pretended solidly for fifteen years so we have something to bond over. I can't decide whether pretending is counterproductive or healthy for our relationship. I suppose it's like faking an orgasm. It may help in that moment to make everyone feel gratified but it harms things in the long run because they now assume you like it when they put their finger there and leave their socks on.

I got really good at throwing in buzzwords to seem knowledgeable. 'Hairpin!' I would say with disbelief. 'Rubens Barrichello?' was always another favourite bit of jargon to throw in. It's only recently I discovered he retired in 2011, which made me realise Dad has probably been faking it this entire time too. The Grand Prix, not orgasms. I wouldn't be here if he faked those.

My dad and I had become much closer recently. A few years ago I got the standard Sunday call. We both pretended to like the Grand Prix for a bit and I threw in the absolute gem of 'traction control'. Eventually the conversation ran its course, he had satisfied the terms of the divorce and we were just about to wrap up.

'Oh, I should probably tell you – I have prostate cancer,' he said casually, like he was saying 'I'm making casserole for dinner' or 'Rubens Barrichello used traction control in the hairpin'. I did a double-take even though I was on the phone. I was almost about to brush over it and say goodbye then my brain backtracked and processed what he had actually just said.

'What?!'

'I've got prostate cancer,' he told me in the same casual manner, not feeling the need to up the level of severity.

I was half expecting him to shout 'You've been Duuunnnnneeeeeed!' but it never came. He informed me that he had caught it early and would have it operated on in a matter of weeks, so there was nothing to worry about.

It was hard to penetrate Dad's relaxed persona and understand how badly he was really affected by this. Was he not worried? Or was he worried but pretending not to be worried? Either way I was worried.

I deal with things in the same way; it's clearly something I've adopted from him. I always think there is nothing to worry about until you know you have something worry about. Unfortunately this doesn't settle the frantic minds of those around you.

Having cancer is obviously a huge life-changing experience for anyone to undergo, no matter how severe it is. The horrific realisation of the fragility of life must make you appreciate everything and everyone you have around you. I realised this when I got a phone call from him a few months after the operation, which had thankfully gone without a hitch.

'Hey, Dad, are you OK?' I asked, ready to jump straight into some sweet F1 buzzwords.

'Yep! Just had my first erection since the operation!' he said proudly. I did the same double-take on the phone I'd done a few months before. We'd gone from a regular stilted chat about a sport we were both pretending to like to overly familiar erection chat in a matter of months. I then realised he'd phoned me on a Saturday.

All it took was a little taste of potential death. Since then we have thankfully found a wonderful happy medium.

His bed and breakfast is beautiful. I don't really see the benefits as he's always cooked and put fresh sheets on the bed for me anyway. Basically other people pay to be his son for the day.

I was looking forward to some hearty countryside cooking then relaxing on the sofa and watching a good DVD which Dad would almost definitely fall asleep in the middle of. I've tried for years to make him watch a feature-length film without drifting away and experiencing better CGI in his sleepy thoughts but he's quite happy with missing key plot points and details.

If you're with someone who falls asleep in the middle of a movie at home just as it's getting to the good parts, then feel free to do the following for fun. Get up silently, tiptoe towards the TV making sure you don't wake them, flick quietly through the DVD selection and change the film to something – and this detail is important – with the same lead actor in it. Obviously if you're watching on Netflix this process becomes infinitely easier but it does take out the fun of sneaking around. Who doesn't love a good tiptoe?*

After you've swapped the film, gently sit back down next to the slumbering couch potato and after about twenty minutes or so, wake them up and act as if absolutely nothing has changed. 'Try to stay awake for the rest of the film,' you must say sincerely, to give the impression it means something to you. Then out of your periphery, just watch the confusion slowly happening on their face as they desperately try to work out what happened in the nap gap.

Once Dad and I were watching *Cast Away* with Tom Hanks in it and I changed it to *Philadelphia*. 'How unlucky is that guy?' Dad said, angry at the frankly ridiculous narrative. 'He finally gets off the island and now he's got AIDS?' he added, utterly bewildered why this won an Oscar.

Here are some suggestions if you want to try it yourself. Change Sandra Bullock's film *Speed* with her Oscar-winning performance in *Gravity* and it feels like she just has terrible luck getting stuck on very different types of transport. Matt Damon in sci-fi films *Interstellar* and *The Martian* are wonderfully interchangeable as he's a man stuck alone on a planet in both. Strangely it actually makes *Interstellar* make more sense. Heath Ledger in *Brokeback Mountain* can be swapped to his turn as the Joker in *The*

---

* Some people call it 'tippy toes' and those people can go fuck themselves.

Dark Knight. A gay cowboy who can't deal with his suppressed homosexual urges snaps, paints his face and tries to kill Batman. I also found if you switch Will Smith's *Independence Day* with *I Am Legend*, it actually makes both films better.

One of the many stops on the way to Crewkerne was Woking. I have never been but I was hugely disappointed to find out from Google that there's no Chinese restaurant within it called Wok King. Another huge missed opportunity.

The train shuddered to a halt. The unnecessarily loud beeping rang out over the half-empty weekend carriage and the doors prised open.

A lady floated onto the train in a long white dress that almost touched the floor yet somehow wasn't dirty. She had long ginger hair and the starkest, whitest skin I'd ever seen. It was impossible not to look at her, a striking vision of red and white. She could have easily represented the England national football team without painting her face.

Time seemed to slow as she swept onto the carriage like an ethereal, sexy spectre. She was carrying a briefcase. Like a proper clichéd briefcase. The hard ones with the gold number locks on top that drug dealers use to put wads of cash in. I wasn't sure whether it was the latest craze or if it was just handcuffed to her wrist for a 'special delivery'.

Every twin seat she walked past was occupied by one person spreading themselves and their luggage purposefully across both spaces to scare away any new passengers who might think of sitting next to them. There were two seats free on the opposite side of my table.

She glanced at me, held my gaze for a moment then looked away. Was that an interested gaze or an uninterested gaze? It's so difficult to decipher. Gays on the other hand are so good at their gazes. There's no guessing game in a gay's gaze.

With no other options, she sat down across the table.

It was almost like we were on a date. Maybe we should have more train dates. Then at least if you don't get on, you get home. Can someone design that app, please? I can't be bothered.

She put her black briefcase on the seat next to her. She wasn't handcuffed to it so it must have been a craze. A leather label hung down with some details on it. I momentarily peeked at it. It said: 'ERICA CEDAR'. A mobile number was written below what I assumed was her name. Unless it wasn't hers and she had stolen the briefcase from a banker or drug dealer.

She got a thick book out of her bag and started to read. She was a woman who doesn't let a page count get in the way of a good novel.* I wanted to talk to her but also didn't want to ruin her journey by assuming she wanted to be hassled. There's nothing worse than sitting opposite a hassler.

After an hour in complete silence I decided to do the romantic thing that people do on trains when they see someone beautiful. I let her leave and regretted it. If only it

---

* One day people will read this on trains. Are you on a train now? If so just do me a favour, just chuckle and say aloud, 'Great book!' It will really help with the sales.

were 1940 I could have lit her cigarette, but nowadays women are allowed their own lighters.

Real life and films are so different. When characters wake up in movies they roll around, rub their face, slowly open their eyes and look beautiful. In real life we just open our eyes and look straight at our phone. No film has ever shown someone wake up and immediately see if anyone's sent them a WhatsApp in the night.

In a film people meet on a train, sit opposite each other, light a cigarette then have to move to the rear of the train to touch each other's rears. In real life you just sit opposite each other, one of you reads a book, then they leave.

She alighted the same way she boarded, floating like a hipster on Heelys. She gave me a small glance on the way out. It could have been to me, it could have been to check that she hadn't left anything on her seat. I couldn't be sure.

Was a small search of her hanging label name on Facebook a terrible violation of her rights? Is a name search on Facebook worse than a whistle from a building site? Again, I wasn't sure.

I finally finished my pilgrimage to Crewkerne and arrived at the comfort of my Dad's B&B. We hugged because that's what we do now and I sat down to a colossal parental luncheon.

'I sneaked a glance at a girl's name tag on her bag. Should I find her online and message her?' I asked over my second helping of roast chicken.

'Oh yes! Find her. It'll be like that film, *Taken*. The one with Liam Neeson, where he tries to save his daughter, then it goes black and white and he saves loads of Jews!'

I was going to find her. Either that or tell Erica Cedar that a ginger girl from Woking had nicked her briefcase.

I typed in her name on Facebook.

I don't use Facebook often because I'd rather not know about people's achievements, Donald Trump, family deaths or birthdays. Talking about Facebook in my word book feels shortsighted. It's like mentioning Friends Reunited in your 2004 novel assuming it's going to last forever. There's a reason that Shakespeare's work has lasted so long: it's because he didn't mention Myspace.

There were a few people of the same name, but only one with a thumbnail that could be mistaken for a marshmallow on fire. Was there another Joel Dommett? I typed in my name. I came up, obviously, and one other of my kind. It's not a common name; we are a rare breed. There may be more who are not on Facebook but they will surely die soon. The other one lives in Milton Keynes so I already win.

'Your name is Joel Dommett. My name is Joel
Dommett. Let's go for a Starbucks?'

I thought Starbucks would be a good choice because they would call out our name when our coffee was ready and we would both answer and laugh.

'No.'

No explanation, no pleasantries, just no. Maybe he thought that I was going to kill him so I could become the only living Joel Dommett.

I messaged Erica. It's difficult to ask a stranger out online without sounding creepy at the best of times, particularly when you are essentially saying, 'I saw you on a train, stared at you for most of the journey and made note of your personal information.'

I attempted to soften it by asking her on a double date. 'It's less creepy if there're more witnesses,' I thought, then realised there's nothing more sinister than the word 'witnesses'. I hadn't even thought about who the other two people would be. The only thing more creepy than using the word 'witnesses' is when the witnesses don't turn up.

She replied and agreed. It was frustratingly easy. It made me think I probably should have just leaned over and talked to her when she was sitting two feet away across a table. Maybe this was number forty? It was certainly a good ending to the story. I was very excited to meet the mysterious train girl.

Naturally I messaged Lily as my nominated double-date mate. Double dates are great. It alleviates the awkwardness if your date is bad because you can just ruin someone else's. Lily was going to bring the preppy guy from the nightclub who she'd been texting.

I was excited for her; it was the first time she'd been on a date since Peter parked her (I gave myself a pat on the back for this) and she was understandably nervous. It was due to be a beautiful Sunday so I decided to take the initiative and organise a picnic. I told Lily and Erica the plan: I would sort the food but they should feel free to bring any alcohol. I went to the supermarket and stacked the snacks neatly in the hamper. I got the usual suspects: strawberries, grapes, ham, pork pies, champagne and of course some Orangina. I bought dates because I thought there's probably a joke in there somewhere to break the ice. I also bought ice. I would make a joke about that too.

I love picnics because I love hampers. Unfortunately you have to have a picnic to use a hamper as it's the only time it's acceptable to use one. I've tried using one to take stuff to the gym and everyone looks at you weirdly.

We organised to meet in Richmond Park because it was close to Erica's house and she didn't seem keen on getting on the train. It's understandable, there are lots of weirdos on trains these days.

I found a good spot. The further I walked from the road the more it felt like an abduction so I kept it simple and sent a WhatsApp pin to the girls. I unravelled and flicked the blanket flat like a posh waiter setting a serviette. Then I opened the tightly organised hamper, set it all out and ate dates while I waited for the dates to arrive.

Another picnic couple set up shop fairly close. A little too close for my liking. I picked this picnic place and you nicked it. While they sat and snogged on their blanket I was sitting alone with four times as much food and a bottle of champagne on ice. I looked like I'd been stood up for a wedding proposal.

Lily arrived first. She looked wonderful, continuing her newfound outgoing freedom from marriage and Ugg boots. She wore a white dress with flowers dotted upon it. If I'd told her when she was eleven she would be wearing a flowery frock when she was thirty-two she would've grabbed me in a headlock and given me a severe wedgie. I've never felt underdressed for a picnic before. I regretted my casual choice of double denim. I greeted her with the customary fist-bump and told her she looked incredible.

'You're wearing a lot of denim,' Lily replied. It's true, I was. I was trying to look like a hipster but I was starting to think I looked more like a French exchange student. 'Double date, double denim,' I said, very pleased with myself.

'Well, don't look at me for another double D, you perv.' We both then simultaneously laughed at the word 'perv'.

The nearby picnic couple seemed glad that someone else had finally turned up but I'm sure it still seemed strange that we were not showing any affection towards each other. Now it looked like a wedding proposal but she'd said no.

Preppy turned up next. He parked his posh car on the road with the stereo blasting out of the open window. It reminded me of myself in my Citroën Saxo when I was a teenager. If he had been blasting out Les Mis I think I would have immediately liked him more. Unfortunately he'd picked a song from the universally hated yet wonderfully catchy Pitbull. He knew we were looking and he wanted us to see car he drove. Sports cars annoy me. They do everything they can to be seen so that you know how much money the owners have. It's the vehicle equivalent to Louie Spence walking round with money stapled to his jacket. If you didn't happen to be looking at it because of its angry sexy design then it makes sure it catches your eye with an intense bright colour to make it stand out from the Vauxhall Corsas. If you do happen to be looking completely in the other direction then it has a loud exhaust to make sure you turn around to see it. I think the thing that annoys me most about sports cars is that despite me hating everything about them I still bloody want one. A part of me wishes I were Prep.

He walked towards us, locking his car behind him with his key fob without looking back. He knew it looked cool, you could tell. He was only locking his car without looking but he clearly felt like he was in a movie walking away from an explosion. Prep had a white polo shirt on with the collar popped. I didn't realise people were still doing the popped-collar thing as it only really looks good on cricketers or Cantona. He was clearly a bit of a playa. By that I mean someone who pulls lots of women, not a sportsman or a Spanish beach.

'Oi oi!' he shouted while cupping his hand to his mouth for extra amplification. This confirmed my playa suspicions. It's the call of the playing lad, like the mockingbird whistle in *The Hunger Games*. I tend to quickly form a dislike of anyone who uses 'oi' in any capacity. It's also always shouted and never whispered, just like 'Pile on!'

The double 'oi oi' is a phrase commonly used by lads who are displaying their manly nature and punctuating a particularly laddy endeavour. 'I shagged a girl in the plane toilet and definitely didn't lose my erection oiiiii oiiiiiiiiiiii' is a perfect example.

The triple 'oi' is used by frustrating Australian lads who are responding to the call of 'oggy oggy oggy!' and any more than three is used by someone breaking up a fight.

'I'm John,' Prep said, introducing himself to me then kissing Lily directly on the mouth, which took us all by surprise. If he were foreign you could have excused his bold-ness as a greeting native to his homeland but he was clearly

English so he was just a bellend. He was a big, slightly muscly, slightly doughy guy. He clearly went to the gym but thought because he did bench presses three times a week that he could eat pizzas constantly. His polo shirt was a good few sizes too small, accentuating his barrel chest. He either bought it that size on purpose or put it on when he was ten and slowly grew into it. He had the look of an amateur-level model. Someone in those photos in the windows of shit barber shops. (In the window, not on the wall, there's a difference.) We sat down and Prep immediately started eating the picnic spread. I know that's what it was there for but he was unapologetically going for it.

Erica was really late even though she lived the closest. I assumed it must take a while to float places. If Google Maps says it's a fifteen-minute walk, that's probably a good twenty-five-minute float. After a while my legs started to hurt. The frustrating thing about picnics is you slowly remember how uncomfortable sitting cross-legged is. It transports me back to the dull days of education where you would sit for hours on a school floor singing hymns or listening to Jon Snow.

Eventually, around forty minutes late, I saw her on the crest of the hill, her hair glistening like a burning beacon in the sunlight. She was holding the same briefcase while wearing a white dress similar to the one she wore on the train. It was clearly her vibe to look like an office-job Jesus.

She was holding a Starbucks coffee cup as white as her complexion and she glided towards us (should that be glid?) like sex on a Segway. She clearly chose to grab a coffee instead of being less late. We unfolded our legs from our picnic yoga and stood to greet her. She kissed us all on the cheek then laid her briefcase on the rug. It felt like we were doing a dodgy deal exchanging cash for fresh strawberries. The picnic neighbours were looking over, intrigued by the addition of someone who looked like they'd walked out of a religious version of *The Apprentice*. I am never one to judge too harshly on appearances but she was wearing Crocs. I couldn't decide whether it was cool or horrific. If you turn up fashionably late in Crocs, I'm sorry but you're just late.

'I really hate picnics,' Erica said as she sat on the blanket. Wow. What an opener. That's what she chose instead of apologising for her tardy arrival and was something she maybe should've brought up when I suggested going for a picnic in the first place. I don't think she shared my love for wicker food baskets. Strangely this bluntness felt mesmerising. She was so fucking cool. She didn't care what anyone thought of her and I think I liked it.

Four (mostly) strangers sat in the sun. The flower dress divorcée, the French exchange, the cricketer and the ginger Jehovah. We all exchanged the niceties and the double denim double date began. Lily was nervous. I could tell because she was swearing a lot which she always did when she was panicking. If she ever has to do a eulogy at a funeral it will be horrific. It must be so odd being with someone for so long then having to go back out in the world and start again like 5ive on their reunion tour when there were only four of them.

'What did you um, fucking, do today?' Lily asked Erica, attempting to be polite.

'It's my day off but I went to the library and read like, four books,' Erica answered as if she just couldn't resist a little bit of learning. Lily and I both laughed and then realised she was actually being serious.

It was time for a prepared joke to lift the mood and get Erica to laugh and, fingers crossed, fancy me. 'This date is terrible,' I said while knowingly eating a date. Lily laughed. The other two didn't get it. They clearly didn't know what a date was and just thought it was a massive sultana. The picnic didn't feel easy so far but it was still early days. I was really wanting it to work.

I noticed Prep was slowly shuffling towards Erica. I knew his game. He was trying to swap dates mid-date. Lily noticed it too and we gave each other a glance of disbelief.

'What's your favourite food?' I asked Erica, desperately trying to distract her from Prep's wandering hands. Damn it. I was already scraping the barrel with 'what's your favourite' questions.

'Peas,' she answered with absolutely no hint of sarcasm. Imagine your favourite food being the little green things that taste of absolutely nothing.

We all sat on the tartan mat politely. I was doing all the legwork trying to make it comfortable, in both the conversation and my seating position. 'It's still early days,' I kept saying to myself. A silence arrived while we all picked at the food that I had paid for. It felt like it went on forever. Prep was chomping at crisps unbelievably loudly while still slowly and slyly working his way towards my date. I couldn't bear the chomping. If I can hear it that loudly I dread to think how loud it must be in his own head. I needed to break this chomp-filled silence. Say something, Joel, anything. Do it.

'I went to Auschwitz recently,' I said, immediately regretting what had passed my lips. Out of everywhere I have been in my life that was a terrible choice to mention, what the hell was I thinking? It was true I had, but that wasn't the point. I'd been there to do some gigs. Poland not Auschwitz obviously. My phone rang in the unbelievably moving bit where there's thousands of pairs of stolen shoes and I've honestly never felt more horrific. It didn't help that my ringtone is Usher's 'Yeah'.

'What's Auschwitz?' Erica asked. Lily and I laughed again, then again realised that she was being serious.

I honestly couldn't believe she didn't know and it wasn't the place to teach her about it now. She clearly hadn't seen the film *Taken*. I started to think she wasn't as smart as she wanted everyone to think she was. Maybe the huge book on the train was hollow with a snow globe inside which she stared at blankly for two hours. If you have a book that big, in hardback, you're either really smart or you're stupid but want people to think you're smart.* Was that a smart thing to say?

I didn't mind that she wasn't the smartest. I'm the first to admit I'm not the most intelligent; maybe we matched each other's intellect perfectly. I suppose the difference is I own up to it. I'll happily admit I'm in the blue group whereas I think Erica wanted to let everyone think she was in the red group when she was obviously with me in the blue.

'What do you do for a living, Lily?' Prep asked politely. It seemed out of character but then I realised it was to distract

---

* It's OK, if you're reading my book in public people are just looking at you like you're a super-cool legend.

the conversation away from him so he could slide further towards Erica. They were basically touching by this point and Erica didn't seem to be doing anything to stop him or move away.

'I'm a teacher,' Lily replied. Erica sniggered to herself but loud enough that we all heard. Did she just laugh at the fact Lily was a teacher? Surely not.

'Those who teach can't teach or do anything else – what's that phrase?' Erica said, petering out.

'Those who can't – teach,' Prep supplied and they both laughed together. They were openly being mean to Lily and I didn't really understand why. Lily was hurt, I could tell. Maybe they just had a different idea of what was funny to us. Lily and I have a very strange sense of humour and if we're together it can be odd to try and fit in. Maybe that was Erica's way of trying to be funny, I thought. I forgave her for it cautiously. Also one thing I know about Lily is that she can easily defend herself.

'It's actually, those who don't teach – cunt,' Lily said, looking towards Erica on the C of the C word. I stifled a laugh and the other two grunted, unamused.

Prep was almost spooning Erica on the rug by now. Lily and I looked at each other in utter disbelief. The sheer confidence of this man was blowing my mind. Classic 'Spanish beach'. Erica didn't seem to care too much. She was someone who reacted to confidence not courtesy. It seemed being rude and direct worked for her and polite conversation was a bore. It felt like a swingers' night where we'd all put our keys in the middle and swapped partners.

There was another lengthy silence. Prep had entirely

polished off the Pringles so he swapped to the strawberries, which made for a wetter open-mouth chomp. He'd eaten most of the food by this point. All I'd eaten during the whole date was a whole date. Fill the chomp silence again, Joel. Do it. Anything.

'What are your thoughts on marriage?' I said, immediately regretting what had come out of my mouth for the second time. Where were these terrible thoughts coming from in my mind?

'I disagree with it,' Erica said confidently like it was something she'd read today in her library session. At last, something that we agreed on. I told her my reasons. I ended it by saying 'I don't want to be told by someone when to save a date' while eating a second date. It went as badly as expected.

'I agree with it, and I've been married,' Lily said boldly, stepping in on our naysaying. Erica reacted with disgust. 'You got divorced? Why?' Lily politely explained that Peter had had an affair and this was her first date since. Erica's response changed everything. It flipped me and the date immediately on its head. 'Men are going to find satisfaction from somewhere. If I was married I would make sure that it was from me.'

I snapped. I really never snap but I snapped. I kinda almost shouted. I couldn't understand why anyone would be so horrible to Lily. I don't remember exactly what I said but it started on me saying, 'I'm pretty sure Lily is the best at blowjobs,' and ended with me saying, 'I would much rather be with Lily than you, Erica.' Then as the last mic-drop moment I said 'this date is over' while attempting to grab a date and eat it but unfortunately Prep had already eaten them all. I was disappointed in myself that I hadn't jumped to her rescue earlier. I just sat there lifeless and pathetic like a terrible friend, blinded and transfixed by a horrible floaty ginger girl. I don't think I'd ever reacted this way to anything. Before this the most angry I'd ever got was closing my curtains testily when I found out I'd been catfished but this was another level.

I realised Erica herself was a pea and she was essentially saying she loves herself. By that I mean, she looks great in a group, brightens up any plate but alone she is bland and not good at picnics.

I suddenly understood that Erica was just an idiot and being horrible was her way of clambering up the socio-economic ladder and make her feel better than other people. She was clearly the good-looking bully in school who'd say something needlessly horrible and John would be the tagalong friend who stood just behind her waving his fist adding 'Yeah!' Her meanness reminded me of Violet but Erica's sharp tongue had no fun jokey edge.

I realised a cool person doesn't care what you think of them, whereas a horrible person doesn't care what you think about anything and Erica was one of those. It was tense on the rug. The nearby picnickers were filming us, hoping for it to go viral. Then the tension was broken wonderfully by Prep.

'If you hit me I'm gonna hit you back . . . That's quantum physics.'

Lily and I broke from anger to laughter in a split second. The change was as quick as what a contestant experiences on *The X Factor* when Simon says, 'I'm sorry, it's bad news . . .'

then adds, 'You are going to have to quit your job as a plumber because you have made it to the finals!'

He was clearly trying to link his lad lifestyle to science, trying to bring in Newton's Third Law – 'Every action has an equal and opposite reaction' – but just slightly missing the mark.

Erica obviously didn't laugh. Physics clearly wasn't written in her snow globe.

'I love you, Prep,' I said while literally ROFLing. I think it was the first time I had ROFLed since I tried to buy Lily every seat on a Megabus. Say what you like about picnics, it makes for an easy ROFL. Then I realised that 'Prep' was my inside brain nickname for him and hadn't been shared with the group. This made me laugh and roll more.

Erica and Prep excused themselves and walked off together, him with his chest pumped defending her dignity and her walking like a floating shit that won't flush.

Lily and I lay on the rug and looked up at the beautiful clear blue sky as our laughter slowly petered out.

'I don't know what quantum physics is either,' I said, which started us off again.

I clearly missed that day at school too.

'Would you actually rather be with me than Erica?' Lily asked. I nodded. I really did. I thought Erica was the great ending to my romcom story. The girl I found on a train was the one, my number forty. But maybe I'd been trying to desperately find something when it was under my nose the entire time. Like when you're looking for your mobile phone and you realise you're already talking on it.

Lily and I looked at each other in a way we'd never looked at each other before and while lying in the sun on a rug, strewn with empty food wrappers, we leaned in, and instead of pulling away and saying 'I completely misread the situation', we kissed. It felt uncomfortably strange yet . . . right. The couple nearby were transfixed. They'd basically witnessed an entire episode of *Hollyoaks*.

To cut a long story short, Lily and I had sex. She was number forty.

In her house that evening, not in the park. I think I may have actually cut the story too short there. I will fill in a little bit of the gap for you. We packed up our things and headed home. We probably would have had sex there but the peeping toms were still watching. The sex was great. It felt like we were trying a bit too hard to take it seriously but it was good. We lay there afterwards, post-coital, both of us not really sure of the implications of what had just happened. Neither of us knew what to do or say.

'You want to slow-dance?' I asked. Lily smiled and nodded. We put on Crazy Town's 'Butterfly' and slow-danced naked in her room. This was it. This was the ending I'd been looking for. It was my perfect romcom diary story, the best friend had become The One. The classic story arc, the perfect punchline. She was my number forty.

'It doesn't feel right,' Lily said, moving away from me before Shifty Shellshock kicked into the second verse. The moment stopped abruptly like a needle slipping off a vinyl record. Although obviously Crazy Town was on Spotify so that continued to play. Lily put on some clothes and sat on the edge of the bed. 'I've always dreamt of doing this with the man I loved. And I'm sorry if I'm being a dick but I really don't think it's you.' For a moment the feeling of rejection burned in my chest. Then I realised, she was right. It did feel odd. It felt like I was slow-dancing with my sister. Urrgh! I HAD SEX WITH MY SISTER. I had been so obsessed with my perfect romcom story I'd failed to think about the characters within it. Maybe it wasn't about the story. This was the biggest anti-climax of my life.

We sat on the edge of the bed and fist-bumped. It felt odd as I was still very much naked. I hurriedly gathered my scattered clothes, put them on, then we fist-bumped again.

'Sorry, I completely misread the situation,' Lily said and we laughed.

My story had no end. No punchline. Forty had come and gone.

'So last night you had sex with your best friend of twenty years?' Hannah asks and I nod.

'You really didn't see forsee this happening? Because I'll be honest, I saw it coming as soon as you started talking about Lily about five hours ago.'

It hasn't been a normal date, but I've strangely enjoyed it in a masochistic way, kinda like a bad gig. You learn so much more about yourself and what to change at the bad ones.

Going into a date knowing we're not going on another one has been liberating. We haven't been selling ourselves, we've just *been* ourselves.

We share a cocktail that doesn't have a firework in it while looking out over London's incredible night skyline and I realise how easy this whole date has been. I've never been this honest, and she has been honest back and we still like each other. I feel like we have nothing else to hide. I've got all my secrets and hidden demons out of the locked cupboard and it feels like if we did go on another date I would have absolutely nothing to hide from her.

On the way back down in one of the world's fastest lifts I grab her instead of the rail and we share a kiss, then we go home our separate ways.

I get a tweet the day after my date from the tapas restaurant saying they recognised me from *I'm a Celebrity Get Me Out of Here!* and that we hadn't paid for our meal. They ask me to do a tweet saying how good the food was in return for the free meal. The worst meal I have ever had somehow ends in me telling 100,000 people that it was incredible. I do it but add #rodrigofuckyourself.

23 December 2017

Hey JD
It has now been a year since that first kiss – almost to the day. Lily has since found a guy who slow-dances with her and she's really into it. As for me I've enjoyed the most incredible year of my life. I went on a mammoth 130-date tour selling nearly 100,000 tickets so I can almost afford to spell out my name with my furniture, I finally got my picture on the wall of an Indian restaurant, I've written an entire book and my childhood dream came true – I sold out the

Hammersmith Apollo. However, above all of that, I managed to fall in love.

She was number forty-one. This was my imperfect end to my tale. I'm obsessed with her not the story.

It's just easy. So fucking easy.

She is more beautiful than anyone I've ever met, seen, or Skyped – inside and out. She makes me a better person and I want her to keep me forever.

I really didn't understand the point of marriage until I met her and everything changed because I'm not scared or even slightly fazed by a future together.

I hope our grandkids read this in seventy years' time and imagine us meeting up for the first time, the same way I read about my grandpa at Young Farmers, and I hope while driving around in their hover cars they are a little bit proud of us.

We're just two tiny people in this huge world trying to connect and when we did, we created a reaction far greater than that of its size. That's quantum physics.

A year ago I was more honest than I'd ever been on a first date because I assumed there wasn't going to be a second. We continued that honesty and it's now the foundation of our relationship, which is what makes it work so well.

I've attempted to have sex in a plane toilet, swapped it for a snowboard, had it with my best friend, been vomited and pissed on, and had my penis put everywhere on the internet. I don't regret any of it because it led me to her.

There is no one else. There is no forty-two. She. Is. It. That's why I have decided to end this book by asking her:

Hannah Aukje Cooper – will you marry me?
Sincerely, Joel